REQUIREMENTS
Engineering

WORLDWIDE
SERIES IN
COMPUTER
SCIENCE

Series Editors   **Professor David Barron, Southampton University, UK**
Professor Peter Wegner, Brown University, USA

The Worldwide Series in Computer Science has been created to publish textbooks which both address and anticipate the needs of an ever evolving curriculum thereby shaping its future. It is designed for undergraduates majoring in Computer Science and practitioners who need to reskill. Its philosophy derives from the conviction that the discipline of computing needs to produce technically skilled engineers who will inevitably face, and possibly invent, radically new technologies throughout their future careers. New media will be used innovatively to support high quality texts written by leaders in the field.

Published titles   Ammeraal, *Computer Graphics for Java Programmers*
Goodrich & Tamassia, *Data Structures and Algorithms in Java*
Winder & Roberts, *Developing Java Software*

Forthcoming
titles   Ben-Ari, *Ada for Software Engineers*
Gollman, *Computer Security*
Lowe & Hall, *Hypertext and the Web: An Engineering Approach*

REQUIREMENTS
Engineering
PROCESSES AND TECHNIQUES

Gerald Kotonya
Computing Department, Lancaster University

and

Ian Sommerville
Computing Department, Lancaster University

JOHN WILEY & SONS
Chichester · New York · Weinheim · Brisbane · Singapore · Toronto

Copyright © 1998 by John Wiley & Sons Ltd,
Baffins Lane, Chichester,
West Sussex PO19 1UD, England

National   01243 779777
International   (+44) 1243 779777
e-mail (for orders and customer service enquiries): cs-books@wiley.co.uk
Visit our Home Page on http://www.wiley.co.uk or
                        http://www.wiley.com

Reprinted February and October 2002

Other Wiley Editorial Offices

John Wiley & Sons, Inc., 605 Third Avenue,
New York, NY 10158–0012, USA

Weinheim • Brisbane • Singapore • Toronto

Library of Congress Cataloging-in-Publication Data
Kotonya, Gerald
     Requirements engineering : processes and techniques / Gerald
Kotonya and Ian Somerville.
      p. cm. – (Worldwide series in computer science)
      Includes bibliographical references and index.
      ISBN 0-471-97208-8 (hbk. : alk. paper)
      1. Software engineering. I. Sommerville, Ian. II. Title.
   III. Series.
   QA76.758.K69   1997
   005.1–dc21   98–4756
                                                   CIP

British Library Cataloguing in Publication Data
A catalogue record for this book is available from the British Library

ISBN 0 471 97208 8

Typeset from the authors' disks by Florencetype Ltd, Stoodleigh, Devon.
Printed and bound by CPI Antony Rowe, Eastbourne
This book is printed on acid-free paper responsibly manufactured from sustainable forestry, in which at least two trees are planted for each one used for paper production.

Contents

Preface

In spite of new and effective software engineering techniques, software system development projects are still prone to failure. All too often complex software systems are delivered late, over-budget and do not meet the real needs of either the system end-users or of the organisation which is paying for the system. In the vast majority of cases, these system failures are not due to incompetent staff or poor software engineering. Rather, they are a consequence of problems with the requirements for the system.

System requirements are specifications of the services the system should provide, the constraints on the system and background information which is necessary to develop the system. Requirements engineering is the systematic process of eliciting, understanding, analysing and documenting these requirements. Although it may seem strange to call this an 'engineering' process, the term engineering is used to indicate that this is a practical, systematic process where trade-offs have to be made to find the best solution

There are many different aspects of requirements engineering and different books interpret the subject in different ways. Some authors focus on the early stages of the process and mostly discuss the human and organisational problems of discovering what people want from a system. Others take a different approach and describe the detailed modelling of a system using structured methods or formal mathematical methods. In contrast to these books which have concentrated on parts of the topic, we have tried to provide comprehensive coverage of the whole of the requirements engineering process from initial requirements elicitation through to requirements validation. We supplement this with a description of a range of techniques which may be applied, including viewpoint-oriented techniques and techniques for modelling the requirements for interactive systems

Our emphasis on a broad coverage of requirements engineering means that we do not discuss particular approaches such as object-oriented analysis or formal specification in depth. This is not just for reasons of space but also because we believe that there is no single requirements engineering technique which is applicable to all types of system. Requirements engineers need to know about a range of different techniques and should select the technique which is appropriate to their application.

After the introductory chapter, the book is split into two logical parts. The first part is process-oriented and describes different activities in the requirements engineering process. These include requirements elicitation and analysis, requirements validation and requirements management. The second part of the book focuses on requirements engineering techniques. It covers the use of structured methods in requirements engineering, viewpoint-oriented approaches, the specification of non-functional requirements and the specification of interactive systems, Finally, we present a case study which illustrates the application of a viewpoint-oriented approach to requirements engineering. This is based on a real system which is currently being developed for users of a group of university libraries.

It is always difficult when writing a book of this nature to find the right balance between tried and tested techniques and new, promising research work. The majority of the material in this text is based on good requirements engineering practice but the chapters on viewpoints and interactive system specification represent recent research which is not yet in widespread use. We have tried to ensure the relevance of this by basing our description on real system descriptions which demonstrate the applicability of the approach.

The book is primarily intended as a student text for senior undergraduate and graduate students studying computer science, software engineering or systems engineering. It can be used to support a one or two-semester course in requirements engineering or as a supplement to other software engineering texts. Possible ways in which the book may be used include the following

1. In a short introductory course in requirements engineering, Chapters 1 and 2 may be used to provide an overview of requirements engineering and RE processes. This can then be supplemented by the material from Chapters 6 and 8 which summarise structured methods for requirements engineering and the problems of specifying non-functional requirements.

2. A more extensive course, lasting a semester, might either develop this material with either a process or a techniques focus. If the orientation of the course is towards processes, then Chapters 3, 4 and 5 which cover elicitation, validation and requirements management might be covered in addition to the introductory material. If the course is more concerned with advanced techniques for requirements engineering, then Chapters 7 and 9 which are concerned with viewpoint-oriented approaches might be covered.

3. A full two-semester course in requirements engineering could make use of all the chapters in the book. After an introduction and process overview (Chapters 1 and 2), elicitation and analysis (Chapter 3) might

be covered along with structure and viewpoint-oriented approaches (Chapters 6 and 7). This would lead naturally to a discussion of requirements validation (Chapter 4) and non-functional requirements (Chapter 8). Finally, requirements management (Chapter 5) may be discussed along with a detailed case study (Chapters 9 and 10).

Software and systems engineers in industry may also find the book useful if they are new to requirements engineering. Experienced requirements engineers may find the description of some techniques useful, particularly if the book is read in conjunction with its companion text *Requirements Engineering: A Good Practice Guide* (Ian Sommerville and Pete Sawyer, Wiley, 1997).

There is very little overlap between the material here and *Requirements Engineering: A Good Practice Guide*. That book is also concerned with requirements engineering processes but it is aimed specifically at practitioners and managers who are already involved in requirements engineering. It assumes that readers already have an understanding of the problems of requirements engineering and requirements process improvement. That book proposes a set of specific guidelines for requirements engineering process improvement, information on formal methods for safety-critical systems specification and an alternative viewpoint-oriented approach to that presented here. Although designed for practising requirements engineers, students who have worked through this book may find the practical advice on process improvement useful.

Finally, we would like to thank our families for their support while this book was being written, and the members of the EDDIS consortium for their permission to use the case study material in Chapter 10.

Gerald Kotonya,
Ian Sommerville

April 1998

PART ONE

The Requirements Engineering Process

◆ **Summary**

The goal of this part of the book is to introduce the processes involved in eliciting, analysing, validating and managing requirements for complex systems. The focus of this part is on 'what' is involved in requirements engineering, in contrast to Part Two, which focuses on 'how' specific techniques may be applied during these processes. Chapter 2 introduces processes in general and discusses models of the overall requirements engineering process. Chapter 3 covers requirements and associated requirements analysis, and Chapter 4 discusses the validation of requirements after an initial version of the requirements document has been issued. Finally, Chapter 5 discusses the critically important process of managing requirements which are evolving as the customer's business and priorities change.

▌ Introduction

◆ **Contents**

1.1 FAQs about requirements

1.2 Systems engineering

1.3 The requirements document

◆ **Summary**

This chapter introduces the notions of system requirements and requirements engineering. We give some examples of requirements and answer
some 'frequently asked questions' about requirements and the requirements
engineering process. Requirements engineering is discussed in the context of
a broader systems engineering process concerned with developing systems
(software, hardware, processes) as a whole. Finally, we discuss the organisation of the requirements document, the definitive statement of the system
requirements. We briefly describe standards in this area and present brief
guidelines for writing clear and concise requirements.

◆

The development of computer-based systems has been plagued with problems
since the 1960s. Too many systems have been delivered late and over budget.
They don't do what users really want and they are often never used to their
full effectiveness by the people who have paid for them. There is rarely a single
reason (or a single solution) for these problems but we know that a major
contributory factor is difficulties with the system requirements.

   As the name implies, system requirements define what the system is
required to do and the circumstances under which it is required to operate.

In other words, the requirements define the services that the system should provide and they set out constraints on the system's operation. Here are some examples of requirements for a library system.

1. The system shall maintain records of all library materials including books, serials, newspapers and magazines, video and audio tapes, reports, collections of transparencies, computer disks and CD-ROMs.

2. The system shall allow users to search for an item by title, author, or ISBN.

3. The system's user interface shall be implemented using a World-Wide-Web browser.

4. The system shall support at least 20 transactions per second.

5. The system facilities which are available to public users shall be demonstrable in 10 minutes or less.

These requirements are written in a typical way and, of course, they need to be supplemented with more detailed information in a complete specification of the system. You can see from these examples that requirements are of different types.

1. Very general requirements, such as 1 above, which set out in broad terms what the system should do.

2. Functional requirements, such as 2, which define part of the system's functionality.

3. Implementation requirements, such as 3, which state how the system must be implemented.

4. Performance requirements, such as 4, which specify a minimum acceptable performance for the system.

5. Usability requirements, such as 5, which specify the maximum acceptable time to demonstrate the use of the system.

Because there are so many different types of requirement, it isn't possible to describe a standard way of writing requirements or to define the 'best' way to specify requirements. It depends on who is writing the requirements, who is likely to read the requirements, the general practices of the organisation developing the requirements and the application domain of the system.

As well as statements of what is required of the system, the description of the system requirements may include other information which must be incorporated in the implementation of the system but which isn't expressed in terms of system services or constraints. This information may include general information about the type of system which is being specified (domain information), information about standards which must be followed when the system is developed, information about other systems which interact with the system being specified and so on. We will see examples of these types of requirement later in the book.

As we have said, many systems engineering problems stem from problems with the system requirements. Common 'requirements' problems which arise are that:

1. the requirements don't reflect the real needs of the customer for the system

2. requirements are inconsistent and/or incomplete

3. it is expensive to make changes to requirements after they have been agreed

4. there are misunderstandings between customers, those developing the system requirements and software engineers developing or maintaining the system.

We can see an example of requirements incompleteness in the simple requirements for the library system. Look carefully at this requirement.

1. The system shall allow users to search for an item by title, author, or by ISBN.

This seems a sensible requirement for a library system but what if the 'item' that the user is searching for is a CD-ROM. It will certainly have a title but it may not have an author; it certainly won't have an ISBN (International Standard Book Number). This requirement has been written so that it only applies to books and not to other items in the library. If this anomaly was not discovered, the system implementors would either have to make their own decisions on what it meant for non-book items or would have to spend time clarifying the requirement with library staff.

The problems of writing requirements are universal and there will never be a complete solution to these problems. However, good requirements engineering practice, as described in this book, can reduce the number of problems and minimise their impact on the final system. These problems therefore underlie almost all of the chapters in the book and we will look at some of them again as we introduce particular requirements engineering techniques.

1.1 FAQs about requirements

Before you can start to understand requirements engineering, you need some basic information and definitions. We present this information in this section in the form of a frequently asked questions (FAQs) list. This style of presentation is increasingly used on the Internet to help people who are new to an area. In essence, what we have tried to do is to anticipate your questions and provide some answers to them. The questions and answers are summarised in Figure 1.1.

1.1.1 What are requirements?

Requirements are defined during the early stages of a system development as a specification of what should be implemented. They are descriptions of how the system should behave, application domain information, constraints on the system's operation, or specifications of a system property or attribute. Sometimes they are constraints on the development process of the system. Therefore a requirement might describe:

Figure 1.1
Requirements
FAQs.

Question	Answer
What are requirements?	A statement of a system service or constraint
What is requirements engineering?	The processes involved in developing system requirements.
How much does requirements engineering cost?	About 15% of system development costs
What is a requirements engineering process?	The structured set of activities involved in developing system requirements
What happens when the requirements are wrong?	Systems are late, unreliable and don't meet customers' expectations
Is there an ideal requirements engineering process?	No – processes must be tailored to organisational needs
What is a requirements document?	The formal statement of the system requirements
What are system stakeholders?	Anyone who is affected in some way by the system
What is the relationship between requirements and design?	Requirements and design are inter-leaved. They should, ideally, be separate processes but in practice this is impossible
What is requirements management?	The processes involved in managing changes to requirements

1. a user-level facility (e.g. 'the word processor must include a spell checking and correction command')

2. a very general system property (e.g. 'the system must ensure that personal information is never made available without authorisation')

3. a specific constraint on the system (e.g. 'the sensor must be polled 10 times per second')

4. how to carry out some computation (e.g. 'the overall mark is computed by adding the student examination, project and coursework marks based on the following formula 'total_mark = exam_mark + 2 * project_mark + 2/3 * coursework_mark')

5. a constraint on the development of the system (e.g. 'the system must be developed using Ada').

Some people suggest that requirements should always be statements of what a system should do rather than a statement of how it should do it. This is an attractive idea but it is too simplistic in practice:

1. The readers of a document are often practical engineers who can relate to implementation descriptions much better than they can understand very abstract problem statements. You must write requirements which are understandable to the likely readers of the document.

2. In almost all cases, the system being specified is only one of several systems in an environment. To be compatible with its environment, and to conform to standards and with organisational concerns, you may have to specify implementation policies which constrain the options of the system designers.

3. The specifiers of the system are often experts in the application domain where the system is to be used. The requirements may be descriptions of how to carry out a computation using application domain data.

Therefore, requirements invariably contain a mixture of problem informtion, statements of system behaviour and properties and design and manufacturing constraints. This can cause difficulties because the design and manufacturing constraints may clash with other requirements. Nevertheless, it is a reality of requirements engineering so the requirements engineering process must include activities to find and resolve the resulting problems.

1.1.2 What is requirements engineering?

Requirements engineering is a relatively new term which has been invented to cover all of the activities involved in discovering, documenting, and maintaining a set of requirements for a computer-based system. The use of the term 'engineering' implies that systematic and repeatable techniques should be used to ensure that system requirements are complete, consistent, relevant, etc. Requirements engineering has much in common with 'systems analysis' – the analysis and specification of business systems. In principle, systems analysis should focus on the business rather than the system but, like requirements engineering, it is often concerned with both business and system concerns.

In this book, we are mostly concerned with the requirements engineering process for software systems. However, the processes and methods used for developing and analysing software requirements are often more generally applicable to systems requirements i.e., requirements which apply to the system as a whole and not just to the software components of the system.

1.1.3 How much does requirements engineering cost?

This depends on the type and size of system being developed and exactly what activities are included under the heading of requirements engineering. In some cases, the system requirements are not developed in detail; in others, a formal specification may be produced. Clearly, the costs of these will differ significantly.

The surveys which have been carried out so far suggest that, for large hardware/software systems, about 15% of the total budget is taken up by requirements engineering activities. This excludes the costs of detailed system specification. For smaller systems which are mostly software, the requirements costs are usually less than this, around 10% of the total budget of the system.

1.1.4 What happens when the requirements are wrong?

There are a number of consequences which arise when the system requirements are wrong.

1. The system may be delivered late and cost more than originally expected.

2. The customer and end-users are not satisfied with the system. They may not use its facilities or may even decide to scrap it altogether.

3. The system may be unreliable in use, with regular system errors and crashes disrupting normal operation.

4. If the system continues in use, the costs of maintaining and evolving the system are usually very high.

The costs of fixing requirements errors are, typically, much greater than fixing errors which arise at later stages of the development process. Fixing requirements problems may require rework of the system design, implementation and testing. Consequently, the costs are high. It has been estimated that the cost of fixing a requirements error can be up to 100 times the cost of fixing a simple programming error.

1.1.5 What is a requirements engineering process?

A requirements engineering process is a structured set of activities which are followed to derive, validate and maintain a systems requirements document. Process activities include requirements elicitation, requirements analysis and negotiation and requirements validation. A complete process description should include what activities are carried out, the structuring or schedule of these activities, who is responsible for each activity, the inputs and outputs to/from the activity and the tools used to support requirements engineering.

Very few organisations have an explicitly-defined and standardised requirements engineering process. The people involved in the process are responsible for deciding what to do and when to do it, what information they need, what tools they should use, etc. However, we anticipate that this situation will change over the lifetime of this book and that organisations will pay more attention to defining and improving requirements engineering processes.

1.1.6 Is there an ideal requirements engineering process?

There is no single process which is right for all organisations. Each organisation must develop its own process which is appropriate for the type of systems it develops, its organisational culture, and the level of experience and ability of the people involved in requirements engineering. There are many possible ways to organise requirements engineering processes and they don't transfer well from one organisation to another. To define a good requirements engineering process, organisations need to involve people who are actually involved in requirements engineering. They may have to ask for outside help from consultants as they can take a more objective perspective than those involved in the process.

Most of the standards which have been developed for requirements engineering are concerned with process outputs such as the structure of requirements documents. Within general software engineering standards such as the US DoD standard 2167A, there is some mention of requirements engineering activities but nothing like a standard process description.

1.1.7   What is a requirements document?

The requirements document is an official statement of the system requirements for customers, end-users and software developers. Depending on the
organisation, the requirements document may have different names such as
the 'functional specification', 'the requirements definition', 'the software
requirements specification (SRS)', etc. We use the term 'requirements document' in this book to cover all of these. The organisation of requirements
documents is discussed in section 1.3.

1.1.8   What are stakeholders?

System stakeholders are people or organisations who will be affected by the
system and who have a direct or indirect influence on the system requirements.
They include end-users of the system, managers and others involved in the
organisational processes influenced by the system, engineers responsible for
the system development and maintenance, customers of the organisation who
will use the system to provide some services, external bodies such as regulators
or certification authorities, etc.

For example, say an automated railway signalling system is to be developed. Possible stakeholders are:

◆   train company operators responsible for running the signalling system
◆   train crew
◆   railway managers
◆   passengers
◆   equipment installation and maintenance engineers
◆   safety certification authorities

You need to identify the important stakeholders in a system and to discover
their requirements. If you don't do so, you may find that they insist on
changes during the system development or after it has been delivered for use.

1.1.9   What is the relationship between requirements
and design?

There is usually a complex relationship between requirements and design.
Some people (Jackson, 1995) suggest that they are quite separate activities;
requirements are mostly concerned with the problem to be solved; design is
concerned with the solution to the problem. That is, requirements engineering
is about what has to be done; design is about how it should be done.

We do not agree with this separation. It would be nice if it were true and
would certainly make life easier for both the specifiers and the designers of
systems. However, in reality, requirements engineering and design are inter-
laced activities. There are a number of reasons for this.

1. Systems are always installed in some environment and, nowadays, there are always other systems in that environment. These other systems usually constrain the design of the system. For example, a design constraint for a new system may be that the system to be developed must obtain its information from an existing database. This has already been designed and parts of its design specification will usually be included in the requirements document.

2. For large systems, some architectural design is necessary to identify subsystems and their relationships. Requirements for these subsystems may then be specified. Identifying the subsystems means that the requirements engineering process for each subsystem can go on in parallel.

3. For reasons of budget, schedule or quality, an organisation may wish to reuse some or all of existing software systems in the implementation of a new system. This constrains both the system requirements and the design.

4. If a system has to be approved by an external regulator (e.g. systems in civil aircraft), it may be necessary to use a standard 'certified' design which has been tested in other systems.

1.1.10   What is requirements management?

Requirements management is the process of managing changes to the system requirements. Requirements for a system always change to reflect the changing needs of system stakeholders, changes in the environment in which the system is to be installed, changes in the business which plans to install the system, changes in laws and regulations, etc. These changes have to be managed to ensure that they make economic sense and contribute to the business needs of the organisation buying the system. The technical feasibility of change proposals must be assessed and it must be possible to make the changes within budget and schedule.

The principal requirements management activities are change control and change impact assessment. Change control is concerned with establishing and executing a formal procedure for collecting, verifying and assessing changes; change impact assessment is concerned with assessing how proposed changes affect the system as a whole. Where changes apply to specific requirements, it is important to check which other requirements are likely to be affected by the change. Requirements management requires traceability information to be recorded, i.e. specific links between requirements, the sources of requirements and the system design. We discuss requirements management in more detail in Chapter 5.

1.2 Systems engineering

The focus of this book is software requirements engineering but, for many types of system, it is impossible to separate the requirements for the software from broader requirements for the system as a whole. As well as software, the system may include computer hardware, other types of hardware device which are interfaced to the computer and the operational processes which are used when the system is installed in some working environment.

Computer-based systems fall into two broad types.

1. User-configured systems where a purchaser puts together a system from existing software products. This book is being written on such a system where products such as a word processor, a drawing package and a file exchange program are installed on a Macintosh to create a 'writing system'. The vast majority of personal computer systems are of this type. 'Systems engineering' is the responsibility of the buyer of the software which is installed on a general-purpose computer. Normally, there are no explicit system requirements. The software requirements are created by the companies which develop the different software products from customer requests and from their perception of what is marketable.

2. Custom or bespoke systems where a customer produces a set of requirements for a hardware/software system and a contractor develops and delivers that system. The customer and the contractor may be different divisions within the same organisation or may be separate companies. The system requirements describe services to be provided by the system as whole and, as part of the systems engineering process, the specific requirements for the software in the system are derived. The discussion of systems engineering in this section is concerned with this type of system.

Custom systems range in size from very small embedded systems in consumer devices such as microwave ovens, to gigantic command and control systems such as military messaging systems. These large systems may involve a network of thousands of computers located all over the world.

There are three important classes of system which are developed specially for customers.

1. **Information systems**
    These are systems which are primarily concerned with processing information which is held in some kind of database. They are usually implemented using standard computer hardware (e.g. mainframe computers, workstations, PCs) and are built on top of commercial

operating systems. For these systems, requirements engineering is primarily software requirements engineering.

2. **Embedded systems**
    These are systems where software is used as a controller in some broader hardware system. They range from simple systems (e.g. in a CD player) to very complex control systems (e.g. in a chemical plant). They often rely on special-purpose hardware and operating systems. Requirements engineering for these systems involves both hardware and software requirements engineering.

3. **Command and control systems**
    These are, essentially, a combination of information systems and embedded systems where special-purpose computers provide information which is collected and stored in a data base and then used to help people make decisions. These systems usually involve a mix of different types of computer which are networked in some way. Within the whole system, there may be several embedded systems and information systems. The largest and most complex systems such as air traffic control systems, railway signalling systems, military communication systems, etc. are usually of this type. Requirements engineering for these systems includes hardware and software specification and a specification of the operational procedures and processes.

A characteristic of all systems is that they have a set of emergent properties. Emergent properties are properties of the system as a whole and they only emerge once all of the individual sub-systems have been integrated. Examples of emergent properties for computer-based systems are reliability, maintainability, performance, usability, security, etc. The system requirements are often concerned with these emergent properties and are therefore not solely concerned with the system's functionality.

Although the processes used to develop systems vary dramatically according to the type and size of system being developed and the organisations developing the system, there are broad activities which are common to all types of system engineering. Figure 1.2 shows one possible generic systems engineering process.

Figure 1.2 shows the process after a decision has been made to acquire a system. Before that, there are activities which are concerned with establishing the business need for the system, assessing the feasibility of developing the system, and setting the budget for the system development. The specific activities shown in Figure 1.2 are described in Figure 1.3.

We can see from Figure 1.2 and Figure 1.3 that the complete requirements engineering process spans several activities from the initial statement of system requirements through to the more detailed development of specific

Figure 1.2
The systems
engineering
process.

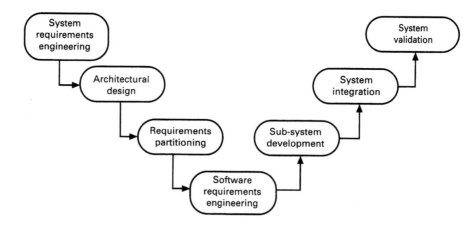

Activity	Description
System requirements engineering	The requirements for the system as a whole are established. These will usually be expressed in a fairly high-level fashion and written in natural language. Some detailed constraints (such as compatibility constraints) may be included if these are critical for the success of the system.
Architectural design	The system is decomposed into a set of independent sub-systems.
Requirements partitioning	The requirements are partitioned to these sub-systems. At this stage, decisions may be made about whether requirements should be hardware or software requirements.
Software requirements engineering	The high-level software requirements are decomposed into a more detailed set of requirements for the software components of the system.
Sub-system development	The hardware and the software subsystems are designed and implemented in parallel.
System integration	The hardware and software subsystems are put together to complete the system.
System validation	The system is validated against its requirements.

Figure 1.3
Systems
engineering
process
activities.

software requirements. It actually includes some initial design activity where the overall structure (architecture) of the system is defined. This has to be carried out at this stage to help structure the system requirements and to allow the requirements for the different sub-systems to be developed in parallel.

1.3 The requirements document

The system and software requirements are usually documented in a formal document which is used to communicate the requirements to customers, system and software engineers and managers of the systems engineering process. As we have said, there is no standard name for this document. In different organisations, this document may have different names such as the requirements document, the functional specification, the system requirements specification, etc.

The requirements document describes the following.

1. The services and functions which the system should provide.

2. The constraints under which the system must operate.

3. Overall properties of the system, i.e. constraints on the system's emergent properties.

4. Definitions of other systems which the system must integrate with.

5. Information about the application domain of the system, e.g. how to carry out particular types of computation.

6. Constraints on the process used to develop the system.

For systems which are primarily software systems, the requirements document may include a description of the hardware on which the system is to run. The document should always include an introductory chapter which provides an overview of the system and the business need that it is intended to support and a glossary which defines the technical terms used in the document. The glossary is particularly important as different system stakeholders from different backgrounds will read the requirements document and use it in different ways (see Figure 1.4). The glossary is essential to ensure a common understanding of the terms used in the requirements document.

There are many different ways to structure requirements documents, depending on the type of system which is being developed, the level of detail included in the requirements, organisational practice and the budget and schedule for the requirements engineering process. To ensure that all essential information is included, organisations may define their own standard for requirements documents which sets out the sections which must be included.

A number of different large organisations such as the US Department of Defense and the IEEE have defined standards for requirements documents. Probably the most accessible of these standards is the IEEE/ANSI 830–1993 standard (IEEE, 1993) which suggests the following structure for requirements documents.

1. **Introduction**
    1.1 Purpose of the requirements document
    1.2 Scope of the product
    1.3 Definitions, acronyms and abbreviations
    1.4 References
    1.5 Overview of the remainder of the document

2. **General description**
    2.1 Product perspective
    2.2 Product functions
    2.3 User characteristics
    2.4 General constraints
    2.5 Assumptions and dependencies

Figure 1.4
Users of a
requirements
document.

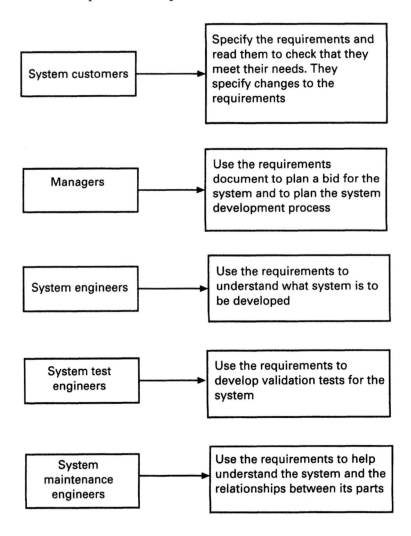

3. **Specific requirements**
   covering functional, non-functional and interface requirements. These should document external interfaces, functionality, performance requirements, logical database requirements, design constraints, system attributes and quality characteristics.

4. **Appendices**

5. **Index**

Although the IEEE standard is not ideal, it contains a great deal of good advice on how to write requirements and how to avoid problems. It is therefore a good starting point for defining a structure for a requirements document. The first two parts in the standard are introductory chapters which set out the background for the system and describe it in general terms. The third section is the major section of the document, namely the detailed specification of the requirements. The standard recognises that this varies considerably depending on the type of system which is being specified and it suggests alternative ways to organise specific requirements.

A requirements document standard must allow for differences between systems. It should be possible to omit parts of the document and to add new sections if necessary. Part of the document standard should therefore be an introductory page which explains allowed variances from the defined standard.

To allow for different types of document, a requirements document standard may include a list of stable and variant parts. Stable parts are those chapters (such as an introduction and a glossary) which should appear in all requirements documents. Variant parts are those chapters which may but need not be included and whose contents may vary depending on the system being specified.

Here is an example of a possible organisational standard for requirements documents which is based on the IEEE standard. Notice that this specifies that the third part of the IEEE standard should be instantiated as several chapters and optional appendices should be included with detailed information. Assume that the organisation is involved in the production of computer-controlled scientific instruments.

Organisation XYZ. Standard Structure for Requirements Documents

1. **Preface**
   This should define the expected readership of the document and describe its version history including a rationale for the creation of a new version and a summary of the changes made in each version.

2. **Introduction**
    This should define the product in which the software is embedded, its expected usage and present and overview of the functionality of the control software.

3. **Glossary**
    This should define all technical terms and abbreviations used in the document.

4. **General user requirements**
    This should define the system requirements from the perspective of the user of the system. These should be presented using a mixture of natural language and diagrams.

5. **System architecture**
    This chapter should present a high-level overview of the anticipated system architecture showing the distribution of functions across system modules. Architectural components which are to be reused should be highlighted.

6. **Hardware specification**
    This is an optional chapter specifying the hardware that the software is expected to control. It may be omitted if the standard instrument platform is used.

7. **Detailed software specification**
    This is a detailed description of the functionality expected of the software of the system. Where appropriate, it may include details of specific algorithms which should be used for computation. If a prototyping approach is to be used for development on the standard instrument platform, this chapter may be omitted.

8. **Reliability and performance requirements**
    This chapter should describe the reliability and performance requirements which are expected of the system. These should be related to the statement of user requirements in Chapter 4.

9. The following appendices may be included where appropriate:
    hardware interface specification
    software components which must be reused in the system implementation
    data structure specification
    data-flow models of the software system
    detailed object models of the software system

10. **Index**

1.3.1 Writing requirements

In most organisations, system requirements are written as paragraphs of natural language (English, French, Japanese, etc.), supplemented by diagrams and equations. Natural language is the only notation that we have which is generally understandable by all potential readers of the requirements for a system.

Here are some examples of natural language requirements which have been taken from different requirements documents.

1. The user will be offered an initial set of databases to search. The set of databases which can be searched will be determined by the PERMISSION_VECTOR of the account to which the user has logged in (from a requirements document for a library system).

2. The database shall support the generation and control of configuration objects; that is, objects which are themselves groupings of other objects in the database. The configuration control facilities shall allow access to the objects in a version group by the use of an incomplete name (from a requirements document for a programming support environment).

3. The inverse transition S1→S2 takes place when the front of the train has just crossed an exit towards a non-equipped zone (from the requirements document for a train protection system).

These requirements have been included to illustrate that natural language can be used in almost all circumstances for requirements description. In principle, they are universally understandable but, in practice, the meaning of requirements is not always obvious.

Natural language can be used to describe requirements clearly. All too often, however, natural language requirements are difficult to understand. Natural language requirements can be ambiguous, surprisingly opaque and is often misunderstood. Common problems are that:

1. the requirements are written using complex conditional clauses (if A then if B then if C . . .) which are confusing

2. terminology is used in a sloppy and inconsistent way

3. The writers of the requirement assume that the reader has specific knowledge of the domain or the system and they leave essential information out of the requirements document.

These problems make it difficult to check the set of requirements for errors and omissions. Different interpretations of the requirements may lead to contractual disagreements between the customer and the system engineering contractor.

To address these difficulties, some organisations have developed special-purpose notations for writing requirements (Alford, 1985) and the natural requirements may be supplemented by system models which may either be graphical models or mathematical models (Rumbaugh et al., 1991; Delisle and Garlan, 1990). However, special-purpose notations have never become widely accepted and system models are often too low-level to communicate essential information to people who need not analyse the requirements in detail. Therefore, there is always a need for well-written, natural language statements of requirements.

Irrespective of the level of detail in a requirements description, there are three essential things you should bear in mind when writing requirements.

1. Requirements are read more often than they are written. Investing effort in writing requirements which are easy to read and understand is almost always cost-effective.

2. Readers of requirements come from diverse backgrounds. If you are a requirements writer, you should not assume that readers have the same background and knowledge as you.

3. Writing clearly and concisely is not easy. If you don't allow sufficient time for requirements descriptions to be drafted, reviewed and improved, you will inevitably end up with poorly written specifications.

Different organisations write requirements at different levels of abstraction from deliberately vague product specifications to detailed and precise descriptions of all aspects of a system. You must decide for yourself on the level of detail that you need. This depends on the type of requirements (stakeholder, system or process requirements), customer expectations, your organisational procedures, and external standards or regulations which you may have to follow.

Detailed guidelines for using natural language for writing requirements are given by Sommerville and Sawyer (1997). These guidelines are summarised in Figure 1.5.

Guideline	Description
Define standard templates for describing requirements	You should define a set of standard format for different types of requirements and always express requirements using that format. This makes is less likely that important information will be missed out and makes it easier for the reader to understand the different parts of the requirement
Use language simply, consistently and concisely	Don't write requirements using convoluted language but follow good writing practice such as using short sentences and paragraphs, using lists and tables and avoiding jargon wherever possible.
Use diagrams appropriately	You should not develop complex diagrams but should use diagrams to present broad overviews and to show relationships between entities.
Supplement natural language with other descriptions of requirements	Don't try to write everything in natural language. If readers of the requirements document are likely to be familiar with other types of notation (e.g. equations), you should not hesitate to use these.
Specify requirements quantitatively	Wherever possible, you should specify your requirements quantitatively. This is often possible when you are specifying the properties of a system such as reliability, usability or performance.

Figure 1.5
Guidelines for writing requirements.

◆ Key Points

◆ The requirements for a system set out the services that the system should provide, define constraints on the system and the process of developing the system and provide domain information to system developers.

◆ Problems with requirements result in late delivery of systems, customer dissatisfaction and requests for changes after the system goes into service.

◆ The requirements engineering process is the structured set of activities concerned with eliciting, analysing and documenting the system requirements. The output of this process is the system requirements document.

◆ Systems engineering is concerned with the development of systems as a whole including hardware, software and operational processes. This book is mostly concerned with requirements engineering for custom systems, i.e. systems which are specified and designed to support specific work practices.

◆ The requirements document is the definitive specification of system requirements for customers, engineers and managers of the development process.

◆ The requirements document should always include an overview of the system, a glossary, a statement of the functional requirements and the operational constraints on the system.

◆ Exercises

1.1 Explain the problems which might arise if the following requirements were included in a requirements document for a library system.

The system shall provide an easy-to-use graphical interface based on MS Windows 95. Accredited users should have privileged access to the cataloguing facilities of the system.

The system software shall be implemented using separate modules for cataloging, user access and archiving.

1.2 Why is it sometimes necessary for requirements documents to include information about the design of a system?

1.3 List the possible stakeholders for a library cataloguing system.

1.4 Using your knowledge of software engineering processes, compare these with the systems engineering process described in section 1.2. What do you think are the key differences between systems engineering and software engineering processes?

1.5 Systems integration is an important systems engineering activity. Suggest the problems which might arise when subsystems from different suppliers are integrated.

1.6 Using examples from your own experience, explain why communication problems arise when people use technical terminology.

1.7 Suggest the uses which each of the stakeholders that you have identified in 1.3 might make of a requirements document for a library system.

1.8 Suggest how the following requirements might be rewritten in a quantitative way. You may use any metrics you like to express the requirements.

The library system shall be easy-to-use.

The library system shall provide reliable service to all classes of user.

The library system shall provide a rapid response to all user requests for book information.

◆ References

Alford, M. W. (1985). SREM at the Age of Eight: The Distributed Computing Design System. *IEEE Computer* **18**(4): 36–46.

Delisle, N., and Garlan, D. (1990). A Formal Specification of an Oscilloscope. *IEEE Software* **7** (5): 29–36.

IEEE (1993). IEEE Recommended Practice for Software Requirements Specifications. *Software Requirements Engineering*. Eds R. H. Thayer and M. Dorfman. Los Alamitos, California, IEEE Computer Society Press.

Jackson, M. A. (1995). *Requirements and Specifications*. Wokingham: Addison Wesley.

Rumbaugh, J., Blaha, M., et al. (1991). *Object-oriented Modeling and Design*. Englewood Cliffs, New Jersey: Prentice-Hall.

Sommerville, I., and Sawyer, P. (1997). *Requirements Engineering: A Good Practice Guide*. Chichester: John Wiley and Sons.

◆ Further reading

There are many books on requirements engineering written from different perspectives and with different emphases. For readers getting started in this field, we particularly recommend the following.

Software Requirements: Objects, Functions and States (A. Davis, Prentice-Hall, 1993). This is probably the best known book in this area. Its orientation is towards the use of structured methods for requirements engineering. It is quite long (more than 500 pages) and of most interest to practitioners who already have well-developed requirements engineering practices. It is very good on system modelling but weak on areas such as requirements validation and management.

Software Requirements Engineering (2nd edition) (R. H. Thayer and M. Dorfman, IEEE Computer Society Press, 1997). An excellent tutorial volume of research papers in requirements engineering.

For requirements engineering practitioners in industry, we recommend the following.

Standards, Guidelines and Examples on System and Software Requirements Engineering (M. Dorfman and R. H. Thayer, IEEE Computer Society Press, 1990). This is a comprehensive set of standards which are relevant to requirements engineering.

For readers who are primarily interested in requirements engineering research, we recommend.

System Requirements Engineering (P. Loucopoulos and V. Karakostas, McGraw-Hill, 1995). A short book which presents an overview of requirements engineering intended for students taking courses in this topic. It mostly describes problems and current research in this area rather than practical requirements engineering solutions.

2 Requirements Engineering Processes

◆ **Contents**

◆ **Summary**

This chapter is a general introduction to requirements engineering processes. It sets the scene for the more detailed process descriptions in the following three chapters. We introduce the general notion of processes, describe the inputs and outputs to requirements engineering processes and explain why these processes often vary from one organisation to another. Different approaches to modelling requirements engineering processes are suggested and we explain why human, social and organisational factors are important influences on these processes. We briefly describe tool support for requirements engineering then go on to cover more general process improvement issues. Finally, we introduce the notion of requirements engineering process maturity and explain how this can be used as the basis of an improvement model for requirements engineering processes.

A process is an organised set of activities which transforms inputs to outputs. Processes are part of all aspects of life and are an essential mechanism for coping with complexity in the world. Descriptions of processes are very important because they allow knowledge to be reused. Once someone has worked out how to solve a problem, they can document they way in which that solution was derived as a process. This then helps other people faced with similar problems to get started on their own solutions.

Processes are fundamental to human activities and we often communicate details of these activities by describing the associated processes.

1. An instruction manual for a kitchen dishwasher describes the process of using that machine to clean dishes. The input to this process is a pile of dirty dishes and a dishwasher; the output is a dishwasher full of clean dishes.

2. A cookery book describes a set of processes to prepare and cook various different types of meal. The inputs to these processes are raw ingredients; the outputs are cooked meals.

3. A procedures manual in a bank describes the ways in which different banking processes such as agreeing a personal loan, correcting errors, etc. should be carried out. The inputs and outputs here are less tangible. The input, perhaps, is a customer request for some service plus various customer details; the output is the delivered service although it may be difficult to separate this from the process itself.

4. A quality manual for software development describes the processes which should be used to assure the quality of the software. It may include descriptions of standards which are the basis for the quality checking. The inputs here are documents and programs to be checked and the quality standards which must be followed; the outputs are reports of the quality assurance activities.

In some cases, processes are defined at a very fine level of detail and the steps in the process must be carried out exactly as described. However, this usually only applies to very simple processes such as making a telephone call from a payphone (lift receiver, insert coins or card, dial number). For more complex processes, the description is usually less detailed and it is up to the person or team who are executing the process to carry it out (enact the process) in their own environment.

Different people usually enact the process in different ways. Sometimes the same person will enact the same process in different ways at different times. The reason for this is that enacting the different activities in the process depends on the background of the people involved and the particular circumstances in which the process is enacted. For example:

1. People with experience may change the order of stages in a process or combine stages because they understand the consequences of what they

are doing. However, inexperienced people follow the stages as described because they don't have this background knowledge.

2.   Different process support software may be available in different environments so the processes in these environments may be adapted to suit the available software.

3.   Other processes or activities in an environment may interact with a process and affect the way it is enacted. If the people who are enacting the process are working to a tight deadline, they may take various short-cuts to reduce the time required to complete the process.

4.   The process description may be incorrect or inappropriate for a particular situation, some inputs may be missing or incomplete, or different outputs from those assumed by the process description may be required.

Design processes are processes which involve creativity, interactions between a wide range of different people, engineering judgement and background knowledge and experience. Generally, the inputs to these processes are not precisely defined. There are many possible outputs which may result to satisfy these inputs. Unlike some kinds of manufacturing process, this type of process cannot be automated nor can it be specified in detail. Different people tackle intellectual tasks in different ways and they adapt the process to suit their own way of thinking.

Examples of design processes are as follows.

1.   The process of writing this book: the inputs are background knowledge and experience plus other books and papers, and the output is the book that you are reading.

2.   The process of organising a conference: the inputs are background experience plus details of the type of conference, the expected size, details of local hotels, etc. and the outputs are a conference programme, hotel reservations for delegates and so on.

3.   The process of designing a processor chip: the inputs are background knowledge and experience, details of current processors (compatibility is essential), details of fabrication technology, and the outputs are a processor design specification, a system simulator, etc.

The requirements engineering process is a design process with inputs and outputs as shown in Figure 2.1.

Figure 2.1
Inputs and
outputs of the
requirements
engineering
process.

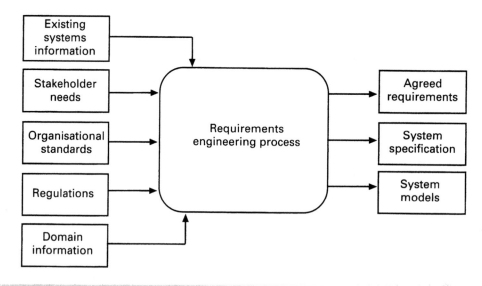

Input or output	Type	Description
Existing system information	Input	Information about the functionality of systems to be replaced or other systems which interact with the system being specified
Stakeholder needs	Input	Descriptions of what system stakeholders need from the system to support their work
Organisational standards	Input	Standards used in an organisation regarding system development practice, quality management, etc.
Regulations	Input	External regulations such as health and safety regulations which apply to the system.
Domain information	Input	General information about the application domain of the system
Agreed requirements	Output	A description of the system requirements which is understandable by stakeholders and which has been agreed by them
System specification	Output	This is a more detailed specification of the system functionality which may be produced in some cases
System models	Output	A set of models such as a data-flow model, an object model, a process model, etc. which describes the system from different perspectives

Figure 2.2
Input/output
description.

Figure 2.2 expands on Figure 2.1 by providing more detail of the inputs and outputs of the requirements engineering process. Although the requirements engineering process inevitably varies from one organisation to another and may even vary within the same organisation, the inputs and outputs are similar in most cases.

To make this more concrete, let us look at some examples of the different types of information which may be inputs to the requirements engineering process. These have been taken from a library information system (LIS).

1. **Existing system information**
    Assume that the system has to interface with a bar code reader system which has already been installed and which generates a queue of bar codes for processing and associated transaction requests. An example of a requirement from this system might be:

    > The LIS shall poll the bar code reader system and process all of the transaction requests every two seconds.

2. **Stakeholder needs**
    Assume that the stakeholder is a visitor to the library who has no previous experience of using the system. An example of a stakeholder need might be:

    > The system should provide a help facility which will explain the facilities of the system to new users. This help facility should be accessible from all user interface screens.

3. **Organisational standards**
    Assume that the library uses a hardware platform for all of its systems. A requirement from this might be:

    > The system shall run on a Sun server running the Solaris 2.0 operating system.

4. **Regulations**
    Regulations such as health and safety regulations are unlikely to have much impact on this type of system. However, data protection laws do apply to it. A requirement for data protection might be:

    > The system shall include a facility to print all of the personal information which is maintained for a library user.

5. **Domain information**
    This is general information which is applicable to all or most library systems. An example of a domain requirement might be:

    > Books are uniquely identified by an International Standard Book Number which is a 10 digit identifier

Examples of the outputs of the process, namely requirements, specifications and system models, are given in later chapters of the book.

The requirements engineering process itself is presented as a 'black box' in Figure 2.1. In practice, RE processes are very variable. They range from very unstructured processes which are almost solely reliant on the experience of the people involved, to systematic processes based on the application of some analysis methodology. These systematic processes are, in principle, more independent of the people involved, although they still require a good deal of individual judgement.

There are a number of factors which contribute to the variability of requirements engineering processes.

1. **Technical maturity**
   The technologies and methods used for requirements engineering vary from one organisation to another.

2. **Disciplinary involvement**
   The types of engineering and managerial disciplines involved in requirements engineering vary from one organisation to another.

3. **Organisational culture**
   The culture of an organisation has an important effect on all business processes and, as the culture varies, so too does the requirements engineering process.

4. **Application domain**
   Different types of application system need different types of requirements engineering process.

The variability of RE processes is often there for a very good reason, and it makes no sense to talk about 'ideal' requirements engineering processes or to define some (technically sound) process and impose it on an organisation. Rather, organisations should start with a generic RE process such as that documented in Figure 2.3 and instantiate this into a more detailed process which is appropriate to their own needs.

2.1 Process models

A process model is a simplified description of a process. It is usually produced from a particular perspective so that there may be several different models of the same process. No single model gives you a complete understanding of the process. When describing processes in detail it is usual to produce several different types of model giving different process information.

We have already seen an example of a process model in Chapter 1 where the systems engineering process was described. The model there was one of the most commonly used types of process model namely a coarse-grain activity model which shows the major activities involved in a particular process and their *approximate* sequencing. The sequencing is approximate because, in reality, processes overlap and are interleaved – they rarely follow a simple sequential pattern.

The types of process model which may be produced depend on the use which you anticipate for these models. You may want to produce a model to help explain how you have organised process information, you may want a model in order to understand and improve a process, you may be required to produce a model to satisfy some quality management standards, etc. Examples of different types of model which may describe processes and the areas where they may be used are:

1. **Coarse-grain activity models**

   Figure 2.3 is an example of such a model. It shows the principal requirements engineering process activities and their (approximate) sequencing. This type of model doesn't tell us how to enact a process but provides an overall picture of the process. This type of model is often constructed as a starting point for a process description with separate sections covering each box in the model.

   Coarse-grain activity models describe the context of the different activities in the process. They show other processes which provide inputs to and consume outputs from a specific process. We can see this in Figure 2.4, which is an example of a software life cycle model which shows the context of the software requirements engineering process in the whole of the software development process.

2. **Fine-grain activity models**

   These are more detailed models of a specific process. They may be used for understanding and improving existing processes. We do not include these detailed models in this chapter but later chapters of this section present more detailed models of specific requirements engineering activities within the general requirements engineering process.

3. **Role-action models**

   These are models which show the roles of different people involved in the process and the actions which they take. These models may be helpful for process understanding and automation.

4. **Entity-relation models**

   These models show the process inputs, outputs and intermediate results and the relationships between them. They may be used in a quality management system and to supplement models of process activities.

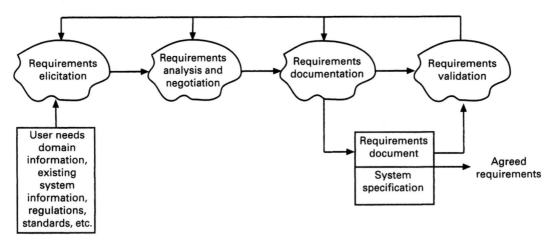

Figure 2.3
Coarse-grain
activity model
of the
requirements
engineering
process.

Different organisations tackle requirements engineering in radically different ways. An aerospace company which is specifying very complex hardware/software systems will not use the same requirements engineering process as a company which is building consumer products for personal computers. However, the differences between these processes usually emerge at the level of detailed process description. At an abstract level, most requirements engineering processes can be described by the coarse-grain activity model shown in Figure 2.3.

In Figure 2.3, we have shown requirements engineering activities using cloud icons. These have been chosen to indicate that there are no distinct boundaries between these activities. In practice, the activities are interleaved and there is a great deal of iteration and feedback from one activity to another.

The activities in the requirements engineering process are as follows.

1. **Requirements elicitation**
    The system requirements are discovered through consultation with stakeholders, from system documents, domain knowledge and market studies. Other names for this process are requirements acquisition or requirements discovery.

2. **Requirements analysis and negotiation**
    The requirements are analysed in detail and different stakeholders negotiate to decide on which requirements are to be accepted. This process is necessary because there are inevitably conflicts between the requirements from different sources, information may be incomplete or the requirements expressed may be incompatible with the budget available to develop the system. There is usually some flexibility in requirements and negotiation is necessary to decide on the set of agreed requirements for the system.

3. **Requirements documentation**

   The agreed requirements are documented at an appropriate level of detail. In general, there needs to be a requirements document which is understandable by all system stakeholders. As discussed in Chapter 1, this usually means that the requirements must be documented using natural language and diagrams. More detailed system documentation, such as system models (see Chapter 6), may also be produced.

4. **Requirements validation**

   There should be a careful check of the requirements for consistency and completeness. This process is intended to detect problems in the requirements document before it is used as a basis for the system development.

Requirements elicitation and analysis processes are discussed in Chapter 3, requirements modelling processes are covered in Chapter 6 and requirements validation processes are described in Chapter 4.

In parallel with all of the above processes is a process of requirements management which is concerned with managing changes to the requirements. Changing requirements are inevitable as business priorities change, as errors or omissions in the requirements are discovered and as new requirements emerge. Requirements management is intended to keep track of these changes and ensure that changes are made to the requirements document in a controlled way. The process of requirements management is discussed in Chapter 5.

The traditional 'waterfall' model for computer-based systems development (shown in Figure 2.4) suggests that software requirements engineering follows system requirements engineering and is itself followed by a software design process. This model was originally developed in the early 1970s as an overall activity model for software engineering. It is helpful to structure descriptions of the software process. There are many different variants of this model but, in all cases, the outputs from one process activity cascade to the following activity – hence the name 'waterfall model'.

If we view the waterfall model as an overall description of the activities in the software engineering process, it is a useful model. However, you must understand that the reality of software systems development is much more complex than is implied by this model. There are no neat phases with clearly defined boundaries between them; the different documents describing the software system are not necessarily completed before the next stage of the process begins; there is a lot of feedback between process activities. The software requirements change during the system design process, the design is modified during implementation as problems are discovered, testing reveals design and, sometimes, requirements errors, etc.

If we consider only the requirements engineering activities in the waterfall model, there is rarely a clear boundary between system and software

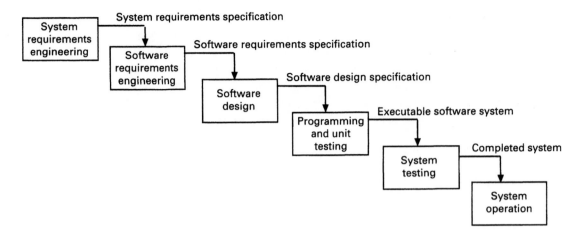

Figure 2.4 A waterfall model of the software process.

requirements engineering and design. Furthermore, requirements engineering is also influenced by a more general systems acquisition or procurement processes which are concerned with the commercial, legal and contractual issues of acquiring a system for an organisation. There are two-way information flows between these processes as they are enacted and the detailed activities in these processes change depending on this information (Figure 2.5).

Figures 2.4 and 2.5 illustrate that, even at very abstract levels, there are different ways to look at processes. Neither Figure 2.4 nor Figure 2.5 is an 'incorrect' model but each presents different possible ways in which the RE process interacts with other processes. The nature of models is that they hide information. When you try to understand process models you must realise that they will never present a complete (or unbiased) picture of whatever process is being described.

Figure 2.5 The context of the requirements engineering process.

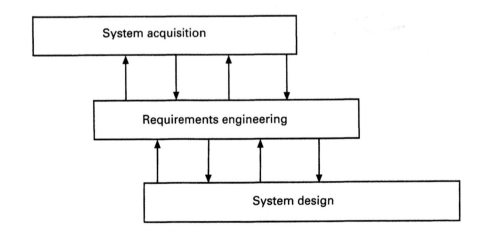

Activity models of processes such as Figure 2.3 and Figure 2.4 often show a sequence of phases with the implication that phases follow each other. They may show feedback from one phase to another and may suggest that phase boundaries are blurred as in Figure 2.3. As information is fed back from one activity to another, obviously the phase receiving the information must be re-entered in some way. An alternative way to present activity models which makes this repetition of activities more explicit is as a spiral model as shown in Figure 2.6.

Figure 2.6 shows that the different activities in requirements engineering are repeated until a decision is made that the requirements document should be accepted. If a draft of the requirements document is found to have problems, the elicitation, analysis, documentation, validation spiral is re-entered. This continues until an acceptable document is produced or until external factors such as schedule pressure or lack of resources mean that the requirements engineering process should end. A final requirements document should then be produced. Any further changes to the requirements are then part of the requirements management process.

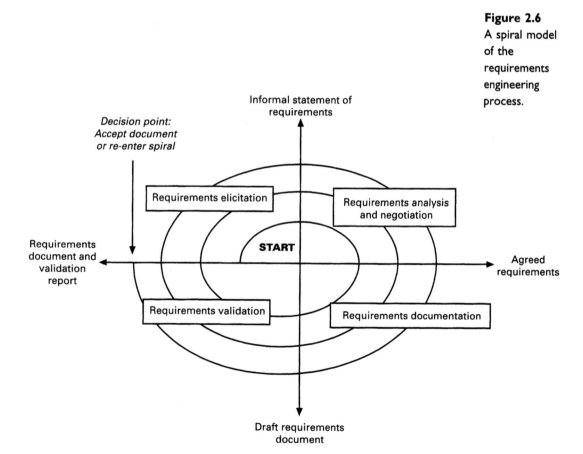

Figure 2.6
A spiral model of the requirements engineering process.

2.2 Actors in requirements engineering processes

The actors in a process are the people who are involved in carrying out that process. Normally actors are identified by their roles, e.g. project manager, purchasing director, system engineer rather than as individuals. It is often useful when modelling a process to identify the roles which would normally be associated with activities in that process.

A characteristic of the requirements engineering process is that it involves people who are primarily interested in the system as a way to help them solve particular problems or support particular activities, as well as people who are primarily concerned with solving the technical problems of developing the system. In addition, another group of people, such as health and safety regulators for a safety-critical system, maintenance engineers and managers, may be affected by the existence of the system. They may also participate in the requirements engineering process. As explained in Chapter 1, the generic term stakeholder is used to refer to all of these people.

Role-action diagrams are process models which show the actors associated with different process activities. These models are not particularly useful at the coarse-grain level but become more valuable when a process is described in more detail. They are particularly important when some automated process support or workflow system is available as they help the support system designer understand the information needs of the different people involved in the process.

To illustrate this type of diagram, consider Figure 2.7, which is a model of part of the requirements elicitation process where a prototype software system is being developed.

Figure 2.7
Role-action
diagram for
software
prototyping.

The roles which are identified in Figure 2.7 are described in Figure 2.8.

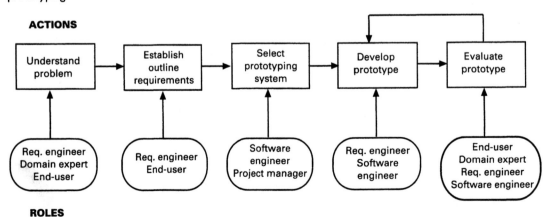

Role	Description
Domain expert	Responsible for providing information about the application domain and the specific problem in that domain which is to be solved
System end-user	Responsible for using the system after delivery
Requirements engineer	Responsible for eliciting and specifying the system requirements
Software engineer	Responsible for developing the prototype software system
Project manager	Responsible for planning and estimating the prototyping project

Figure 2.8
Roles in the prototyping process.

2.2.1 Human, social and organisational factors

Requirements engineering processes are dominated by human, social and organisational factors because they always involve a range of stakeholders from different backgrounds and with different individual and organisational goals. This is in contrast to other software processes, such as system testing, where the majority of the people involved in the processes have a common technical background and a shared goal of demonstrating that the system meets its specification.

Stakeholders in a system may or may not have a technical background. They may come from different engineering disciplines. They may be responsible for management and may be internal or external to an organisation. Examples of these different stakeholder types are:

◆ software engineers responsible for system development
◆ system end-users who will use the system after it has been delivered
◆ managers of system end-users who are responsible for their work
◆ external regulators who check that the system meets its legal requirements
◆ domain experts who give essential background information about the system application domain

Typically, these people come from different departments in an organisation and they are usually responsible for many other things apart from the requirements engineering of a system. They will not necessarily give priority to the requirements engineering process. It is likely that each group of stakeholders will have different goals. They will try to influence the requirements so that their goals are met without necessarily taking the goals of other stakeholders into account. Whether or not a stakeholder succeeds in influencing the requirements often depends on personality and status and not necessarily on reasoned argument.

To illustrate this, consider a simple situation where an end-user has a requirement for some system facility which is clearly difficult to implement. The software engineers responsible for the system may attempt to change that requirement because they think that it will cause them to overrun their agreed development schedule.

If the end-user is in a fairly junior position and is opposed by a senior software manager then it is likely that the software manager's views will prevail. However, if the end-user has managerial support and comes from a department which is politically influential in an organisation then their requirement will probably be accepted. Personalities are also important. If the end-user has an aggressive and persistent personality, the engineers may agree to accept their requirement simply to get rid of them. They may then, however, deliberately give this a low priority so that they can later demonstrate that this was an unreasonable requirement.

Within an organisation, different departments and individuals have differing degrees of political influence. This influence depends on the individuals involved, the priorities of the organisation and the success or otherwise of the departments and individuals in meeting their goals. People try to influence system requirements so that they can maintain or increase their own political influence in the organisation. For example, in a university, there is a constant tension between administration and academic departments. If a budget information system is planned, the administration is likely to propose requirements which give them more power. However, the academic departments are likely to oppose this and suggest system requirements which mean that they increase their responsibility for their own financial management.

2.3 Process support

The need to provide some automated support for software processes has been recognised since the 1980s. This led to the development of a large number of CASE (Computer-Aided Software Engineering) tools which supported various process activities such as software design, configuration management and testing. Some over-optimistic commentators predicted that this automated process support would lead to orders of magnitude improvement in software productivity. In fact, the scale of improvement was much less than predicted. Although CASE tools have an important role to play in supporting software processes, they rarely lead to very large increases in productivity or quality.

CASE tool support has tended to develop around those parts of the software process which are common to all organisations and which are relatively well-understood. Therefore, there are mature tools for programming support (editors, compilers, debuggers, etc.), for activities such as configuration management and project planning, for the support of structured methods based around functional and object-oriented design and for software testing. Activities which vary significantly between organisations or which are less mature, have poorer tool support.

As we have discussed, requirements engineering is variable and, until relatively recently, there were few products which were specifically designed to support this process. A number of large companies had developed their own tool support which was oriented towards their own RE process but there was no consensus as to the most effective way to support requirements engineering.

There are, essentially, two types of tools which are available to support the requirements engineering process.

1.   Modelling and validation tools support the development of system models which can be used to specify the system and the checking of these models for completeness and consistency. The tool package which supports this book includes this type of tool.

2.   Management tools help manage a database of requirements and support the management of changes to these requirements.

Modelling tools may be based around structured methods such as SADT (Ross, 1977; Schoman and Ross, 1977) or around specialised requirements modelling languages such as RSL (Alford, 1977; Alford, 1985). Basically, they are model editors and checkers. It is possible to create graphical or textual models of the requirements and to carry out some kinds of consistency checks. For example, the tools can check if names are duplicated, if there are unlinked entities in a model and if the same entity at different levels is always linked to the same things. However, as requirements engineering is a more variable process than software design, structured methods with guidelines and rules are less appropriate. Consequently, the range of model checks is fairly limited.

If a mathematical model of the requirements is developed using a notation such as VDM (Jones, 1980; Jones, 1986) or Z (Spivey, 1992), then more extensive validation checkers may be used. Mathematical requirements modelling has been proposed as a way of developing concise and unambiguous system specifications and there have been a number of successful experiments in formal specification (Hall, 1990; Hall, 1996; Delisle and Garlan, 1990). However, pragmatic requirements engineers have shown little enthusiasm for these methods. It seems likely that their use in future will be confined to the area of critical systems where safety, security and reliability considerations are paramount.

Validation tools based on formal models of requirements rely on the fact that the semantics of the notation is formally defined. They can analyse the description for mathematical inconsistencies which imply either mistakes in the formal specification or requirements errors.

Tools for requirements management have been developed because of the problems of managing the large amount of data which is collected during the requirements engineering process and the volatility of the requirements. As well as data storage and retrieval facilities, these tools provide a change management system which can record change proposals, link these to the requirements affected and keep track of the status of the changes. Requirements histories can be constructed, and some traceability support which allows the impact of changes to be assessed is usually provided.

At the time of writing, there are several commercial CASE products available for requirements management such as DOORS, RML, RDD-100 and Requisite Pro. Links to the suppliers of these tools are included in the book's web pages. Typically, these systems support interfaces to commercial word processor systems such a Microsoft Word and provide some support for converting natural language requirements into their proprietary database format.

Figure 2.9 illustrates some of the facilities which may be provided by a requirements management system. Round-edged rectangles represent system components; rectangular boxes represent data in the requirements management system.

Requirements management tools collect together the system requirements in a database or repository and provide a range of facilities to access the information about the requirements. These facilities may include:

1. a requirements browser so that readers of the requirements can browse
   · the database

2. a requirements query system so that tool users can retrieve specific requirements or requirements which are related in some way

Figure 2.9
A requirements management system.

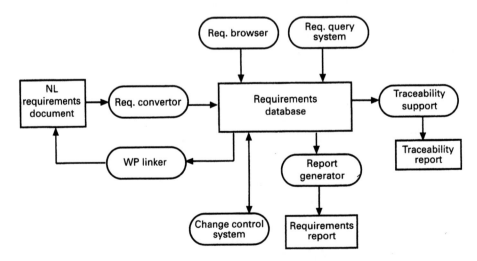

3.   a traceability support system which can be used to generate traceability information (see Chapter 5)

4.   a more general report generator which can generate various different types of reports about the requirements such as requirements from specific stakeholders, etc.

5.   a requirements converter and a word processor linker which can convert requirements in a word processor document into the requirements database format and which can maintain links between the database and the natural language representation of the requirements

6.   a change control system which can maintain information about requested requirements changes and links to the requirements affected by the changes.

Requirements management systems have been designed as general tools which may be used in many different requirements engineering processes. They do not, generally, impose their own model of the requirements engineering process.

One area of requirements engineering where support is currently very limited is the area of elicitation. This is a difficult area to support because of the wide range of different stakeholders who may be involved in the process, the different notations and vocabularies used by these stakeholders and the incompleteness of the requirements at this stage. There is some scope for using tools for managing unstructured information during the elicitation process (Sommerville, Rodden et al., 1993). In practice, however, we have found that putting a computer between the requirements engineering and the system stakeholders often inhibits the elicitation process.

2.4   Process improvement

Since the late 1980s, the importance of processes and their role in a business has been increasingly widely recognised. In many cases, analyses of business processes showed that they included redundant activities, unnecessary duplication of information and inefficient flow of work from one process participant to another. There may be scope for process 'improvement' where the process is modified to meet some improvement objectives.

Process improvement objectives may include the following.

1.   **Quality improvement**
      The outputs produced by the process are of higher quality. In the case of requirements, this means that they may contain fewer errors, may be

more complete or may better reflect the real needs of system stake-holders.

2. **Schedule reduction**

The outputs from the process are produced more quickly. In the case of requirements, this means that less time is needed to produce the final version of the requirements document.

3. **Resource reduction**

Fewer resources such as staff time are needed to enact the process. Therefore, a smaller team of requirements engineers can produce the final requirements document.

These are general improvement dimensions but individual organisations might have more specific improvement objectives such as more reuse of requirements across different systems, more involvement of end-users in the requirements engineering process, etc.

Process improvement came to prominence in the 1980s with the notion of business process re-engineering (Hammer, 1990). Supporters of business process re-engineering argue that, in many cases, processes are inefficient because they were originally developed in a different business environment. They maintain that improvements are best achieved by completely re-thinking the nature of processes and re-designing these processes to be at least an order-of-magnitude more efficient. However, in many cases, the scope for drastic process re-engineering is quite limited although the general principle that processes can be modified for improvement is still valid.

Another improvement approach has been adopted by many Japanese companies and, increasingly, in organisations in the West. Rather than revolutionary improvement, this approach is based on long-term process evolution where continuous small improvements are made in the process. The Japanese word *Kaizen* is sometimes used to refer to this approach. An approach to process improvement based on this approach is described by Sommerville and Sawyer (1997).

This evolutionary approach has been suggested because it isn't realistic to expect organisations to invest a lot of time and money in new processes whose value is difficult to assess. Revolutionary approaches to process improvement cost too much and are far too risky for most organisations. We think that a better approach to improvement is an iterative approach where small changes are made to the process and the results observed. If mistakes are made, the damage caused by these 'improvements' is limited. Small-scale improvements with a high returns should be introduced before expensive new techniques.

Process improvement is sometimes seen simply as the introduction of new methods or techniques. Because these are more advanced technically than existing methods, you might think that these will necessarily lead to process improvements. A good example of this was the widespread investment in CASE technology in the late 1980s and early 1990s. Many organisations which invested in CASE tools found that they had no significant effect on the productivity or quality of their products. The CASE tools changed the process but did not address the real problems (such as requirements engineering problems) faced by these organisations.

There are four questions which should be answered when planning process improvements.

1. **What are the problems with current processes?**
    These may be identifiable problems such as late delivery of products, budget over-runs, poor quality, products, etc. They may be less tangible problems such as poor staff morale, a reluctance in people to take responsibility or a meeting-dominated process where people spend too much time in meetings. Alternatively, the key problems might be problems of process understanding – no-one actually knows what processes are followed.

2. **What are the improvement goals?**
    These should normally be related to the identified problems. For example, if an organisation has quality management problems, its goal may be to improve quality management procedures to satisfy the ISO 9000 certification standard (Ince, 1994). If there are problems with budget-overruns, the goal may be to reduce the amount of rework which is required in a process. Goals must be realistic. There is no point in setting unrealisable goals or having unrealistic expectations about the benefits of new techniques or methods.

3. **How can we introduce process improvements to achieve these goals?**
    This involves assessing the existing requirements engineering processes to find out the activities which cause most problems and identifying changes to these which will contribute to the improvement goals.

4. **How should improvements be controlled and managed?**
    Procedures to collect feedback on improvements, which may be either quantitative measurements of the process or informal comments on the improvements, must be put in place. You should also ensure that action is taken in response to this feedback to correct any identified problems.

Requirements engineering processes may suffer from many different kinds of problem which result in consequential problems with the system and software requirements. Some examples of fairly common problems are as follows.

◆ **Lack of stakeholder involvement**
The process does not identify and take into account the real needs of all of the different stakeholders in the system. This problem can be addressed by including explicit process activities concerned with stakeholder identification and by using viewpoint-oriented methods of requirements engineering as described in Chapter 7.

◆ **Business needs are not considered**
The requirements engineering process is seen as a technical rather than a business process and is dominated by technical concerns. This can mean that the requirements do not satisfy the real needs of the business which is acquiring the system. This problem should be addressed by including an explicit stage where business needs are identified and by the involvement of business stakeholders in the process.

◆ **Lack of requirements management**
The process does not include effective techniques of requirements management. This means that changes to the requirements may be introduced in an *ad hoc* way and that a great deal of time and effort may be required to understand and incorporate these requirements changes. These problems can be addressed by introducing a change management process as discussed in Chapter 5.

◆ **Lack of defined responsibilities**
The different people involved in the requirements engineering process do not understand their individual responsibilities. This means that some tasks may not be carried out because everyone assumes that someone else is responsible for it. This can be addressed by developing responsibility or role-action models as part of the RE process.

◆ **Stakeholder communication problems**
The different stakeholders in the system (end-users, managers, engineers, etc.) fail to communicate effectively so that the resulting requirements document is not understandable (and hence checkable) by all stakeholders. This results in incorrect or incomplete requirements which may only be discovered after the system has been implemented. This can be addressed by using shared notations for requirements description, defining a glossary explicitly as part of the process, involving all stakeholders in review meetings, etc.

There is no standard set of process improvements which should be introduced nor is there a standard requirements engineering process which all organisations should be aiming for. Rather, the appropriate improvements depend on the type of organisation and the organisational culture. For example, improvements which depend on introducing more disciplined processes may not be acceptable to small informal organisations but may be more appropriate for large companies with a workforce spread over several different sites.

2.4.1 Process maturity

A particularly important factor which affects process improvement is the level of process maturity in an organisation. Process maturity can be thought of as the extent that an organisation has defined its processes, actively controls these processes and provides systematic human and computer-based support for them. Therefore, an organisation which has a defined a set of standards for processes and provides tool support for these standards is more 'mature' than an organisation with only informal process definitions.

The idea of 'process maturity' came about through the work of the US Department of Defense's Software Engineering Institute (Humphrey, 1988; Humphrey, 1989; Paulk, Curtis et al., 1993; Paulk, Weber et al., 1995). They developed a method of assessing the capabilities of companies bidding for defence contracts and this has become known as the 'Capability Maturity Model' (CMM). This model rates organisations on a scale from 1 to 5. The higher the rating, the higher the maturity of the organisation. The assumption is that the more mature the process used to develop software, the better the software systems will be.

The basic idea underlying the CMM approach is that organisations should assess their maturity then introduce process changes which will enable them to progress up the maturity 'ladder' in a five stage process. The steps in this maturity ladder are shown in Figure 2.10.

The five levels in the SEI's capability maturity model are as follows.

1. **Initial level**
    organisations have an undisciplined process and it is left to individuals to decide how to manage the process and which development techniques to use.

2. **Repeatable level**
    organisations have basic cost and schedule management procedures in place. They are likely to be able to make consistent budget and schedule predictions for projects in the same application area.

3. **Defined level**
    the software process for both management and engineering activities is documented, standardized and integrated into a standard software process for the organisation.

Figure 2.10
Process maturity
levels.

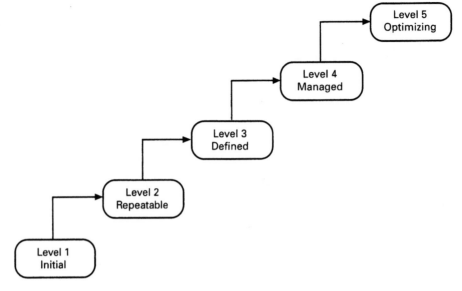

4. **Managed level**
   detailed measurements of both process and product quality are collected and used to control the process.

5. **Optimizing level**
   the organisation has a continuous process improvement strategy, based on objective measurements, in place.

   At each of these levels, a set of 'Key Practices' have been defined. Once all of the practices at one level have been introduced in an organisation, it has reached that level of maturity and moves up to the next level. Examples of practices include requirements management (repeatable level), configuration management (repeatable level), peer reviews (defined level), quantitative and process management (managed level).
   The SEI's Capability Maturity Model has been very influential and has spawned other models, such as the Bootstrap and SPICE models, of process maturity and process improvements (Koch, 1993; Kuvaja, Similä et al., 1994; El Amam, Drouin et al., 1997) Many organisations are assessing their processes using the CMM and have the declared objective to move to a given level of maturity (usually either 2 or 3) within some defined timescale. Experience has shown that moving from one level to another takes several years in most organisations. As yet, few organisations have reached the higher levels of the model.

2.4.2 A requirements engineering process maturity model

Requirements engineering process maturity is the extent to which an organisation has a defined requirements engineering process based on good requirements engineering practices. An organisation with a mature RE process will have this process explicitly defined. It will use appropriate methods and techniques for requirements engineering, will have defined standards for requirements documents, requirements descriptions, etc. The organisation may use automated tools to support process activities. It will have management policies and procedures in place to ensure that the process is followed and may use process measurements to collect information about the process to help assess the value of process changes.

The SEI's Capability Maturity Model is mostly concerned with the management of software development processes and does not cover system requirements engineering. However, a comparable model of requirements engineering process maturity has been designed and is described in the companion text to this book (Sommerville and Sawyer, 1997). The requirements process maturity model is a three-level model. The first two levels are roughly comparable to the first two levels of the SEI model. The third level encompasses all of the higher levels in that model. This is illustrated in Figure 2.11.

1. **Level 1: Initial level**

   Level 1 organisations do not have a defined requirements engineering process and often suffer from requirements problems such as excessive requirements volatility, unsatisfied stakeholders and large rework costs when requirements change. They do not use advanced methods to support their requirements engineering processes. They often fail to produce good quality requirement documents on time and within budget. They

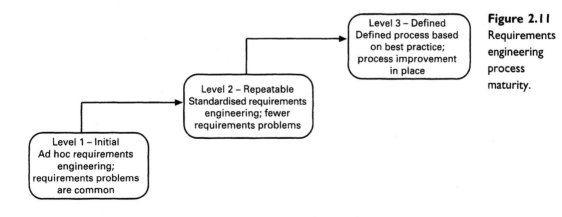

Figure 2.11
Requirements engineering process maturity.

are dependent on the skills and experience of individual engineers for requirements elicitation, analysis and validation.

2. **Level 2: Repeatable level**

Level 2 organisations have defined standards for requirements documents and requirements descriptions and have introduced policies and procedures for requirements management. They may use some advanced tools and techniques in their requirements engineering processes. Their requirements documents are more likely to be of a consistent high quality and to be produced on schedule.

3. **Level 3: Defined level**

Level 3 organisations have a defined requirements engineering process model based on good practices and techniques. They have an active process improvement programme in place and can make objective assessments of the value of new methods and techniques.

The general approach proposed for process improvement is based on the incremental adoption of good practice guidelines which describe good requirements engineering practice at each of these levels. An organisation should identify and prioritise its process problems then introduce the best practices which can address the highest priority problems. Once a set of these guidelines has been introduced (an improvement cycle), the improvement process begins again and further potential improvements are identified. Examples of good practice guidelines which are appropriate to each of the above levels are shown in Figure 2.12.

Guideline	Level	Description
Define a standard document structure	Initial	Define a standard for requirements documents which includes all relevant system information.
Uniquely identify each requirement	Initial	Make sure that each requirement has a unique identifier and that this identifier is always used to refer to that requirement.
Define policies for requirements management	Initial	Have an explicitly defined change management processes and put procedures in place to assure that this process is followed.
Use checklists for requirements analysis	Initial	Develop checklists of potential problems and explicitly check off these problems during the requirements validation process.
Use scenarios to elicit requirements	Repeatable	Develop a set of usage scenarios and use these with stakeholders to elicit their specific requirements.
Specify requirements quantitatively	Repeatable	Where it is appropriate, specify requirements such as reliability requirements in terms of system attributes which can be objectively measured.
Use prototyping to animate requirements	Repeatable	Develop an executable prototype of a system based on outline requirements and get stakeholders opinions of the prototype facilities.
Reuse requirements	Defined	Wherever possible, reuse requirements from previous systems as these will (to some extent) have already been validated.
Specify systems using formal specification	Defined	If you are involved in the development of critical systems, use a mathematical specification language to specify the functionality of the system.

Figure 2.12
Examples of good practice guidelines

◆ Key Points

◆ The requirements engineering process is a structured set of activities which leads to the production of a requirements document which specifies a system.

◆ Inputs to the requirements engineering process are information about existing systems, stakeholder needs, organisational standards, regulations and domain information.

◆ Requirements engineering processes vary radically from one organisation to another but most processes involve requirements elicitation, requirements analysis and negotiation and requirements validation.

◆ Requirements engineering process models are simplified process description which are presented from a particular perspective. Examples of RE process models include activity models, role-action models and entity-relation models.

◆ A spiral model of the requirements engineering process illustrates that the process is iterative and involves repetition of elicitation, analysis and validation activities.

◆ Human, social and organisational factors are important influences on requirements engineering processes. These often dominate technical considerations.

◆ Requirements engineering process improvement is difficult and is best tackled in an incremental way. Organisations which are interested in improving their processes should have clear improvement goals and an incremental plan to achieve these goals.

◆ Requirements engineering processes can be classified according to their degree of maturity. At the initial level, processes are unstructured; at the repeatable level, processes are standardised; at the defined level, processes include best practice and active process improvement is in place.

◆ Exercises

2.1 Explain why there is a great deal of variability in the requirements engineering processes used in different organisations.

2.2 Define an activity model of the processes of checking a book out of a library, making an omelette and installing some new software on your computer (this can be very challenging!). You should choose an appropriate level of granularity for the models.

2.3 Explain why both coarse-grain and fine-grain activity models of a process should be produced in an organisation.

2.4 Explain why the waterfall model of the software process is not an accurate reflection of the detailed software processes in most organisations. Why is a spiral model more realistic?

2.5 Why is it important to understand the roles of people involved in requirements engineering processes?

2.6 Suggest four reasons why CASE tools have not been as effective in improving productivity as was suggested in the 1980s. Do these reasons apply to CASE tools for requirements engineering?

2.7 What are the key questions which must be answered when planning improvements to business processes? What factors are likely to be particularly significant when considering requirements engineering process improvement?

2.8 Apart from the practices shown in Figure 2.12, suggest other good practices which might be incorporated into requirements engineering processes.

◆ References

Alford, M. W. (1977). A Requirements Engineering Methodology for Real Time Processing Requirements. *IEEE Transactions on Software Engineering* **SE-3**(1): 60–9.

Alford, M. W. (1985). SREM at the Age of Eight: The Distributed Computing Design System. *IEEE Computer* **18**(4): 36–46.

Delisle, N., and Garlan, D. (1990). A Formal Specification of an Oscilloscope. *IEEE Software* **7** (5): 29–36.

El Amam, K., Drouin, J., et al. (1997). *SPICE: The Theory and Practice of Software Process Improvement and Capability Determination*. Los Alamitos, California: IEEE Computer Society Press.

Hall, A. (1996). Using Formal Methods to Develop an ATC Information System. *IEEE Software* **13**(2): 66–76.

Hall, J. A. (1990). Using Z as a specification calculus for object-oriented systems. In: *VDM and Z – Formal methods in Software Development*. Eds D. Bjorner, C. A. R. Hoare and H. Langmaack. Heidelberg, Springer-Verlag: 290–318.

Hammer, M. (1990). Reengineering Work: Don't Automate, Obliterate. *Harvard Business Review* **July–August**: 104–112.

Humphrey, W. (1989). *Managing the Software Process*. Reading, Massachusetts: Addison Wesley.

Humphrey, W. S. (1988). Characterizing the Software Process. *IEEE Software* **5**(2): 73–79.

Ince, D. (1994). *ISO 9001 and Software Quality Assurance*. London: McGraw-Hill.

Jones, C. B. (1980). *Software Development – A Rigorous Approach*. London: Prentice-Hall.

Jones, C. B. (1986). *Systematic Software Development using VDM*. London: Prentice-Hall.

Koch, G. (1993). Process assessment: the 'BOOTSTRAP' approach. *Information and Software Technology* **35**(6/7): 387–403.

Kuvaja, P., Similä, J., et al. (1994). *Software Process Assessment and Improvement: The BOOTSTRAP Approach*. Oxford: Blackwell Publishers.

Paulk, M. C., Curtis, B., et al. (1993). Capability Maturity Model, Version 1.1. *IEEE Software* **10**(4): 18–27.

Paulk, M. C., Weber, C. V., et al. (1995). *The Capability Maturity Model: Guidelines for Improving the Software Process*. Reading, Massachusetts: Addison-Wesley.

Ross, D. T. (1977). Structured Analysis (SA). A Language for Communicating Ideas. *IEEE Transactions on Software Engineering*. **SE-3**(1): 16–34.

Schoman, K. and Ross, D. T. (1977). Structured Analysis for Requirements Definition. *IEEE Transactions on Software Engineering*. **SE-3**(1): 6–15.

Sommerville, I., Rodden, T., et al. (1993). Integrating ethnography into the requirements engineering process. *RE'93*, San Diego California, IEEE Computer Society Press.

Sommerville, I., and Sawyer, P. (1997). *Requirements Engineering:A Good Practice Guide*. Chichester: John Wiley & Sons.

Spivey, J. M. (1992). *The Z Notation: A Reference Manual*, 2nd edition. London: Prentice-Hall.

◆ Further reading

Exploring Requirements: Quality before Design (D.C. Gause and G. M. Weinberg). This book does not specifically discuss the requirements engineering process as such but focuses on non-technical issues and human factors. This gives the reader a different perspective on the practicalities of requirements engineering.

3 Requirements Elicitation and Analysis

◆ **Contents**

◆ **Summary**

This chapter describes the activities in the requirements engineering process which are concerned with discovering requirements, analysing requirements for incompleteness, inconsistency, relevance and practicality and negotiating the final requirements for the system. The processes of elicitation and analysis are described and elicitation techniques such as interviewing, software systems analysis, scenario analysis and ethnography are explained. Prototyping is introduced as a technique for helping stakeholders understand their requirements and we describe several different approaches to prototyping. Finally, we discuss requirements analysis and negotiation and show how these activities are normally interleaved with requirements elicitation.

◆

Requirements elicitation is the usual name given to activities involved in discovering the requirements the system. System developers and engineers work with customers and end-users to find out about the problem to be solved, the system services, the required performance of the system, hardware constraints, and so on. This doesn't just involve asking people what they want; it requires a careful analysis of the organisation, the application domain and business processes where the system will be used.

Requirements analysis and negotiation are processes which are closely linked with requirements elicitation. The objective of requirements analysis and negotiation is to establish an agreed set of requirements which are complete and consistent. These requirements should be unambiguous so that they can be used as a basis for system development. During the analysis process, missing requirements, requirements conflicts, ambiguous requirements, overlapping requirements and unrealistic requirements are normally discovered. If there are requirements conflicts or if the requirements proposal seems to be too ambitious, stakeholders must negotiate and agree on modifications and simplifications to the system requirements.

The term requirements elicitation suggests that the process is a simple knowledge transfer process where requirements engineers elicit and document existing customer knowledge. In reality, the process is much more complex. Customers rarely have a clear picture of their requirements, different people in an organisation have conflicting requirements; there are usually technological limitations on the requirements, and so on. Elicitation is not, therefore, a process of 'fishing' for requirements. Rather, it is a complex negotiation process involving all system stakeholders, including the developers of the system. We prefer the term 'requirements discovery' to reflect the uncertainties in the process. However, as elicitation is more commonly used, we shall stick to this name here.

Davis (1993) avoids the term elicitation and equates this discovery process to a process of problem analysis and understanding. He defines problem analysis as follows:

> Problem analysis is the activity that encompasses learning about the problem to be solved (often through brainstorming and/or questioning), understanding the needs of potential users, trying to find out who the user really is, and understanding all the constraints on the solution

The term problem analysis can also be misleading, however, as it implies that the activity is only concerned with understanding the details of a specific problem which requires some kind of systems solution. In fact, there are four dimensions to requirements elicitation as shown in Figure 3.1.

1. **Application domain understanding**
    Application domain knowledge is knowledge of the general area where the system is applied. For example, to understand the requirements for a cataloguing system, you must have a general knowledge of libraries and how libraries work; to understand the requirements for a railway signalling system, you must have background knowledge about the operation of railways and the physical characteristics of trains.

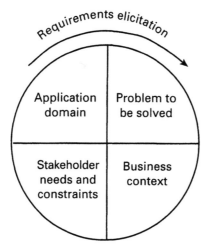

Figure 3.1
Components of
requirements
elicitation.

2. **Problem understanding**

   The details of the specific customer problem where the system will be
   applied must be understood. Therefore, for a cataloguing system, you
   must understand how a particular library organises its collection; for a
   railway signalling system, you must know the way in which speed limits
   are applied to particular track segments. During problem understanding,
   you specialise and extend general domain knowledge.

3. **Business understanding**

   Systems are generally intended to contribute in some way to the development of a business or organisation. You must understand how these
   systems interact and affect the different parts of the business and how
   they can contribute to overall business goals.

4. **Understanding the needs and constraints of system stakeholders**

   System stakeholders are those people who are affected in some way by
   the system. They may be end-users of the system, managers of departments where the system is installed, etc. You must understand, in detail,
   their specific needs for system support in their work. In particular, you
   must understand the work processes that the system is intended to
   support and the role of existing systems in these work processes.

   Effective requirements elicitation is very important. If the customer's real
requirements are not discovered, they are unlikely to be satisfied with the
final system. The acceptability of the system depends on how well it meets
the customer's needs and supports the work to be automated. It is not always
easy to assess this as there may be a wide range of stakeholders who benefit

directly or indirectly from the system. They all may use different criteria to judge the system's acceptability.

The multi-dimensional nature of requirements elicitation, as shown in Figure 3.1, is reflected in the problems faced by requirements engineers when trying to understand system requirements.

1. Application domain knowledge is not collected neatly in one place. It exists in a variety of different sources such as in textbooks, operating manuals and in the heads of the people working in that area. It usually involves specialist terminology which is not immediately understandable by the requirements engineer.

2. People who understand the problem to be solved are often too busy solving the problem without any new system. They can't spend a lot of time helping requirements engineers understand the requirements for a new system. They will not necessarily be convinced of the need for a new system so may not want to be involved in the requirements engineering process.

3. Organisational issues and political factors may influence the system requirements. These factors may not be apparent to the system end-users who have their own requirements. Higher management may influence the system requirements in ways that satisfy their personal agendas. For example, they may want to move some functions to their department so propose requirements which integrate the support for these functions with support for operations that they already provide.

4. Stakeholders often don't really know what they want from the computer system except in the most general terms. Even when they have a clear idea of what they would like the system to do, they often find this difficult to articulate. They may make unrealistic demands because they are unaware of the costs of their requests. Different stakeholders have different requirements and may express these in quite different ways. Analysts must discover all potential sources of requirements and should expose requirements commonalities and conflicts.

Requirements elicitation is further complicated by the fact that the economic and business environment in which the analysis takes place is constantly changing. It inevitably changes during the elicitation process. Hence, the importance of particular requirements may change. Requirements emerge from new stakeholders who were not originally consulted. The people consulted at some stage in the process may change jobs so that they are no longer available for further consultation.

All of these factors mean that structured methods are not very useful for requirements elicitation. In general, most of these methods can only be used to support analysis after some initial elicitation has been carried out. To use a method, you need a general understanding of the application domain and the problem to be solved. Methods do have a place in the elicitation process but their use must always be supplemented by a more general understanding of the requirements from the problem domain and system stakeholders.

3.1 Elicitation and analysis processes

Requirements elicitation and requirements analysis are closely linked processes. As requirements are discovered during the elicitation process, some analysis is inevitably carried out. Problems may be immediately recognised, discussed with the source of the requirements and resolved. We discuss analysis as if it is a separate activity which follows elicitation. However, you should bear in mind that, in reality, they are interleaved processes.

Requirements analysis and negotiation are concerned with the high-level statement of requirements elicited from stakeholders. Requirements engineers and stakeholders negotiate to agree on the definition of the requirements to be included in the requirements document. In some organisations, these requirements will then be developed in more detail as a system specification or model (see Chapter 6). Developing these models often reveals further contradictions and incompleteness in the requirements. The elicitation, analysis and negotiation phases may have to be re-activated to discover more information to resolve the problems which have been discovered.

You can therefore think of requirements elicitation, analysis and negotiation processes as segments in a spiral, as shown in Figure 3.2.

Typically, a requirements engineer discovers some information about requirements. This is analysed, a negotiation takes place and then another round of the spiral begins. This continues until schedule pressure forces system development to begin (the normal terminating condition) or until all stakeholders are satisfied with the requirements.

There are many possible requirements elicitation processes and different organisations use different processes. A very general elicitation process model which covers many of these different processes is shown in Figure 3.3.

A good requirements elicitation process should include four critical activities.

1. **Objective setting**

    The overall organisational objectives should be established at this stage. These include general goals of the business, an outline description of the problem to be solved and why the system may be necessary and the constraints on the system such as budget, schedule and inter-operability constraints.

Figure 3.2
The elicitation,
analysis and
negotiation
spiral.

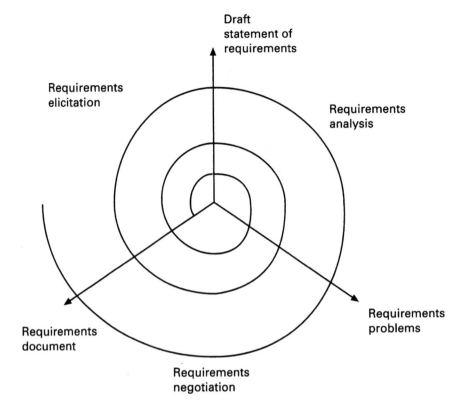

2. **Background knowledge acquisition**
    This is a very important stage where the requirements engineers gather and understand background information about the system. This includes information about the organisation where the system is to be installed, information about the application domain of the system and information about any existing systems which are in use and which may be replaced by the system being specified.

3. **Knowledge organisation**
    The large amount of knowledge which has been collected in the previous stage must be organised and collated. This involves identifying system stakeholders and their roles in the organisation, prioritising the goals of the organisation and discarding domain knowledge which does not contribute directly to the system requirements.

4. **Stakeholder requirements collection**
    This stage is what many people think of as elicitation. It involves consulting system stakeholders to discover their requirements, and deriving requirements which come from the application domain and the organisation which is acquiring the system.

Establish objectives Understand background Organise knowledge Collect requirements

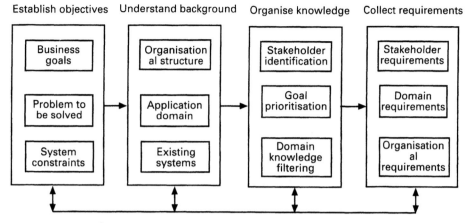

Figure 3.3
A generic requirements elicitation process.

Although Figure 3.3 is a reasonable depiction of requirements elicitation activities, it is an idealised process model. The reality of requirements elicitation tends to be much messier. The activities identified in Figure 3.3 are usually mixed up with each other. In many cases, the critical early activities of establishing objectives for the system are not carried out. This often results in significant analysis problems as there are no objectives and business goals which may be used to prioritise the requirements.

The output from the requirements elicitation process should be a draft document which describes the system requirements. This document is then analysed to discover problems and conflicts in the requirements definition. Conflicts and overlaps are almost inevitable so there then must be a negotiation stage, involving the different system stakeholders, to resolve these conflicts and agree on a set of requirements. A general model for this analysis and negotiation process is shown in Figure 3.4.

The goal of requirements analysis is to find problems in the draft requirements document. Although this is shown as a sequence of discrete activities, in reality, the analysis activities are interleaved. The activities which are typically part of requirements analysis are as follows.

1. **Necessity checking**
   The need for the requirement is analysed. In some cases, requirements may be proposed which don't contribute to the business goals of the organisation or to the specific problem to be addressed by the system.

2. **Consistency and completeness checking**
   The requirements are cross-checked for consistency and completeness. Consistency means that no requirements should be contradictory; completeness means that no services or constraints which are needed have been missed out.

Figure 3.4
The
requirements
analysis and
negotiation
process.

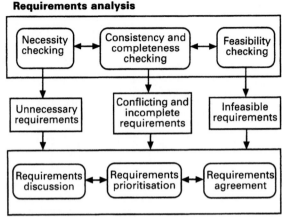

Requirements analysis

Requirements negotiation

3.   **Feasibility checking**
      The requirements are checked to ensure that they are feasible in the
      context of the budget and schedule available for the system development.

   These activities result in the identification of a set of requirements which
are discussed in the requirements negotiation process. Whether a requirement
is necessary or feasible is often a matter of opinion and different engineers
may disagree on this. Conflicts have to be resolved by discussing which of
the requirements which conflict must be changed and the extent of the
changes to be made.
   The requirements negotiation process also has a number of interleaved
process steps which are also shown in Figure 3.4.

1.   **Requirements discussion**
      Requirements which have been highlighted as problematical are
      discussed and the stakeholders involved present their views about the
      requirements.

2.   **Requirements prioritisation**
      Disputed requirements are prioritised to identify critical requirements
      and to help the decision making process.

3.   **Requirements agreement**
      Solutions to the requirements problems are identified and a compromise
      set of requirements is agreed. Generally, this will involve making
      changes to some of the requirements.

   In many cases, of course, the analysis process will raise questions which cannot be answered and it may not be possible to reach agreement about changes

to the requirements. In essence, this means that insufficient information is available for the negotiation. Another round of the spiral shown in Figure 3.2 must start to collect more information about the system requirements.

3.2 Elicitation techniques

As we have discussed, requirements elicitation involves discovering information about the application domain of the system, the specific problem to be solved, the business which is buying the system and the specific needs of system stakeholders. In general, requirements engineers may need to use different techniques to discover all this information. We describe four complementary approaches to requirements elicitation in this section.

Much of the knowledge in requirements elicitation comes from reading documents about the system and talking to the people who are involved with the system as users, managers, etc. This results in a large volume of information which must be organised to make it understandable. Yeh and Zave (1980) suggest that there are three fundamental ways of structuring this knowledge. Davis, in his book on requirements engineering (Davis, 1993) describes these three structuring mechanisms, as follows.

- **Partitioning**
  This is organisation of knowledge into aggregation relationships where requirements knowledge is described in terms of its parts. For example, in a booking system, a booking record may be defined as a flight reference, a source and destination of the flight, the name and address of the passenger, the fare paid and the date of travel.

- **Abstraction**
  This is the organisation of knowledge according to general/specific relationships. Requirements knowledge is described by relating specific instances to abstract structures. Therefore, in a booking system, the abstraction, Passenger, may be developed and used to refer to all classes of passenger such as children or adults, people paying full-fare or concessionary fares, etc.

- **Projection**
  This is the organisation of knowledge from several different perspectives or viewpoints. Different sources contribute different information about the system and it is often important to explicitly identify these sources during elicitation. For example, viewpoints on a booking system might be travel agents, airline management, check-in desk operators, passengers, a bookings database, etc. This is the basis of viewpoint-oriented requirements engineering, discussed in Chapter 7.

Good requirements engineers use these fundamentals without thinking during requirements elicitation. Analysis methods such as object-oriented analysis are explicitly based around these approaches and may require classification and aggregation relationships to be explicitly specified. Methods which use these techniques are covered in Chapter 6.

Requirements elicitation is a cooperative process involving requirements engineers and system stakeholders. Effective elicitation requires effective cooperation but, in many cases, it is difficult for the requirements engineers and the stakeholders to form good working relationships. Some of the problems they may face are as follows.

1. **Insufficient time has been allowed for the requirements elicitation**
    Stakeholders are busy people with a job to do and they do not have a great deal of free time to discuss new systems with requirements engineers.

2. **Requirements engineers do not prepare themselves properly for the elicitation process**
    Developing an understanding of an application domain is essential for effective elicitation. Sometimes, however, requirements engineers either don't or can't learn about the domain before talking to stakeholders. This makes stakeholders impatient and results in misunderstandings because specialised terms are used which are unfamiliar to requirements engineers.

3. **Stakeholders may not want a new system**
    In many cases, buying and installing a new system is an organisational decision and the people who are affected by the system are not consulted. They may feel that a new system is unnecessary and they don't see why they should cooperate in its specification.

Some of the many system failures which have been reported are a direct consequence of these problems. Requirements engineers must be sensitive to the needs of stakeholders and the demands made on their time. They should not always assume that the specification of a system is a high-priority activity for them.

3.2.1 Interviews

Interviews are a very commonly used technique of requirements elicitation. The requirements engineer or analyst discusses the system with different stakeholders and builds up an understanding of their requirements. There are, basically, two types of interview:

1. closed interviews where the requirements engineer looks for answers to a pre-defined set of questions.

2. open interviews where there is no pre-defined agenda and the requirements engineer discusses, in an open-ended way, what stakeholders want from the system.

In reality, of course, the boundary between these types of interview is blurred. A requirements engineer may start with a pre-defined set of questions but, as different issues arise, these are discussed in an open-ended way. Similarly, a completely open-ended discussion is usually simpler when there are some simple questions to structure the interview.

Interviews can be very effective for developing an understanding of the problem and for eliciting very general system requirements. End-users are usually happy to describe their work and the difficulties they face, although they may have unrealistic expectations about the computer support which can be provided. However, interviews are much less effective for understanding the application domain and for understanding organisational issues which affect the requirements.

There are two essentials for effective interviewing.

1. The interviewer must be open-minded and willing to listen to stakeholders. There is no point in holding interviews if the requirements engineer is unwilling to change his or her mind about the real needs of stakeholders.
2. Stakeholders must be given some kind of starting point for discussion. This can be a question, a requirements proposal, or an existing system. Saying to people 'tell me what you want' is unlikely to result in useful information. People find it much easier to talk in a defined context rather than in general terms.

Interviews should be part of all requirements elicitation processes. In many cases, apart from information from documents, they may be the only source of information about the system requirements. However, they are rarely completely adequate for requirements elicitation. Wherever possible, interviewing should be used in conjunction with other requirements elicitation techniques.

Application domain knowledge is difficult to elicit during interviews for two reasons:

1. Most application domains have their own terminology and stakeholders find it very difficult to discuss the domain without using this terminology. In many cases, they do so in a precise and subtle way and it is easy for requirements engineers to misunderstand these descriptions.

2. There are some types of domain knowledge which stakeholders either find very difficult to explain or is so familiar that they never think of

explaining it. For example, for a librarian, it goes without saying that all acquisitions are catalogued before they are shelved. However, this may not be so obvious to a requirements engineer.

Organisational knowledge is also difficult to elicit during interviews primarily because of political and social factors. In all organisations, there are subtle power and influence relationships between the different people in the organisation. Stakeholder requirements are influenced by these but stakeholders may be (understandably) reluctant to discuss them. Published organisational structures often don't match reality but stakeholders may not wish to discuss these with a stranger from outside their own department.

3.2.2 Scenarios

End-users and other system stakeholders find it easier to relate to real-life examples rather than abstract descriptions of the functions provided by a system. For this reason, it is often useful to develop a set of interaction scenarios and to use these to elicit and clarify system requirements. Scenarios are examples of interaction sessions which are concerned with a single type of interaction between an end-user and the system. End-users simulate their interaction using the scenario. They explain to the requirements engineering team what they are doing and the information which they need from the system to carry out the task described in the scenario.

In addition, the process of developing a scenario, even without considering user interaction, can help with requirements understanding. Discovering possible scenarios exposes the range of possible system interactions and reveals system facilities which may be required. Scenarios are a basic part of some object-oriented analysis methods (Jacobsen, Christerson et al., 1993; Fowler and Scott, 1997). Potts, Takahashi et al. (1994) and Gough, Fodemski et al. (1995) give good descriptions of a scenario-based approach to requirements analysis.

Scenarios can be thought of as stories which explain how the system is used. They are primarily useful for adding detail to an outline requirements description. Once you have a basic idea of the facilities that a system should provide, you can develop usage scenarios around these facilities. You can identify scenarios by initial discussions with stakeholders who interact with the system. For complex systems, a fairly large number (tens or hundreds) of scenarios will usually be required.

Scenarios can be written in different ways but they should at least include the following information.

1. a description of the state of the system before entering the scenario

2. the normal flow of events in the scenario

3. exceptions to the normal flow of events

4. information about other activities which might be going on at the same time

5. a description of the state of the system after completion of the scenario.

To illustrate this, consider the following scenario which describes what happens when a user interacts with the EDDIS system to order a report from a different library.

If a report is not available from their local library users may log on to the EDDIS system to order that report from another library. The steps involved are as follows.

1. The user logs on to the EDDIS system.

2. The order document command is issued

3. The reference number of the document which is required is entered on the order form.

4. The user selects one of the delivery options from the delivery menu.

5. The user logs out from EDDIS.

This is a simple scenario but it doesn't cover what should happen if something unexpected happens. We could add this to the natural language scenario by including if clauses with each step. For example, step 3 could be amended.

3. The reference number of the document which is required is entered on the form. The system checks this number and, if it is incorrect, offers the user the opportunity to re-enter the document reference or to invoke the EDDIS help system to give the advice on how to recover from the error.

This gives more detail but information such as some inputs and outputs are still missing. These could also be added but as more and more information is included in the natural language scenario, it becomes harder and harder to understand. As an alternative, a graphical representation of the scenario may be developed as shown in Figure 3.5. In this case, the system is idle before and after the scenario.

In Figure 3.5, the 'normal' flow of events is from left to right in the top group of boxes. Each box shows some user action. Therefore, a user logs in to the system, selects the 'order document' command, inputs the identifier of the document required, confirms delivery and then logs out of the system.

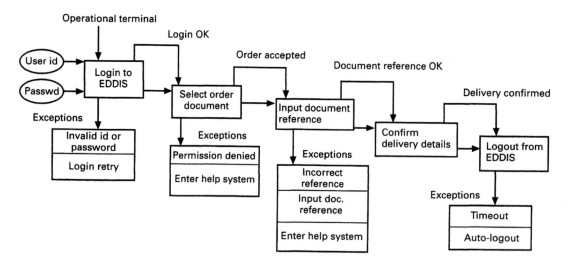

Figure 3.5
Library scenario.

The arrows at the top indicate control and show the conditions that must be fulfilled before control can move to the next action box. Therefore, a valid user identifier and password must be input before an order can be placed, the user must have permission to place and order, etc. If a control condition is not satisfied then progress to the next stage is impossible.

Exceptions which may occur are shown beneath the associated action. The exception boxes briefly set out the exception in the top part of the box and describe the associated action in the bottom part of the box. Therefore, if the user inputs an invalid document reference, he or she can retry or can enter the help system to find out about document references.

Applying a scenario involves the requirements engineer and the system end-user working through the scenario together with the engineer taking notes of the user's comments, problems and suggestions. The end-user simulates the use of the system, following the scenario and points out areas where the scenario is incorrect, simplistic, variable etc. The requirements engineer may ask questions at various points about current user actions, how tasks are carried out, who is involved in tasks, and what would happen if some alternative approach was taken.

Scenarios take time to develop as they involve interaction with stakeholders to understand what should happen. However, once available, they can be reused in different systems. It may take 1 or 2 days to develop each scenario depending on the complexity of the interaction. In an experiment with this method, it was found that 88 scenarios were needed to describe interaction with a medical system (Gough, Fodemski et al., 1995). Several months of effort may therefore be needed to develop scenarios for a complex system. However, scenario-based elicitation does not seem to require significantly more effort that other approaches to elicitation for systems of a comparable size.

ELICITATION TECHNIQUES **67**

3.2.3 Soft systems methods

Structured methods of requirements analysis, which we discuss in Chapter 6, are not particularly useful for the early stages of analysis where the application domain, the problem and the organisational requirements must be understood. They are based on 'hard' models of the system such as entity-relationship models, data-flow models, etc. These models are inflexible and focus on the automated systems. By contrast, soft systems methods rely on producing less formal models of the whole socio-technical system. They consider the automated system, the people and the organisation.

A number of these soft systems methods have been developed including SSM (Checkland, 1981; Checkland and Scholes, 1990), ETHICS (Mumford, 1989) and Eason's User-Centred Design approach (Eason, 1988). These are all fairly comprehensive methods and we cannot describe them in detail here. Rather, we will give a brief overview of SSM which is probably the best known of these approaches.

SSM (Soft Systems Methodology) was not specifically designed as a technique of eliciting requirements for computer-based systems. Rather, it was developed to help apply 'systems thinking' to problems within organisations. It is concerned with socio-technical systems in the broadest sense including people, procedures and policies, hardware and software, etc. This broad perspective makes the approach usable in requirements elicitation and Bustard et al. (1995) describe how SSM can be combined with other requirements analysis methods.

There are seven fundamental stages in SSM, as shown in Figure 3.6.

The essence of SSM is that recognises that systems are embedded in a wider human and organisational context. It provides a means to understand abstract system requirements by analysing that organisational context, the problem to be solved and existing systems which are in place. It was one of the first methods to introduce the notion of viewpoints (called World Views in SSM) where different viewpoints have different perceptions of the problem and the solution requirements.

SSM and other soft systems methods are not techniques for detailed requirements elicitation. Rather, they are most effective for helping to understand a problem, the organisational situation in which they problem exists and the constraints on the problem solution. They are particularly valuable when there is uncertainty about what kind of system is really needed in a particular context. They produce abstract requirements for a system which need to be fleshed out using other elicitation techniques.

3.2.4 Observation and social analysis

Most work is a social activity which involves teams of people who cooperate to carry out different tasks. The nature of the cooperation is often complex

Method activity	Description
Problem situation assessment	This involves finding out about the situation where some problem exists. It does not rely on pre-conceived problem descriptions but looks at the whole organisational situation with an open mind. It involves finding out who is involved, their perceptions of the situation, existing processes, etc.
Problem situation description	The problem situation is described using 'rich pictures'. Rich pictures are a diagrammatic presentation of the organisation and the problem situation which don't rely on a limited set of symbols but where you can use any appropriate icons (maps, schematic drawings, logos, etc.) to describe the situation.
Abstract system definition from selected viewpoints	One or more so-called 'root definitions' of the system are produced. A root definition is produced from a particular viewpoint of world view and should include information about customers who benefit from the system, actors who are involved, transformations from inputs to outputs, the world view from which the definition was produced, the system 'owner' and constraints on the system coming from its environment.
Conceptual system modelling	Models of the system are produced which match the root definition. These are called human-activity models and, a general method guideline is that the activities in the model should be based on the verbs in the root definition.
Model/real-world comparison	The model produced is compared with the current situation in the real-world. For each activity in the conceptual model, questions such as 'is this a real-world activity?', 'how can it be measured?' are asked.
Change identification	Based on the conceptual models and the model/real-world comparison a set of possible changes to the existing real-world systems are identified. These take into account what is desirable and what is feasible to introduce into the organisation.
Recommendations for action	The identified changes are assessed and a set of action recommendations is produced.

Figure 3.6
The stages of soft systems methodology.

and varies depending on the people involved, the physical environment and the organisation in which the work takes place. People often find it very difficult to explain how they carry out tasks and how they work together in particular situations. Individuals and teams develop improvements to normal ways of working and use tools and documents in an intuitive way. They may not even realise what they are doing. When tasks become routine and people don't have to consciously think about them, it becomes very difficult for them to articulate how work is done.

Goguen and Linde (1993) give a good example of this type of task. They point out that it is very difficult to describe how to tie a shoelace but easy to demonstrate the process. Observation is a better way of understanding this type of task that direct questioning. Therefore, observing people carrying out their normal work is sometimes the best way to understand what support they need from a computer-based system.

Social scientists and anthropologists have used passive observation techniques for many years to develop a complete and detailed understanding of particular cultures. An approach known as ethnography involves an observer spending an extended period in a society or culture, making detailed observation of all their practices. The theory behind this is that a full understanding of a culture emerges when an observer becomes subsumed into it, relates to the people involved and knows the importance of the detailed practices which go on.

It is reasonable to consider a group of workers in a bank or air-traffic controllers (say) as members of a society and to use ethnographic analysis to understand their everyday work and hence derive requirements for computer support. There have now been a large number of studies of this type (Suchman, 1987; Harper, Hughes et al., 1991; Ackroyd, Harper et al., 1992; Heath, Jirotka et al., 1993) and it is clear from these studies that requirements can be discovered which do not emerge from other requirements elicitation techniques.

Ethnographic studies, by their very nature, cannot be carried out according to a formula. They are dependent on the personality of the ethnographer, the type of process being studied and the people involved in the process. To be effective, the ethnographer must be accepted by the people being studied as a 'kindred spirit' and must be sufficiently familiar that they carry on with their normal practices as if he or she wasn't there. If this isn't the case, the ethnographer will not be able to build up a true picture of the work done.

Although we can't define in detail how to carry out an ethnographic study, some guidelines which we have developed from several years of experience in using this technique for understanding requirements for computer system support are as follows.

1. Assume that the people you are studying are good at doing their job and look for non-standard ways of working. These often point to efficiencies which have been introduced through individual experience.

2. It is very important to spend time getting to know the people involved and establishing a relationship of trust. For this reason, ethnography is best carried out by an external organisation. This makes it easier to convince the people involved in processes that the ethnographic study can be objective rather than driven by management requirements.

3. Detailed notes of all work practices should be made during the observation and written up on a regular basis. The ethnographer must analyse

the notes and draw conclusions from them. A fundamental of ethnographic analysis is that we can learn a great deal from the details of how people work and it is only after many of these details have been collected that a coherent picture emerges.

4. Open-ended interviewing, where people are encouraged to talk about their work, can be combined effectively with ethnography and is often essential for the ethnographer to develop an understanding of what is going on.

5. Although video tapes and audio tape records of work can sometimes be useful, they take a long time to process and are therefore very expensive. Large-scale recording is impractical.

6. Regular de-briefing sessions where the ethnographer talks about the work with people outside of the process are essential to identify critical elements in the work.

A fundamental problem with ethnography as far as requirements engineering is concerned is that, as a technique, it is intended to be non-judgmental. Ethnography was developed as a technique for understanding complex societies and not as a technique for making judgements about how ways of working could be improved or supported by computer systems. Therefore, ethnography needs to be used to support other approaches to requirements elicitation rather than as a stand-alone requirements elicitation technique. Figure 3.7 shows one approach to integrating ethnography with system prototyping for interactive systems.

In the approach shown in Figure 3.7, the ethnographic analysis is used to develop an initial understanding of the system and the application domain. The later stages of the ethnography are more focused, and they aim at discovering the answers to questions which are raised during the development of the system prototype.

As an example of how ethnography revealed important system requirements, Bentley et al. (1992) describe an ethnographic study of air traffic controllers. They found that manual processes such as the sorting of paper strips describing aircraft flight plans were important as they helped controllers build a mental map of the airspace. If these were automated, some alternative way must be found to help controllers reinforce their knowledge of the aircraft in their sector. This contradicts the normal intuition that people don't like repetitive processes such as sorting and that these are best automated.

Ethnography involves making detailed records of observations. In practice, it is very difficult for anyone apart from the ethnographer to interpret these records so this limits the use of the raw data, particularly if there is a need to come back to it after the ethnographer has moved on to other things. To

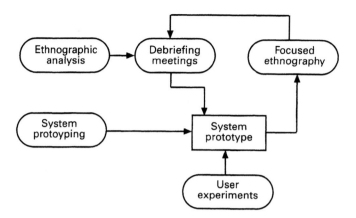

Figure 3.7
Using
ethnography in
requirements
elicitation.

address this problem, viewpoints (discussed in Chapter 7) have been proposed as a mechanism to organise and structure the ethnographic record (Hughes, O'Brien et al., 1995). They suggest that the ethnography may be presented from three viewpoints.

1. **The work setting viewpoint**
    This describes the context and the physical location of the work and how people use objects to carry out tasks. Therefore, in a study of a help desk (say), this would describe the objects which the helper had to hand and how these were organised.

2. **Social and organisational perspectives**
    This tries to bring out the day-to-day experience of work as seen by different people who are involved. Each individual typically sees the work in a different ways and this viewpoint tries to organise and integrate all these perceptions.

3. **The workflow viewpoint**
    This viewpoint presents the work from a series of work activities with information flowing from one activity to another.

This structuring has proved useful in utilising the results of ethnography in requirements engineering. However, the use of ethnography is still immature and it is not easy to incorporate this into a systematic requirements engineering process.

To address this problem, Holtzblatt and Beyer (Holtzblatt and Beyer, 1993) have developed a technique called Contextual Inquiry. This has adapted ethnographic methods so that they can be applied in a short time and with limited resources. It is based on a mixture of open-ended interviewing and workplace observation and, where appropriate, may use prototyping to help elicit requirements. It then involves users in the system design process. This approach seems to have been primarily used for interactive systems design where user interface design is critical. However, the basic principles should be applicable to other types of computer-based system.

3.2.5 Requirements reuse

It is generally good systems and software engineering practice to reuse as much knowledge as possible when developing a new system. While the possibility of reusing system designs and code is easy to understand, it is more difficult to understand what is meant by requirements reuse. Surely all systems are different conceptually and have different sets of stakeholders? This must mean that the system requirements are distinct.

However, while it is clearly the case that some requirements for each system must be distinct, there are a number of situations where reuse of requirements across systems may be possible. Some of these situations are given below.

1. Where the requirement is concerned with providing information about the application domain: many requirements don't actually specify system functionality but rather specify constraints on the system or system operations which are derived from the application domain. For example, the specification of a train braking system will include information about how the mass of the train, its speed, the track gradient, etc. affect the time the train takes to come to a halt. This information is likely to be applicable to all systems concerned with train control and protection.

2. Where the requirement is concerned with the style of presentation of information: insofar as it is possible, it makes sense for organisations to have a consistent 'look and feel' in the user interface for all systems. This means that user errors are less likely when they move from one system to another. Requirements which specify the user interface characteristics may therefore be reusable across different systems.

3. Where the requirement reflects company policies: company policies such as security policies may be reflected in system requirements. Where requirements which embody these policies are developed for one system, they may be reused in later systems. Therefore, if it is a company policy that all personal information should be kept private, a requirement for encryption may be common to a number of different systems.

For many systems, more than 50% of the requirements may fall into these classes so there is considerable scope for cost savings by requirements reuse.

The primary reason why costs are saved is that the reused requirements have already been analysed and validated in other systems. Although some analysis and validation is still required to check that the requirements are appropriate, the time and effort needed should normally be less than for 'new' requirements.

Of course, the danger with requirements reuse is that, when reused in a different context from that in which they were developed, there may be unexpected problems. There may be unanticipated interactions between the reused requirements and 'new' requirements. As the reused requirements have already been analysed, time and resource pressures may mean that analysis may miss these problems. Considerable rework may be required when they come to light at later stages in the process.

Currently, requirements reuse is an informal process which depends on the individual knowledge of requirements engineers. As such, it is widely practised but, clearly, a more systematic approach to requirements reuse is likely to yield larger cost savings. We are not aware of any techniques which have been found to be successful for requirements reuse although the ideas in design 'patterns' (Gamma, Helm et al., 1995) seem to have potential in this area.

3.3 Prototyping

A prototype of a system is an initial version of the system which is available early in the development process. In hardware systems, prototypes are often developed to test and experiment with system designs. In software systems, prototypes are more often used to help elicit and validate the system requirements.

An essential requirement for a prototype is that it should be possible to develop it quickly so that it can be used during the development process. This means that functionality may be left out, normal mechanisms of management and quality assurance may be ignored, non-functional requirements such as performance, security and reliability requirements may be less stringent and so on. Different technologies may be used to develop the prototype than are used for the final system development.

In this chapter, we are primarily concerned with the use of prototypes to help elicit and analyse system requirements. These prototypes are sometimes called 'throw-away' prototypes as they should be discarded when the final system has been developed. This 'throw-away' approach contrasts with evolutionary prototyping, which is an approach to software system development where a system with limited functionality is made available to users early in the development process. This system is then modified and extended to produce the final system.

The distinction between throw-away and evolutionary prototyping is as follows.

♦ Throw-away prototyping is intended to help elicit and develop the system requirements. The requirements which should be prototyped are those which cause most difficulties to customers and which are the hardest to understand. Requirements which are well-understood need not be implemented by the prototype.

♦ Evolutionary prototyping is intended to deliver a workable system quickly to the customer. Therefore, the requirements which should be supported by the initial versions of this prototype are those which are well-understood and which can deliver useful end-user functionality. It is only after extensive use that poorly understood requirements should be implemented.

Of course, there is not a hard and fast division between these different approaches to prototyping. Sometimes, for good business reasons, throw-away prototypes of software may evolve into the final delivered system. This is particularly common when there are problems in meeting the delivery schedule for a re-implementation of the prototype. However, although this can lead to short-term gains, there are usually long-term costs. Prototypes are usually poorly structured so the costs of maintenance and system evolution are high. Consequently, the overall lifetime of the system is relatively short.

The principal benefit of developing a prototype during requirements elicitation is that it allows customers and end-users of the system to experiment with the software. They can develop an understanding of how the system can be used to support their work. People find it difficult to visualise how a written statement of requirements will translate into an executable software system. With a prototype system to demonstrate requirements which they don't fully understand, stakeholders find it easier to discover problems and suggest how the requirements may be improved.

As well as serving as an experimental system, there are other benefits from developing a system prototype during the requirements engineering process.

♦ The prototype may help to establish the overall feasibility and usefulness of the system before high development costs are incurred.

♦ Prototyping is the only effective way of developing system user interfaces. If a prototype has been developed as part of the requirements process, this can reduce later development costs for the system.

♦ It may be possible to use the prototype to develop system tests which can be used later in the system validation process. Executable prototypes can also be used for back-to-back testing with the final system where the same tests are submitted to both prototype and final system. If the outputs are not the same, this suggests that an error or an inconsistency may have been introduced into the software.

◆ Prototype implementation requires careful study of the requirements. This, in itself, often reveals requirements inconsistencies and incompleteness.

There are, of course, costs and problems associated with prototyping and these must be traded-off against the benefits of this approach. These include the following.

1. **Training costs**
   If a company does not have experience of prototype development, developers must be trained in the use of a prototyping environment or in the particular prototyping techniques discussed in the following section.

2. **Development costs**
   These obviously depend on the type of system being prototyped and the prototyping method which is used. They can range from a few person days for small systems to several person-years for very large system prototypes.

3. **Extended development schedules**
   In some cases, developing a prototype will cause the development schedule to be extended so that the final delivery date of the product is delayed. However, if the product which is delivered is more suited to the customer's needs, this is not necessarily a problem. It may also be the case that the time taken for prototyping is less than the time required to fix the development problems that might have arisen without the prototype.

4. **Incomplete prototyping**
   Prototyping can only simulate the functionality or the final system and is of little help in determining the emergent system requirements. In fact, it can mislead users, as they may think that the system as a whole will have the same performance and reliability characteristics as the prototype. They may express their requirements with this in mind.

Most organisations have found that taking the time to develop a system prototype is worthwhile. Although initial development costs are higher, the requirements are more likely to reflect the real needs of the customer. There is less need for requirements rework after the system has gone into service.

3.3.1 Prototype implementation

Prototypes must be available during the requirements elicitation phase which means that they must be implemented quickly. Conventional system development techniques usually take too long, so rapid system development methods have to be used for prototyping. When these are used to develop a simplified system, it is sometimes possible to develop a prototype in a few days where a complete system implementation would take several months.

There are three possible approaches which allow a prototype system to be developed relatively quickly.

1. Paper prototyping, where a mock-up of the system is developed and used for system experiments.

2. 'Wizard of Oz' prototyping, where a person simulates the responses of the system in response to some user inputs.

3. Automated prototyping, where a fourth generation language or other rapid development environment is used to develop an executable prototype.

Paper prototyping is a cheap and surprisingly effective approach to prototype development. No executable software need be developed. Paper versions of the screens which might be presented to the end-user are drawn and various usage scenarios are planned. Analysts and end-users work through these scenarios and simulate how the system might be used. For interactive systems, this is an effective way to find users' reactions to the system, the information they require and how they would normally interact with the system.

'Wizard of Oz' prototyping is also relatively cheap as it does not require much software to be developed. The user interacts with what appears to be the system but his or her inputs are actually channelled to a person who simulates the system's responses. This approach is particularly useful when a new system has to be developed which is an extension of an existing system. Users are familiar with the interface and can see the interactions between it and the system functionality simulated by the 'Wizard of Oz'. The only software required in this case is the user interface software. The underlying functional system need not be developed.

Developing an executable prototype of the system is a more expensive option. It involves writing software to simulate the functionality of the system to be delivered. Because of the need for rapid development, a very high level programming language should be used to develop the prototype. There are several alternatives.

1. Fourth generation languages based around database systems. These are good for prototyping applications which involve information manage-

ment. However, they do have restrictions which are inherent in the interaction facilities which they provide. These limitations may mean that some facilities (e.g. navigation around a database by using a graphical visualisation of the data) may be impossible.

2. Visual programming languages such as Visual Basic or ObjectWorks. These are general purpose programming language which come with a powerful development environment, access to a range of reusable objects and a user interface development system which allows interfaces to the quickly created. These systems are more flexible than 4GLs but not, generally, so good for database-oriented applications.

3. Internet-based prototyping solutions based on World Wide Web browsers and languages such as Java. Here, you have a ready-made user interface. You add functionality to it by associating segments of Java programs with the information to be displayed. These segments (called applets) are executed automatically when the page is loaded into the browser. This approach is a fast way of developing user interface prototypes but there are inherent restrictions imposed by the browser and the Java security model.

Prototyping interactive systems is much easier than prototyping real-time systems. Most prototyping systems are not designed for efficient hardware interaction so you may not be able to access the sensors and actuators which will be used in the final system.

Some requirements are practically impossible to prototype. This is particularly true for 'whole system' requirements which reflect general objectives such as system usability, reliability, etc. In general, because the performance, efficiency, reliability, etc. of a prototype are quite different from those of a finished system, you can only use prototypes to discover the functional requirements for a system.

3.4   Requirements analysis and negotiation

Requirements analysis and negotiation are activities which aim to discover problems with the system requirements and reach agreement on changes to satisfy all system stakeholders. Some analysis is usually inter-leaved with requirements elicitation as problems are sometimes obvious as soon as a requirement is expressed. However, further analysis usually takes place after the initial draft of the requirements document is produced. The analysts involved read the requirements, highlight problems and meet in a requirements review to discuss the requirements. Obviously, requirements analysis has something in common with requirements validation which is described in the following chapter. However, it is a different process. Analysis is concerned with an incomplete set of requirements which has not been discussed by stakeholders. Validation should have an agreed, complete set of requirements as its starting point.

Requirements analysis and negotiation is an expensive and time-consuming process because skilled and experienced people must spend time reading documents carefully and thinking about the implications of the statements in these documents. People do not all think in the same way and different analysts will tackle the process in different ways. It is not possible to turn requirements analysis and negotiation into structured, systematic processes. They are reliant on the judgement and experience of the process participants.

3.4.1 Analysis checklists

A checklist is a list of questions which the analyst may use to assess each requirement. Analysts should check items on this list as they read through the requirements document. When potential problems are discovered, these should be noted either in the margins of the document or on a separate analysis list. Analysis checklists can be implemented as a spreadsheet where the rows are labelled with the requirements identifiers and the columns are the checklist items. You then fill in the appropriate cell with comments about potential problems.

Checklists are useful because they provide a reminder of what to look for and reduce the chances that you will forget some requirements checks. The analysis checklists are an organisational resource which must evolve with experience of the requirements analysis process. The questions on the checklist should usually be general rather than restrictive. If the questions are too specific, they will be irrelevant for most systems. Figure 3.8 shows a possible requirements analysis checklist.

Checklists should not normally include more than 10 items. People can't hold a lot of items in their head, so people forget items on long checklists when reading through a document. Furthermore, long checklists inevitably mean that most questions are irrelevant to most requirements and they will be applied in a perfunctory way. The only exception to this is in critical systems specifications where particularly detailed analysis may be required and there may be a long list of potential checks which should be carried out. In these cases, the additional time needed to use a large number of checklist items is acceptable because of the particularly high costs of specification errors.

3.4.2 Interaction matrices

A very important objective of requirements analysis is to discover the interactions between requirements and to highlight requirements conflicts and

Checklist item	Description
Premature design	Does the requirement include premature design or implementation information?
Combined requirements	Does the description of a requirement describe a single requirement or could it be broken down into several different requirements?
Unnecessary requirements	Is the requirement 'gold plating'? That is, is the requirement a cosmetic addition to the system which is not really necessary.
Use of non-standard hardware	Does the requirement mean that non-standard hardware or software must be used? To make this decision, you need to know the computer platform requirements.
Conformance with business goals	Is the requirement consistent with the business goals defined in the introduction to the requirements document?
Requirements ambiguity	Is the requirement ambiguous i.e. could it be read in different ways by different people? What are the possible interpretations of the requirement? Ambiguity is not necessarily a bad thing as it allows system designers some freedom. However, it has to be removed at some stage in the development process.
Requirements realism	Is the requirement realistic given the technology which will be used to implement the system?
Requirements testability	Is the requirement testable, that is, is it stated in such a way that test engineers can derive a test which can show if the system meets that requirement?

Figure 3.8
Analysis
checklist items.

overlaps. To help with this process, an interaction matrix can be constructed which displays this information. The simplest way to construct an interaction matrix is to use a spreadsheet program and to label the rows and the columns of the spreadsheet with the requirement identifiers. Each requirement is then considered and compared with other requirements. You then fill in values in the spreadsheet cells as follows:

1. For requirements which conflict, fill in a 1
2. For requirements which overlap, fill in a 1000
3. For requirements which are independent, fill in a 0

If you can't decide whether requirements conflict, you should assume that a conflict exists. If you assume a conflict where none exists then it is usually fairly cheap to fix this problem; it can be much more expensive to resolve undetected conflicts.

Figure 3.9 shows an example of an interaction matrix where 6 requirements are compared.

Figure 3.9
An interaction
matrix.

Requirement	R1	R2	R3	R4	R5	R6
R1	0	0	1000	0	1	1
R2	0	0	0	0	0	0
R3	1000	0	0	1000	0	1000
R4	0	0	1000	0	1	1
R5	1	0	0	1	0	0
R6	1	0	1000	1	0	0

In the interaction matrix shown in Figure 3.9, we can see that R1 overlaps with R3 and conflicts with R5 and R6; R2 is an independent requirement; R3 overlaps with R1, R4 and R6 and so on. These overlaps and conflicts have to be discussed and resolved during requirements negotiation.

The advantage of using numeric values for conflicts and overlaps is that you can then sum each row and column to find the number of conflicts (i.e. the remainder when the total is divided by 1000) and the number of overlaps (the total divided by 1000). Requirements which have high values for one or both of these figures should be carefully examined as part of the analysis process. A large number of conflicts or overlaps means that any changes to that requirement will probably have a major impact on the rest of the system.

Interaction matrices only work when there is a relatively small number of requirements as they require each requirement to be compared with every other requirement in the system. The upper size limit is probably about 200 requirements.

3.4.3 Requirements negotiation

All complex systems have many stakeholders and it is inevitable that some of these stakeholders will disagree about the system requirements and put different priorities on different system services. Requirements negotiation is the process of discussing the conflicts in requirements and finding some compromise which all of the stakeholders can live with. The final requirements will always be a compromise which is governed by the needs of the organisation in general, the specific requirements of different stakeholders, design and implementation constraints and the budget and schedule for the system development.

In principle, requirements negotiation should be an objective process. The judgements on the requirements for the system should be based on technical and organisational needs. However, reality is often different. Negotiations are rarely conducted using only logical, technical arguments. They are influenced by organisational and political considerations and the personalities of the people involved. A strong personality may force their priorities on other stakeholders; requirements may be accepted or rejected because they strengthen the political influence in the organisation of some stakeholders; end-users may be resistant to change and may block requirements, etc.

The majority of time in requirements negotiation is usually spent resolving requirements conflicts. A requirements conflict arises when two or more requirements ask for different things. For example, one requirement on a distributed system from organisational managers might be that they have privileged access to local data. However, security staff may have the requirement that only the system manager has privileged access. The conflict here must be resolved in requirements negotiation.

In spite of years of experience, many organisations still don't allow enough time to resolve requirements conflicts. The reason for this is, perhaps, that conflicts are considered as some kind of 'failure' and it is not acceptable to plan for failure. This view is completely wrong. Conflicts are natural and inevitable. They reflect the fact that different stakeholders in the system have different needs and priorities. You cannot produce a system that will completely satisfy everyone. If you do not have open and explicit conflict negotiation, some stakeholders are likely to be disgruntled and hostile to the system.

Meetings are the most effective way to negotiate requirements and resolve requirements conflicts. Conflict resolution meetings should be solely concerned with resolving outstanding requirements problems. The meeting should be attended by analysts who have discovered requirements conflicts, omissions and overlaps and system stakeholders who can help resolve the problems which have been discovered.

The negotiation meeting should discuss those requirements where problems cannot be resolved by informal discussions between stakeholders and analysts. All requirements which are in conflict should be discussed individually. You should not assume that decisions made for one requirement will necessarily apply to related requirements.

The meeting should be conducted in three stages, as follows.

1. An information stage where the nature of the problems associated with a requirement is explained.

2. A discussion stage where the stakeholders involved discuss how these problems might be resolved. All stakeholders with an interest in the requirement should be given the opportunity to comment. Priorities may be assigned to requirements at this stage. This helps the meeting to decide what requirements may be eliminated and what requirements must be included in the final system specification.

3. A resolution stage where actions concerning the requirement are agreed. These actions might be to delete the requirement, to suggest specific modifications to the requirement or to elicit further information about the requirement. If you record requirements rationale, you must remember to modify this to reflect requirements changes made during this meeting.

Meeting participants should be given copies of the results of the analysis (e.g. requirements checklists) and the meeting should be chaired by someone who is not a stakeholder in the system. They should be independent, which makes it easier for them to ensure that the views of all stakeholders are considered.

◆ **Key Points**

◆ Requirements elicitation involves understanding the application domain, the specific problem to be solved, the organisational needs and constraints and the specific facilities needed by system stakeholders.

◆ The processes of requirements elicitation, analysis and negotiation are inter-leaved processes which may be repeated several times before a statement of the system requirements, acceptable to all stakeholders, can be produced.

◆ There are various techniques of requirements elicitation which may be used, including interviewing, scenarios, soft systems methods, prototyping and participant observation. All have strengths and weaknesses and may be used together in a requirements elicitation process.

◆ Many stakeholders find it difficult to relate to and understand abstract system descriptions. For this reason, prototypes are effective for requirements elicitation because stakeholders have something which they can experiment with to find their real requirements.

◆ Checklists are particularly useful as a way of organising the requirements validation process. They remind analysts what to look for when reading through the proposed requirements.

◆ Requirements negotiation is always necessary to resolve requirements conflicts and remove requirements overlaps. Negotiation involves information interchange, discussion and resolution of disagreements.

◆ **Exercises**

3.1 Using examples to support your answer, explain why domain knowledge is important in the requirements elicitation process.

3.2 Explain why it is simplistic to present requirements elicitation, analysis and negotiation as serial, sequential processes. Why is the spiral model shown in Figure 0.2 a better representation of these processes? What is the simplification in this model?

3.3 What are the advantages and disadvantages of interviewing as a requirements elicitation technique. Explain how observation of work processes can be used to supplement the information gained from interviews and discussions of the system with stakeholders.

3.4 Identify possible stakeholders in the following systems.

A stockholding system for oil companies which keeps track of the amount of petrol (gas) at each of its sales outlets and automatically reorders new stock when the tanks fall below a certain level.

A train protection system which will automatically bring a train to a halt if it exceeds the speed limit for a track segment or if it goes through a red signal.

An information system for television schedulers which provides information about viewing figures for all programmes produced by different TV stations as well as other information about major events, such as football matches, which may affect programme scheduling.

3.5 Write plausible scenarios for the following activities:
◆ registering for a university or college course
◆ processing an application for a loan or a credit card
◆ transferring funds from one account to another using an ATM
◆ searching a library catalogue for books on the topic of requirements elicitation. If there are no books with this title, you should extend your search to related areas.

3.6 Explain why the combination of ethnography and prototyping is useful for requirements elicitation.

3.7 What is the critical distinction between throw-away and evolutionary prototyping?

3.8 You have been asked to prototype the requirements for the EDDIS library system which is discussed in Chapter 10. Giving reasons for your answer, suggest an appropriate prototyping method which may be used.

3.9 Suggest two reasons why requirements may be ambiguous? Give examples of possible ambiguities which may arise in a library system, a television scheduling system or a fuel stock control system as described in Exercise 3.4.

◆ **References**

Ackroyd, S., Harper, R., et al. (1992). *Information Technology and Practical Police Work.* Milton Keynes: Open University Press.

Bentley, R., Rodden, T., et al. (1992). Ethnographically-informed Systems Design for Air Traffic Control. *CSCW'92*, Toronto, Canada.

Bustard, D. W., Dobbin, T. J., et al. (1995). Integrating Soft Systems and Object Oriented Analysis. *Proc. ICRE'95*, Colorado Springs, IEEE Press.

Checkland, P. (1981). *Systems Thinking, Systems Practice.* Chichester: John Wiley & Sons.

Checkland, P. and Scholes, J. (1990). *Soft Systems Methodology in Action.* Chichester: John Wiley & Sons.

Davis, A. M. (1993). *Software Requirements: Objects, Functions and States.* Englewood Cliffs, New Jersey: Prentice-Hall.

Eason, K. D. (1988). *Information Technology and Organisational Change.* London: Taylor and Francis.

Fowler, M., and Scott, K. (1997). *UML Distilled: Applying the Standard Object Modelling Language.* Reading, Massachusetts: Addison Wesley.

Gamma, E., Helm, R., et al. (1995). *Design Patterns: Elements of Reusable Object-Oriented Software.* Reading, Massachusetts: Addison-Wesley.

Goguen, J. and Linde, C. (1993). Techniques for Requirements Elicitation. *Proc. RE'93*, San Diego, California, IEEE Computer Society Press.

Gough, P. A., Fodemski, F. T., et al. (1995). Scenarios – An Industrial Case Study and Hypermedia Enhancements. *Proc. RE'95*, York, UK, IEEE Press.

Harper, R., Hughes, J., et al. (1991). Harmonious Working and CSCW: Computer Technology and Air Traffic Control. In: *Studies in Computer-Supported Cooperative Work.* Eds J. M. Bowers and S. D. Benford. Amsterdam, Kluwer: 225–34.

Heath, C., Jirotka, M., et al. (1993). Unpacking collaboration: the interactional organisation of trading in a city dealing room. *ECSCW'93*, Milan.

Holtzblatt, K. and Beyer, H. (1993). Making Customer-Centred Design Work for Teams. *Communications of the ACM* **36**(10): 93–103.

Hughes, J., O'Brien, J., et al. (1995). Presenting Ethnography in the Requirements Process. *Proc. RE'95*, York, UK, IEEE Computer Society Press.

Jacobsen, I., Christerson, M., et al. (1993). *Object-Oriented Software Engineering.* Wokingham: Addison-Wesley.

Mumford, E. (1989). User Participation in a Changing Environment – Why We Need It. In: *Participation in Systems Development.* Ed. K. Knight. London, Kogan Page.

Potts, C., Takahashi, K., et al. (1994). Inquiry-based Requirements Analysis. *IEEE Software* **11**(2): 21–32.

Suchman, L. (1987). *Plans and Situated Actions*. Cambridge: Cambridge University Press.

Yeh, R., and Zave, P. (1980). Specifying Software Requirements. *Proceedings of the IEEE* **68**(9): 1077–85.

◆ Further reading

Requirements Engineering (L. A. Macaulay, Springer, 1996) This book on requirements engineering doesn't really cover the whole process but it focuses on elicitation and understanding the system. As well as some of the techniques discussed here, the author describes various group-based and interactive approaches to elicitation.

The Role of Ethnography in Interactive Systems Design (J. Hughes, V. King, T. Rodden, H. Andersen, *ACM Interactions*, II.2, 56–65, April 1995). A general introduction to ethnography and its use in analysing work processes with a view to understanding their automation requirements.

4 Requirements Validation

◆ **Summary**

Requirements validation is concerned with checking the requirements document for consistency, completeness, and accuracy. This chapter describes a number of different, complementary, approaches to validation. Requirements reviews are the normal validation technique where a group of stakeholders check the requirements document. A prototype system may be developed for validation and we discuss here how prototypes, developed for requirements elicitation, may be extended to support validation activities. We also cover automated model validation where automatic checks may be applied to a structured or formal requirements model of the system. Finally, we discuss the notion of requirements testing where validation involves designing requirements tests and simulating their application to the system.

◆

Requirements validation is the final stage of requirements engineering. As the name implies, the aim of requirements validation is to 'validate' the requirements, i.e. check the requirements to certify that they represent an acceptable description of the system which is to be implemented. The process involves system stakeholders, requirements engineers and system designers who analyse the requirements for problems, omissions and ambiguities.

In this book, we make a distinction between requirements analysis and requirements validation and cover them in separate chapters. Obviously, however, these activities have much in common; they involve analysing the requirements, judging if they are an appropriate description of stakeholder needs and checking for requirements problems. However, there are important differences between these activities so that it makes sense to consider them separately.

1. Requirements analysis is concerned with 'raw' requirements as elicited from system stakeholders. The requirements are usually incomplete and are expressed in an informal and unstructured way. There will probably be a mixture of notations used to describe the requirements. The focus during requirements analysis should be on making sure that the requirements meet stakeholder needs rather than the details of the requirements description.

   In short, requirements analysis should mostly be concerned with answering the question 'have we got the right requirements?'

2. Requirements validation is concerned with checking a final draft of a requirements document which includes all system requirements and where known incompleteness and inconsistency has been removed. The document and the requirements should follow defined quality standards. While the needs of stakeholders must obviously be considered, the validation process should be more concerned with the way in which the requirements are described.

   In short, requirements validation should mostly (but not exclusively) be concerned with answering the question 'have we got the requirements right?'

Analysis should focus on stakeholder needs before the detailed requirements document is produced. Ideally, the requirements document should only include requirements which are acceptable to stakeholders. Inevitably, however, some stakeholder-related problems are inevitably discovered during requirements validation and these must be corrected.

Examples of requirements problems discovered during validation might be:

- lack of conformance to quality standards
- poorly worded requirements which are ambiguous
- errors in models of the system or the problem to be solved
- requirements conflicts which were not detected during the analysis process.

These problems should be solved before the requirements document is approved and used as a basis for system development. In some cases, the problems will simply be documentation problems and can be fixed by improving the requirements description. In other cases, however, the problems result from flaws in the requirements elicitation, analysis and modelling. You may have to re-enter some of the earlier requirements engineering process activities.

The main problem of requirements validation is that there is no existing document which can be a basis for the validation. A design or a program may be validated against the specification. However, there is no way to demonstrate that a requirements specification is 'correct' with respect to some other system representation. Specification validation, therefore, really means ensuring that the requirements document represents a clear description of the system for design and implementation and is a final check that the requirements meet stakeholder needs.

Figure 4.1 shows the inputs and outputs of the requirements validation process.

The inputs to the requirements validation process are as follows.

1. **The requirements document**
   This should be a complete version of the document rather than an unfinished draft. It should be formatted and organised according to organisational standards.

2. **Organisational standards**
   The requirements validation process should check conformance with company standards. Therefore, whatever standards are relevant for the requirements document should be an input to the validation process.

3. **Organisational knowledge**
   This is not a tangible input but is, in practice, very important. The people involved in requirements validation may know the organisation, its particular terminology and its practices and the skills of the people involved in developing and using the system. This implicit knowledge is very important as the same requirements may be closely linked to organisational structure, standards and culture.

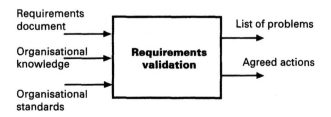

Figure 4.1 Requirements validation – inputs and outputs.

The process outputs are as follows.

1. **A problem list**
    This is a list of reported problems with the requirements document. Ideally, it should be organised into problem type, e.g. ambiguity, incompleteness, etc. In practice, however, it is often difficult to classify problems in this way.

2. **Agreed actions**
    This is a list of actions in response to requirements problems which have been agreed by those involved in the validation process. There is not necessarily a 1:1 correspondence between problems and actions. Some problems may result in several corrective actions; others may simply be noted but with no associated corrective action.

Requirements validation is a prolonged process as it involves people reading and thinking about a lengthy document. Meetings may have to be arranged and experiments carried out with prototype systems. It can take several weeks or sometimes months to validate the requirements for a complex system. This is particularly likely when stakeholders from different organisations are involved.

There is always a natural tendency to rush the validation process so that system development can begin, particularly where the development schedule is very tight. However, if system development starts too early, some rework is almost inevitable as requirements problems emerge. Errors in delivered systems which are a consequence of requirements errors may cost up to 100 times as much to repair as programming errors. If these errors and problems can be discovered during requirements validation, the amount of design and implementation rework is reduced.

4.1 Requirements reviews

Requirements reviews are the most widely used technique of requirements validation. They involve a group of people who read and analyse the requirements, look for problems, meet to discuss these problems and agree on a set of actions to address the identified problems. There is very little published work which focuses specifically on requirements reviews and how these should be conducted. However, there is a lot of evidence that program inspections (Fagan, 1976; Fagan, 1986; Weller, 1993; Barnard and Price, 1994) are a very effective way of discovering problems with code and various ways of organising program inspection processes have been proposed (Gilb and

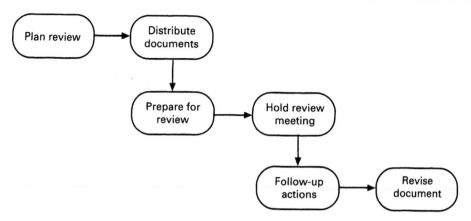

Figure 4.2
The
requirements
review process.

Graham, 1993). The review process model described here is based on this work and on our experience of requirements reviews.

Figure 4.2 shows a simple process model for the requirements review process. The principal stages in the review process are as follows.

1. **Plan review**
   The review team is selected and a time and place for the review meeting is chosen.

2. **Distribute documents**
   The requirements document and any other relevant documents are distributed to the review team members.

3. **Prepare for review**
   The individual reviewers read the requirements document to identify conflicts, omissions, inconsistencies, deviations from standards and any other problems.

4. **Hold review meeting**
   The individual comments and problems are discussed and a set of actions to address the problems is agreed.

5. **Follow-up actions**
   The chair of the review checks that the agreed actions have been carried out.

6. **Revise document**
   The requirements document is revised to reflect the agreed actions. At this stage, it may be accepted or it may be re-reviewed.

The requirements review is a formal meeting. It should be chaired by someone who has not been involved in producing the requirements which are being validated. During the meeting, a requirements engineer presents each requirement in turn for comment by the group and identified problems are recorded for later discussion. One member of the group should be assigned the role of scribe to note the identified requirements problems.

In program inspections, it is normal practice to report errors to the program author for correction. However, in requirements reviews, the review group make decisions on actions to be taken to correct the identified problems. Unlike programming errors, the problems usually require discussion and negotiation to agree on a possible solution.

Actions which might be decided for each problem are as follows.

1. **Requirements clarification**

   The requirement may be badly expressed or may have accidentally omitted information which has been collected during requirements elicitation. The author should improve the requirement by rewriting it.

2. **Missing information**

   Some information is missing from the requirements document. It is the responsibility of the requirements engineers who are revising the document to discover this information from system stakeholders or other requirements sources.

3. **Requirements conflict**

   There is a significant conflict between requirements. The stakeholders involved must negotiate to resolve the conflict.

4. **Unrealistic requirement**

   The requirement does not appear to be implementable with the technology available or given other constraints on the system. Stakeholders must be consulted to decide whether the requirement should be deleted or modified to make it more realistic.

The time taken for a requirements document review obviously depends on the size of the requirements document. There are published figures available for program inspections (about 125 lines of code per hour can be inspected, with the same time required for preparation) but not for requirements reviews. Our guess is that probably about 20–40 requirements per hour could be inspected, depending on the size of the requirements. A comparable time is required for preparation. Therefore, a document with 400 requirements would require a total of 50 person-hours of effort to inspect if a 4-person team were involved.

4.1.1 Pre-review checking

Reviews involve a lot of time and expense so it makes sense to minimise the work of reviewers. Errors which are avoidable and which can be detected without a full review should be removed from the requirements document before it is circulated to the review team. Avoidable errors are usually those errors which can be detected automatically such as spelling mistakes and errors of non-conformance to organisational standards.

Before distributing the requirements document for general review, one person should carry out a quick standards check to ensure that the document structure and the defined requirements are consistent with whatever standards have been defined. They should also process the document with whatever automatic checkers are available to remove spelling mistakes, cross-reference errors, etc. This is illustrated in Figure 4.3.

This is a quick and cheap way to check standards conformance as only one person is needed to carry out this type of check. It is not worth everyone involved in the review process checking the document against the standard and all reporting the same standards deviations. Furthermore, checking against a standard can quickly reveal problems with the requirements. If a requirements document does not conform to company standards, it may indicate large-scale problems with the requirements specification which require management intervention for their solution.

An analyst or an engineer who is familiar with the requirements standards but who has not been involved in the system requirements specification should be responsible for this initial document check. It is not necessary for the document checker to understand the requirements in detail. The checker should compare the structure of the requirement document to the defined standard and should highlight missing or incomplete sections. The search and outline facilities provided with most word processing systems may be used to find parts of the document and display the document structure. Individual requirements should also be checked for standards conformance.

This initial check should also check that all pages in the document are numbered, that all diagrams and figures are labelled, that there are no requirements

Figure 4.3
Pre-review
checking.

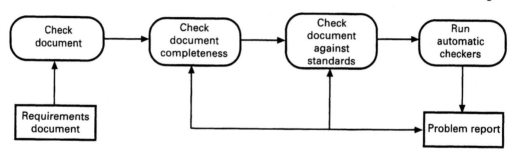

which are unfinished or labelled 'To be completed' and that all required appendices in the document have been included.

After the initial checking process is complete, there are two possible options if deviations from the standard are found.

◆ Return the document to the requirements engineering team to correct deviations from the standards. This option should be chosen if there is enough time to allow for a re-issue of the document.

◆ Note the deviations from the standards and distribute this to document reviewers. This saves the time and cost of creating a new version of the requirements document. However, the deviations from standards may make it harder for reviewers to understand the requirements.

Unless the requirements document is very large, this initial check of the requirements should not normally take more than a day. The saving in time for other document reviewers is therefore significant.

4.1.2 Review team membership

Selecting the right membership for the requirements review team is important. Ideally, the requirements document should be reviewed by a multi-disciplinary team drawn from people with different backgrounds. If possible, the team should include a system end-user or end-user representative, a customer representative, one or more domain experts, engineers who will be responsible for system design and implementation and requirements engineers.

The advantages of involving stakeholders from different disciplines are as follows.

◆ People from different backgrounds bring different skills, domain knowledge and experience to the review. It is therefore more probable that requirements problems will be discovered.

◆ If system stakeholders from different backgrounds are involved in the review process, they feel involved in the requirements engineering process and develop an understanding of the needs of other stakeholders. They are therefore more likely to understand why changes to requirements which they have proposed are necessary.

The review team should include different stakeholders who have been involved in the requirements elicitation. If this is not possible, there should be at least one domain expert and one end-user involved in the process. System developers should become involved at this stage as they may find requirements which are particularly difficult to implement. If these can be discovered and modified before design and implementation, this can save a lot of effort and expense.

Unlike program inspections where 4 or 5 members is the normal team size, requirements reviews may involve a varying number of people ranging from 3 to perhaps 10 people. There is no ideal size – it depends on the type and size of the system and the number of stakeholders who are likely to be affected by the system.

Inspections require a group of people with different skills and responsibilities to read documents. They must get together in the same place at the same time to carry out the inspection. As the people involved may work for different organisations or different parts of the same organisation this can be very difficult. Therefore, it is sometimes necessary to make compromises. A review team which is less than ideal but which can meet fairly quickly to review the requirements may be better than a delayed review.

4.1.3 Review checklists

The use of checklists which describe characteristic and frequently occurring errors is an inherent part of the program inspection process. Program inspectors look at each statement in the code and use the checklist as a prompt to discover the analysis which should be carried out for that statement. This is a very effective technique which can also be used for the individual checking of programs.

This approach works well because programmers often make the same kinds of errors such as failing to de-allocate memory, indexing beyond the end of an array, executing loops one more time than necessary, etc. While requirements engineers may also make comparable mistakes, these are usually hidden by the diversity of different types of system and application domain. It isn't practical to produce very detailed checklists expect perhaps for critical systems (e.g. Leveson's checklist for safety-critical systems (Leveson, 1995)). Rather, requirements review checklists should be more general. They should not be concerned with individual requirements but with the quality properties of the requirements document as a whole and with the relationships between requirements.

Figure 4.4 lists some general quality properties of requirements and requirements documents which may be used to derive requirements checklists.

Organisations should derive their own set of requirements review questions based on their experience and their local standards. These may include more specialised questions which are tailored to the types of system which they develop. Figure 4.5 gives some examples of possible questions which might be associated with the quality attributes described in Figure 4.4.

Checklists should be expressed in a fairly general way and should be understandable by people such as end-users who are not system experts. As

Review check	Description
Understandability	Can readers of the document understand what the requirements mean? This is probably the most important attribute of a requirements document – if it can't be understood, the requirements can't be validated.
Redundancy	Is information unnecessarily repeated in the requirements document? Sometimes, of course, repeating information adds to understandability. There must be a balance struck between removing all redundancy and making the document harder to understand.
Completeness	Does the checker know of any missing requirements or is there any information missing from individual requirement descriptions?
Ambiguity	Are the requirements expressed using terms which are clearly defined? Could readers from different backgrounds make different interpretations of the requirements?
Consistency	Do the descriptions of different requirements include contradictions? Are there contradictions between individual requirements and overall system requirements?
Organisation	Is the document structured in a sensible way? Are the descriptions of requirements organised so that related requirements are grouped? Would an alternative structure be easier to understand?
Conformance to standards	Does the requirements document and individual requirements conform to defined standards? If there is a departure from the standards, is it justified?
Traceability	Are requirements unambiguously identified, include links to related requirements and to the reasons why these requirements have been included? Is there a clear link between software requirements and more general systems engineering requirements?

Figure 4.4
Requirements
quality
attributes.

a general rule, checklists should not be too long. If checklists have more than 10 items, checkers cannot remember all items. They must continually re-consult the checklist to remind themselves about its contents.

Checklists can be distributed and used to remind people what to look for when reading the requirements document. Alternatively, they can be used more systematically where, for each requirement, an indication is given that the checklist item has been considered. This may be done on paper or you can manage this type of checklist completion by using a simple database or a spreadsheet.

4.1.4 Examples of requirements problems

It isn't really possible in a book to give a true impression of the reality of a requirements review meeting. It is often the case that different reviewers will

Checklist question	Quality attribute
Is each requirement uniquely identified?	Traceability, Conformance to standards
Are specialised terms defined in the glossary	Understandability
Does a requirement stand on its own or do you have to examine other requirements to understand what it means?	Understandability, completeness
Do individual requirements use the same term in different ways	Ambiguity
Is the same service requested in different requirements? Are there any contradictions in these requests?	Consistency, redundancy,
If a requirement makes reference to some other facilities, are these described elsewhere in the document?	Completeness
Are related requirements grouped together? If not, do they refer to each other?	Organisation, traceability

Figure 4.5
Examples of
checklist
questions.

disagree about problems in the requirements document. As in any other process involving people, issues of status and personality are often more important in decision-making than technical judgements. All we can do here is to give some examples of the kinds of problem that can be discovered in requirements reviews and suggest the recommendations that a review meeting might make to help solve these problems.

The requirements which we use as examples are some of the initial requirements which were derived for the case study that we describe in Chapter 10. These are requirements for the EDDIS library system which is an interactive system providing access to a large document database and which allows the automated ordering and electronic delivery of documents to local and remote end-users. The style of these requirements is fairly typical of the general way in which initial system requirements are written.

The example requirements here is concerned with the provision of copyright safeguards in the document distribution system. There are complex issues of copyright when document copies are distributed so this requirement allows for this:

4. EDDIS will be configurable so that it will comply with the requirements of all UK and (where relevant) international copyright legislation.

Minimally, this means that EDDIS must provide a form for the user to sign the Copyright Declaration statement. It also means that EDDIS must keep track of Copyright Declaration statements which have been signed/not-signed. Under no circumstances must an order be sent to the supplier if the copyright statement has not been signed.

Figure 4.6 shows some of the problems in this requirement which might be revealed in a requirements review and recommendations which may be agreed in a review meeting.

Other requirements for the EDDIS system are concerned with the user interface. The intention is that distributed access to the system will be provided through World-Wide-Web browsers. We see an example of redundancy and possible conflict in the requirements for the case study when we consider requirements 8 and 11.

Figure 4.6
Problems with
an individual
requirement.

Problem type	Identified problem	Recommendation
Incompleteness	Requirement does not state which international copyright legislation is relevant.	Define all copyright legislation which is applicable in a separate requirement
Incompleteness	What happens to an order if it has been filled in and the copyright declaration statement has not been signed?	Reword requirement so that the copyright declaration must be signed before the order can be completed
Ambiguity	What does 'signing' an electronic form mean? Is this a physical signature on a piece of paper which is given to a person or is it some kind of digital signature.	Define what is meant by 'signature'
Incompleteness	If signature is interpreted as a 'digital signature', how are signatures assigned to individual users.	Introduce a new requirement for signature assignment
Standards	Requirement appears to contain more that 1 requirement. The maintenance of copyright declaration statements and the requirement that documents will not be issued without a signed copyright statement.	Split requirement into at least two and perhaps three separate requirements.

8.(i)   The user interface will be html. Users will access EDDIS via standard web browsers such as Netscape and Internet Explorer.

8.(ii)   EDDIS will be primarily an end-user sysem. Users will use the system within the constraints of the permissions assigned by the administrator to identify, locate, order and receive documents.

11.(i)   Users will communicate with EDDIS mainly via the html interface.

11.(ii)   User input to EDDIS will be via the html interface.

11.(iii)   EDDIS output to the user will be via the html interface, email and print. The print output will mainly be documents supplied which, because of copyright restrictions, must be printed and deleted immediately upon receipt. The email output will be documents, messages from the system and other output.

Figure 4.7 shows some of the problems with these requirements and the associated meeting recommendations.

Problem type	Identified problem	Recommendation
Redundancy	Requirement 8.(i) and Requirements 11.(i) seem to say the same thing.	Remove the first sentence in Requirement 8.(i).
Conflict, Understandability	Requirement 8.(i) states that access is via a standard Web browser; Requirement 11.(ii) states that communication is via html.	Rewrite 11.(i) to make clear that end-users do not actually have to write html directly to communicate with EDDIS
Completeness	Requirement 11.(iii) states that the print output will 'mainly' be documents ..., what else might be printed? What other output will be produced.	Either remove 'mainly' or clarify other print output. Define other output.
Completeness	What versions of html and web browsers are assumed in requirements 8.(i) and 11?	Define the minimal HTML standard and the browser versions supporting that standard.

Figure 4.7
Problems with requirements interactions.

Problems of understandability of requirements may arise because requirements writers have background knowledge about the system because of their involvement in the requirements engineering process. They unconsciously use this knowledge when writing the requirements. A statement which is perfectly clear to them may be incomprehensible without this essential background knowledge which is not explicit in the requirements document.

These problems of understanding may not be detected during requirements analysis because the stakeholders involved may also have the necessary background. However, when developers without this background knowledge are involved in the requirements review, they may find it hard to understand some of the requirements. Consider the following 'requirement' from the EDDIS system:

> 1. Although EDDIS is primarily an end-user system, it was recognised that, because of financial constraints, many of the functions of EDDIS would be mediated by an administrator. It was anticipated that the system would be administered by the Library but this would not always be the case. Furthermore, some of the administrator's functions could be devolved to other users; for example, EDDIS could be configured so that departments would have control of their own budgets.

It is not at all clear what requirement is actually being stated here. It clearly represents some discussions which took place about the system management but without more details of these discussions, the requirement is not understandable. A review meeting should recommend that this 'requirement' should either be deleted or should be more clearly expressed as a number of 'administration' requirements.

4.2 Prototyping

We have already discussed how a system prototype may be used for requirements elicitation and analysis. People find it very difficult to visualise how a written statement of requirements will translate into an executable software system. If you develop a prototype system to demonstrate requirements, stakeholders and other end-users find it easier to discover problems and suggest how the requirements may be improved.

If a prototype has been developed for requirements elicitation, it makes sense to use this later in the requirements engineering process for validation. However, if a prototype system is not already available, it is not likely to be cost-effective to develop a prototype system only for requirements validation.

Prototypes for validation must be more complete than elicitation prototypes. Elicitation prototypes can simply include those requirements which are particularly difficult to describe or understand. They may leave out well-understood requirements. While a validation prototype need not include all system facilities, there must be a sufficient number of facilities implemented in a reasonably efficient and robust way that end-users can make practical use of the system. Otherwise, they won't be able to use the system in a natural way.

Elicitation prototypes usually have missing functionality and may not include changes agreed during the requirements analysis process. It is therefore usually necessary to continue development of the prototype during the requirements validation process as shown in Figure 4.8. This figure also shows the other process activities which should go on in parallel with prototype development.

1. **Choose prototype testers**

   Choosing the right people to act as prototype testers is very important. There is a danger that people who are enthusiastic about the technology will volunteer and these may not be representative of real users. The best testers are users who are fairly experienced and who are open-minded about the use of new systems. If possible, end-users who do different jobs should be involved so that different areas of system functionality will be covered.

2. **Develop test scenarios**

   It is important that the prototype is exercised during the validation in a systematic way. This means that careful planning is required to draw up a set of test scenarios which provide broad coverage of the requirements. End-users will normally have other things to do apart from experiment with the prototype system and so have relatively little time to spend on validation. They shouldn't just play around with the system as this may never exercise critical system features.

3. **Execute scenarios**

   The users of the system work, usually on their own, to try the system by executing the planned scenarios. It is best that users work alone because they are then more likely to use the system in a realistic way and will not be biased by the advice given by requirements engineers. However, requirements engineers should spend some time observing

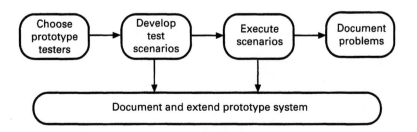

Figure 4.8
Prototyping for requirements validation.

how end-users make use of the system. This can reveal particular problem areas and the coping strategies which users develop for dealing with system features which they find useful but awkward to use.

4.   **Document problems**
      To be effective problems which users encounter must be carefully documented. Its usually best to define some kind of electronic or paper problem report form which users fill in when they encounter a problem or want to suggest some change to the system.

Requirements validation can begin with an incomplete prototype but the system should be extended and developed during the validation process. It is important that the prototype system is reliable. If it crashes regularly, users will quickly become discouraged and will abandon the system. If there are facilities missing, you should tell users about these in advance so that they don't waste time trying them unsuccessfully. User documentation and/or help scripts so that people can find out what to do when things go wrong should be written and available with the prototype system. If you don't provide this information, users will probably give up as soon as they encounter problems.

As well as being useful for requirements validation, a fairly complete prototype system may also be useful at later development stages.

◆   It may be possible to use the prototype to develop system tests which can be used later in the system validation process. Executable prototypes can also be used for back-to-back testing with the final system where the same tests are submitted to both prototype and final system and checked for consistency.

◆   An executable prototype may serve as a stop-gap system which can be delivered if there are delays in implementing the final system. This is important in situations where an organisation has planned other processes around the system and schedule slippage is very expensive.

Prototyping methods have already been discussed in Chapter 3 which covered the use of prototyping in requirements elicitation and analysis. These methods are also appropriate for implementing a prototype for requirements validation.

4.2.1   User manual development

As we discuss in the following section, rewriting the requirements in a different way is a very effective validation technique. To rewrite the requirements you must understand the requirements and the relationships between them. Developing this understanding reveals conflicts, omissions and inconsistencies. One possible alternative form of the requirements which may be produced using the validation process is a draft of the end-user documentation for the system.

The user manuals should include the following information.

1. A description of the functionality which has been implemented and how to access that functionality through the user interface.

2. It should be made clear which parts of the system are not implemented. Manual writers should not leave users to find this out when problems arise.

3. A description of how to recover from difficulties. Users are working with an experimental system and it is inevitable that things will go wrong. Information about how they can get back to a known system state and restart use of the system should be included.

4. If users have to install the prototype themselves, installation instructions should be provided.

If there is insufficient time or resources to build a prototype system for validation, some of the benefits of this approach can be gained by writing a draft user manual. The manual should be written by systematically translating the functionality described in the requirements into descriptions, written in end-user terms, of how to use them. If it is difficult to explain a function to end-users or to explain how to express system functionality, this suggests that there may be a requirements problem.

In some cases, the prototype user manual can be a basis for the final user documentation. However, this may not always be possible. The system development may be cancelled or the system may change to such an extent that a completely new user manual must to be written. The cost of writing the draft manual should be included in the requirements validation costs. Any subsequent saving in documentation costs is a bonus.

4.3 Model validation

Part of the requirements specification for a system may consist of one or more system models as discussed in Chapter 6. These models may be data-flow models of the system's functionality, object models, event models, entity-relation models, etc. The validation of these models has three objectives.

1. To demonstrate that each individual model is self-consistent. That is, the model should include all information which is necessary and there should be no conflicts between the different parts of the model.

2. If there are several models of the systems, to demonstrate that these are internally and externally consistent. That is, entities which are referenced in more than one model should be defined to be the same in each model, comparable items should have the same names and the model interfaces should be consistent.

3. To demonstrate that the models accurately reflect the real requirements of system stakeholders. This is the most difficult model validation task. It involves making convincing arguments that the system defined in the model is the system which stakeholders really need.

If models are expressed using notations which are supported by CASE tools, some of this checking can be automated. CASE tools can check individual models for consistency and can carry out some cross-model checks. However, some consistency checks involving several different models cannot be automated but may be considered in model reviews. An example of the type of check which cannot be automated is where an entity defined in one model is referenced in another but the reference is to the wrong entity.

Checking that the model reflects the real needs of stakeholders can be difficult. You need to get the stakeholders themselves involved in the model validation process. In spite of what some designers say, our experience is that non-technical people do not intuitively understand data-flow diagrams, event diagrams or object models. They prefer working with natural language descriptions even when these say exactly the same thing as a diagrammatic model.

One way to get round this problem is to paraphrase or rewrite the model in natural language. By making this transformation, stakeholders such as end-users, organisational management and regulators can understand and comment on the detailed system specification. Furthermore, the process of explaining the system model in natural language is an effective way to detect errors, inconsistencies and incompleteness in the model.

Converting a system model to natural language text should be done in a systematic way. The actual technique used should depend on the type of system model but we recommend using some kind of form or table where different components in the model are described in different fields or columns. For example, in a data-flow diagram, you might use a template with the following fields to describe each transformation:

1. **transformation name**

2. **transformation inputs and input sources**
    Gives the name of each input to the transformation and lists where that input comes from.

3. **transformation function**

Explain what the transformation is supposed to do to convert inputs to outputs.

4. **transformation outputs**

Gives the name of each output and lists where the output goes to.

5. **control**

Any exception or control information which is included in the model.

Figure 4.9 is an example of a data-flow diagram to document the library function 'Issue' (see Chapter 6). To illustrate how systematic paraphrasing of a model can reveal problems, we have modified this slightly and have left out the 'return date' input to the Issue item function

The paraphrased description of this data-flow diagram is shown in Figure 4.10. In this description, we have used a table with columns for inputs, transformations, outputs and control information.

We receive an immediate hint of a possible problem when we see that the Issue item function has no inputs. Further examination of the description shows that a return date must be associated with each item and this is unavailable. Therefore, it is likely that there is a flaw in the system model and this information is missing.

In some cases, it may be possible to partially automate this process. Some CASE tools will generate reports on the system models which can be a starting point for paraphrasing. However, these are normally fairly stilted. They must be modified to make them more readable and to add information which cannot be automatically derived. You may find that it is actually less effort to ignore the generation facilities and simply work directly from the system model.

Paraphrasing system models is particularly valuable when a mathematical model or formal specification of the system has been developed (as discussed

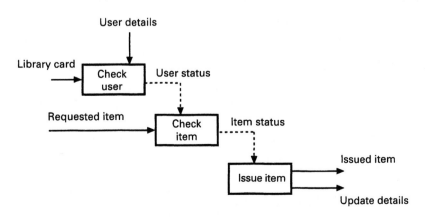

Figure 4.9
Data-flow diagram for the issue function.

Figure 4.10
Paraphrased description of 'Issue' data-flow diagram.

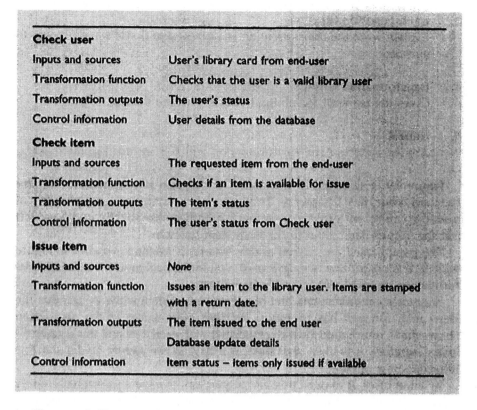

Check user	
Inputs and sources	User's library card from end-user
Transformation function	Checks that the user is a valid library user
Transformation outputs	The user's status
Control information	User details from the database
Check item	
Inputs and sources	The requested item from the end-user
Transformation function	Checks if an item is available for issue
Transformation outputs	The item's status
Control information	The user's status from Check user
Issue item	
Inputs and sources	None
Transformation function	Issues an item to the library user. Items are stamped with a return date.
Transformation outputs	The item issued to the end user
	Database update details
Control information	Item status – items only issued if available

in Chapter 6). These models have several advantages over structured models as they have a much more complete semantics and their consistency can be proved mathematically. However, it is usually the case that only a few people in an organisation can understand formal models so a translation to natural language is essential to validate that they reflect the real requirements of the system.

4.4 Requirements testing

A desirable attribute of requirement is that it should be testable. That is, it should be possible to define one or more tests that may be carried out in the finished system which will clearly demonstrate that the requirement has been met. The execution of the implemented requirement may be simulated using these tests. While the actual tests of a system are carried out after implementation, proposing possible tests is an effective way of revealing requirements problems such as incompleteness and ambiguity. If there are difficulties in deriving test cases for a requirement, this implies that there is some kind of requirement problem. There may be missing information in the requirement or the requirement description may not make clear exactly what is required.

Each functional requirement in the requirements document should be analysed and a test defined which can objectively check if the system satisfies the requirement. The objective of proposing test cases for requirements is to validate the requirement not the system. To define test cases for a requirement, you can ask the following questions about that requirement.

♦ What usage scenario might be used to check the requirement? This should define the context in which the test should be applied.

♦ Does the requirement, on its own, include enough information to allow a test to be defined? If not, what other requirements must be examined to find this information? If you need to look at other requirements, you should record these. There may be dependencies between requirements which are important for traceability (see Chapter 5).

♦ Is it possible to check the requirement using a single test or are multiple test cases required? If you need several tests, it may mean that there is more than one requirement embedded in a single requirement description.

♦ Could the requirement be re-stated so that the required test cases are fairly obvious?

A test record form should be designed and filled in for each requirement which is 'tested'. This should include at least the following information.

1. **The requirement's identifier**
   There should be at least one for each requirement.

2. **Related requirements**
   These should be referenced as the test may also be relevant to these requirements.

3. **Test description**
   A brief description of the test which could be applied and why this is an objective requirements test. This should include system inputs and the corresponding outputs which are expected.

4. **Requirements problems**
   A description of requirements problems which made test definition difficult or impossible.

5. **Comments and recommendations**
   These are advice on how to solve requirements problems which have been discovered.

As an example of how requirements tests can highlight requirements problems, consider the following requirement from the EDDIS system.

> 10.(iv) When users access EDDIS, they will be presented with web pages and all the services available to them

Figure 4.11 shows the requirements test form which documents the test for that requirement:

When designing requirements tests, the test designer need not be concerned with practicalities such as testing costs, avoiding redundant tests, detailed test data definition, etc. It isn't necessary to propose real tests which will be applied to the final system. The tester can make any assumptions that he wishes about the way in which the system satisfies other requirements and the ways in which the test may actually be carried out.

However, wherever possible, it makes sense to try and design tests which can be used as system tests. These are applied after implementation as part of the system verification and validation process. By reusing requirements tests in this way, the overall costs of test planning may be reduced.

There are problems, however, in designing tests for some types of requirement.

1.   **System requirements**

These are requirements which apply to the system as a whole. In general, these are the most difficult requirements to validate irrespective of the method used as they may be influenced by any of the functional require-

Figure 4.11
Requirements
test form.

> **Requirements tested**: 10(iv)
>
> **Related requirements**: 10i), 10(ii), 10(iii), 10(vi), 10 (vii)
>
> **Test applied**: For each class of user, prepare a login script and identify the services expected for that class of user.
>
> The results of the login should be a web page with a menu of available services.
>
> **Requirements problems**: We don't know the different classes of EDDIS user and the services which are available to each user class. Apart from the administrator, are all other EDDIS users in the same class?
>
> Recommendations: Explicitly list all user classes and the services which they can access.

ments. Tests, which are not executed, cannot test for non-functional system-wide characteristics such as usability.

2. **Exclusive requirements**

   These are requirements which exclude specific behaviour. For example, a requirement may state that system failures must never corrupt the system database. It is not possible to test such a requirement exhaustively so, again, confidence simply increases with the number of system tests.

3. **Some non-functional requirements**

   Some non-functional requirements, such as reliability requirements, can only be tested with a large test set. Designing this test set does not help with requirements validation.

◆ **Key Points**

◆ Requirements validation should focus on checking the final draft of the requirements document for conflicts, omissions and deviations from standards.

◆ The inputs to the validation process are the requirements document, organisational standards and implicit organisational knowledge. The outputs are a list of requirements problems and agreed actions to address these problems.

◆ Reviews are the most widely used form of requirements validation. They involve a group of people making a detailed analysis of the requirements.

◆ Review costs can be reduced by checking the requirements before the review for deviations from organisational standards. These may result from more serious requirements problems.

◆ Checklists of what to look for may be used to drive a requirements review process.

◆ Prototyping is effective for requirements validation if a prototype has been developed during the requirements elicitation stage.

◆ System models may be validated by paraphrasing them. This means that they are systematically translated into a natural language description.

◆ Designing tests for requirements can reveal problems with the requirements. If the requirement is unclear, it may be impossible to define a test for it.

◆ Exercises

4.1 Explain why it is useful to involve people from different technical backgrounds in a requirements review team.

4.2 Give four examples of problem types which may be discovered in a pre-review check of a requirements document.

4.3 Using the natural language requirements for the EDDIS system, find examples of problems of ambiguity, completeness and consistency in these requirements.

4.4 A centralised lock control system which controls the locks of all external doors in University buildings is to be implemented. Some requirements for this system are as follows.

    A. Staff and students are issued with a card which provides them with access to those buildings which they are authorised to use after normal working hours.

    B. Access is implemented by wiping a personalised card through a card reader and, if entry is allowed, the door lock is released.

    C. Users must use the card to both enter and leave locked buildings.

    E. If a card is lost, it should be reported to the security office who will issue a new card and arrange for all access rights associated with the old card to be cancelled.

Review these requirements using the checklist suggested in Figure 4.4 and discover possible problems with them.

4.6 Why is it important to choose testers for a prototype rather than simply accept anyone who volunteers for the job.

4.7 What validation problems might arise if a system prototype used in the validation process exhibited very poor performance.

4.8 In checks of object models of a system, give examples of two problems which can be discovered automatically by CASE tools and two problems which can only be discovered by manual inspection.

4.9 Inheritance is considered as a fundamental aspect of object models of a system (see section 6.3). Suggest why the use of inheritance may introduce difficulties when validating a system specification which is expressed as an object model.

4.10 Suggest tests which might be developed to validate the following requirements for a centralised lock control system. Do these tests give any insights into possible requirements problems?

    F. The system shall provide a facility for an administrator to print the names and card numbers of all users of an individual lock.

G. The system shall allow a system administrator to change the access permissions of a user and thus forbid access to some or all rooms.

H. The lock control system shall allow the times at which individual users use individual doors for access to be specified.

◆ References

Barnard, J. and Price, A. (1994). Managing Code Inspection Information. *IEEE Software* **11**(2): 59–69.

Fagan, M. E. (1976). Design and code inspections to reduce errors in program development. *IBM Systems Journal* **15**(3): 182–211.

Fagan, M. E. (1986). Advances in Software Inspections. *IEEE Transactions on Software Engineering* **SE-12**(7): 744–51.

Gilb, T., and Graham, D. (1993). *Software Inspection*. Wokingham: Addison Wesley.

Leveson, N. G. (1995). *Safeware: System Safety and Computers*. Reading, Massachusetts: Addison Wesley.

Weller, E. F. (1993). Lessons from Three Years of Inspection Data. *IEEE Software* **10**(5): 38–45.

Further reading

Twenty-two Tips for a Happier, Healthier Prototype (J. Rudd and S. Isensee, *ACM Interactions*, **1(1)**, 1994). An easy-to-read article which gives good practical advice on developing prototypes which will be acceptable to end-users.

Requirements Engineering – A Good Practice Guide (I. Sommerville and P. Sawyer, Wiley, 1997) This book is written for practising requirements engineers and gives simple, pragmatic advice on requirements engineering. The chapter on requirements validation covers, in more detail, some of the topics introduced here.

5 Requirements Management

◆ **Contents**

◆ **Summary**

Requirements management is the process of managing changes to a system's requirements. Requirements evolve because of changes to a system's environment and as customers develop a better understanding of their real needs. We start by discussing why some types of requirement are more likely to change than others and identify several types of volatile requirement. Techniques for uniquely identifying requirements and storing requirements in a database are discussed. We describe a change management process which may be applied to requirements and the tool support required by the process. Finally, we discuss requirements traceability which is concerned with maintaining links between dependent requirements, requirements and design and requirements and stakeholders who suggested these requirements.

◆

New requirements emerge and existing requirements change at all stages of the system development process. It is often the case that more than 50% of a system's requirements will be modified before it is put into service. Clearly, this can cause serious problems for system developers. To minimise difficulties, requirements management is necessary where changes to the requirements are documented and controlled.

The impact of proposed changes to requirements must be assessed and, as requirements changes are accepted, the system design and implementation must then be modified. If changes are not controlled, low priority changes may be implemented before high priority changes and expensive modifications to the system which are not really necessary may be approved.

Requirements management therefore supports other requirements engineering and system development activities. As explained in Chapter 2, it is carried out in parallel with other requirements engineering processes and continues after the first version of the requirements document has been delivered. The requirements continue to change during system development and these changes must be managed.

A recent European survey of 4000 companies found that the management of customer requirements was one of the principal problem areas in software development and production. These problems were not confined to the management of requirements for external clients. There were also problems of managing requirements change where the system was being specified and developed in the same organisation.

The principal concerns of requirements management are:

1.   managing changes to agreed requirements

2.   managing the relationships between requirements

3.   managing the dependencies between the requirements document and other documents produced during the systems and software engineering process.

Changes to system requirements may be due to errors and misunderstandings in the requirements engineering process, design or implementation problems. New requirements may emerge as stakeholders develop a better understanding of the system. Most commonly, however, requirements change is a result of changing external circumstances. The strategy or priorities of the business buying the system may change as a result of economic changes or new competitors in its market. New information about the system's environment may become available, e.g. new digital maps for a geographic information system. New laws or regulations may be introduced which require system change.

Requirements cannot be managed effectively without requirements traceability. A requirement is traceable if you can discover who suggested the requirement, why the requirement exists, what requirements are related to it and how that requirement relates to other information such as systems designs, implementations and user documentation. Traceability information is used to find other requirements which might be affected by proposed changes.

Good requirements management practices such as maintaining dependencies between requirements have long-term benefits such as better customer satisfaction and lower system development costs. These returns are not immediate so requirements management may sometimes be seen as an unnecessary overhead. This makes it more difficult to make changes to the system on time and within budget. However, if the requirements are not managed, the short-term savings are likely to be swamped by long-term costs.

Problems with requirements management often mean that systems whose requirements do not satisfy the customer are delivered. Systems development schedules may be extended and high costs incurred for rework of the design and implementation to include the requirements changes. The costs of these problems in the long-term usually outweigh the short-term costs of introducing good requirements management practice.

Requirements management is essentially a process of managing large amounts of information and ensuring that it is delivered to the right people at the right time. We have already introduced, in Chapter 2, CASE tools for supporting the requirements management process (see Figure 2.9). These tools may provide facilities such as:

1. a database system for storing requirements

2. document analysis and generation facilities to help construct a requirements database and to help create requirements documents

3. change management facilities which help to ensure that changes are properly assessed and costed

4. traceability facilities which help requirements engineers find dependencies between system requirements.

We discuss each of these later in this chapter. As explained in Chapter 2, there are a number of commercial products available for requirements management. Although quite different in their implementation, these systems offer comparable functionality. We include links to more information about these products in the book's Web pages.

5.1 Stable and volatile requirements

Requirements changes occur while the requirements are being elicited, analysed and validated and after the system has gone into service. Requirements change is unavoidable and does not imply poor requirements engineering practice. It results from a combination of factors such as those shown in Figure 5.1.

Figure 5.1
Factors leading
to requirements
change.

Change factor	Description
Requirements errors, conflicts and inconsistencies	As the requirements are analysed and implemented, errors and inconsistencies emerge and must be corrected. These problems may be discovered during requirements analysis and validation or later in the development process.
Evolving customer/end-user knowledge of the system	As requirements are developed, customers and end-users develop a better understanding of what they really require from a system.
Technical, schedule or cost problems	Problems may be encountered in implementing a requirement. It may be too expensive or take too long to implement certain requirements.
Changing customer priorities	Customer priorities change during system development as a result of a changing business environment, the emergence of new competitors, staff changes, etc.
Environmental changes	The environment in which the system is to be installed may change so that the system requirements have to change to maintain compatibility
Organisational changes	The organisation which intends to use the system may change its structure and processes resulting in new system requirements

Although change is inevitable, it is usually the case that some require-ments are more stable than others. Stable requirements are concerned with the essence of a system and its application domain. They change more slowly than volatile requirements. Volatile requirements are specific to the instantiation of the system in a particular environment and for a particular customer.

For example, consider a system for managing student records in a univer-sity. Such a system will always have to have information about students, the courses they have taken and the assessment of how well they performed in these courses. This are stable features of the system. The system may also maintain information about the students' attendance at classes, recommended course groupings, and standard letters sent to students. Requirements for these are more volatile. Courses may be taught remotely over the Internet so that class attendance then means something completely different, course groupings change as a subject evolves and the standard letters also change both with course groupings and with changes to administration. These are, therefore, volatile features of the system.

There are at least 4 different types of volatile requirement.

1. **Mutable requirements**

    These are requirements which change because of changes to the environment in which the system is operating. For example, the requirements for a system which computes tax deductions evolve as the tax laws are changed.

2. **Emergent requirements**

    These are requirements which cannot be completely defined when the system is specified but which emerge as the system is designed and implemented. For example, it may not be possible to specify, in advance, the details of how information should be displayed. As stakeholders see examples of possible presentations, they may think of new ways of presenting information that would be useful to them.

3. **Consequential requirements**

    These are requirements which are based on assumptions about how the system will be used. When the system is put to use, some of these assumptions will be wrong. Users will adapt to the system and find new ways to use its functionality. This will result in demands from users for system changes and modifications.

4. **Compatibility requirements**

    These are requirements which depend on other equipment or processes. As this equipment changes, these requirements also evolve. For example, an instrument system in a power station control room may have to be modified when a new type of information display is added.

It is good requirements management practice to try to anticipate likely requirements changes. This usually involves classifying different requirements to identify the most volatile and then predicting possible changes. The advantage of doing this is that it provides information to system developers which helps them design the system so that these requirements are implemented by (relatively) independent components. Therefore, when changes are proposed, the influence of these changes on the rest of the system is lessened.

5.2 Requirements identification and storage

An essential pre-requisite for requirements management is that every requirement must have some kind of unique identification. Although this may seem simple and obvious, a surprisingly large number of requirements documents do not uniquely identify the system requirements. Consequently, effective requirements management is impossible.

The commonest approach to requirements identification is based on numbering the requirements according to the chapter and section of the requirements document where the requirement is included. Therefore, the 6th requirement in the 2nd section in Chapter 4 would be number 4.2.6; the 8th requirement in 3rd section of Chapter 2 would be assigned the number 2.3.8; and so on.

There are two problems with this style of requirements identification.

1. It isn't possible to assign a unique number until the requirements document has been finished. The chapter and section organisation must be stable. When a requirement is elicited, it is unclear where it will appear in the requirements document. It can't be assigned a number and therefore can't be referenced by other requirements.

2. Assigning an identifier based on chapter and section numbers implicitly classifies the requirement. It suggests that the requirement is closely related to other requirements with similar identifiers. Document readers may be misled into thinking that there are no other important relationships between that requirement and other requirements elsewhere in the document.

There are alternative approaches to requirements identification which address these problems. Some of these are shown in Figure 5.2. If a require-

Figure 5.2
Techniques for requirements identification.

Identification method	Description
Dynamic renumbering	Some word processing systems allow for automatic renumbering of paragraphs and the inclusion of cross-references. You can therefore assign a number to a requirement at any time. As you re-organise your document and add new requirements, the system keeps track of the cross-reference. It automatically renumbers your requirement depending on its chapter, section and position within the section. All references to the requirement are also renumbered.
Database record identification	When a requirement is identified it is immediately entered in a requirements database and a database record identifier is assigned. This database identifier is used in all subsequent references to the requirement.
Symbolic identification	Requirements can be identified by giving them a symbolic name which is associated with the requirement itself. For example, EFF-1, EFF-2, EFF-3 may be used for requirements which relate to the efficiency of the system. The problem with this is that it is sometimes difficult to classify requirements and assign a meaningful mnemonic to them.

ment has a unique identification number as well as a paragraph number, references to the requirement may use its unique identifier. This allows for easy rearrangement of the requirements document but can sometimes confuse requirements readers who mix-up the requirements identifier and the paragraph number.

A word processing system and drawing package are usually used to create the initial version of the requirements document. The requirements, therefore, are stored as one or more word processor files. Where several people are involved in writing the document, there has to be some master copy held which is used as a reference copy by all writers and which is distributed to readers and reviewers of the requirements document. Changes made by different people are periodically merged and a new master version is created.

The advantages of 'storing' the requirements in the requirements document are that requirements are all stored together, and that it is easy to access them and relatively simple to produce new versions of the requirements document. Most organisations which produce requirements for small and medium-sized systems maintain their requirements in this way.

However, from a requirements management perspective, there are disadvantages of this approach to storing requirements.

1. Information about requirements dependencies (traceability information) has to be externally maintained.

2. The facilities available for searching the requirements are limited to whatever word processor searching facilities are available. It is not usually easy to find groups of requirements which have common characteristics.

3. It is not possible to electronically link requirements with changes which have been proposed.

4. Any version control of the requirements has to be at the level of the whole requirements document or, at least, individual document chapters. It isn't usually possible to maintain different versions of the same requirement.

5. It isn't possible to navigate automatically between related requirements or between different requirements representations (e.g. from a textual representation to a system model).

To provide these facilities, the requirements must be maintained in a database with each requirement represented as one or more database entities. The facilities of the database can be used to link related requirements and it is usually possible to formulate fairly complex database queries to identify requirements groupings. The database may provide some version control facilities (Brown, Earl et al., 1992) or, at least, provision for these facilities to be implemented. Databases usually include facilities for browsing and report generation. Related requirements are linked and simple scripts which scan the database, extract parts of the record for each requirement and generate skeletons of the requirements document may be developed.

Relational databases are now the most commonly used type of database. Relational databases were designed for storing and managing large numbers of records which have the same structure and minimal links between them. A requirements database, however, may have relatively few records (hundreds rather than hundreds of thousands) each of which includes many links such as links to documents, text files and other requirements. Maintaining these links is possible with a relational database but it is inefficient. It requires operations on several different tables. For very large numbers of requirements, this type of database may be too slow.

Object-oriented databases have been developed relatively recently and are structurally more suited to requirements management. They are better than relational databases when there are many different types of entity to be managed and where there are direct links between different entities in the database. They allow different types of information to be maintained in different objects and managing links between objects is fairly straightforward.

Figure 5.3 shows a set of object classes which could be defined in an object-oriented requirements database.

The central class is REQUIREMENT which has 11 associated attributes.

1. **Identifier**
    This is a simple text string which is assigned when a requirement object is created and entered in the database.

Figure 5.3
Object classes for a requirements database.

2. **Statement**
    This is a statement of the requirement which may be natural language text or a graphical description of some kind (e.g. a timing diagram).

SYS_MODELS
Model: MODEL Description: TEXT Next: MODEL I NULL

REQ_LIST
Req: REQUIREMENT Description: TEXT Next: REQUIREMENT I NULL

REQUIREMENT
Identifier: TEXT Statement: TEXT I GRAPHIC Date_entered: DATE Date_changed:DATE Sources: SOURCE_LIST Rationale: REQ_RATIONALE Status: STATUS Dependents: REQ_LIST Is_dependent_on: REQ_LIST Model_links: SYS_MODELS Comments: TEXT

SOURCE_LIST
People: TEXT Documents: TEXT Reqs: REQ_LIST

REQ_RATIONALE
Rationale: TEXT Diagrams: GRAPHIC Photos: PICTURE

3. **Date_entered**
   The date that the requirement was originally entered in the database.

4. **Date_changed**
   The date of the last alteration to the requirement.

5. **Sources**
   This is a reference to one or more of the sources of the requirement. This helps with analysis when changes to the requirement are proposed.

6. **Rationale**
   This is a reference to a set of information which provides a rationale explaining why the requirement has been included. The associated information may include text, diagrams or photographs.

7. **Status**
   This is a variable representing the status of the requirement. The status may be 'proposed', 'under review', 'accepted', or 'rejected'. Rejected requirements should be maintained in the database as they may be proposed again in future. The analysis of the new proposal is simplified if previous information is available.

8 **Dependants**
   This is a list of references to requirements which are dependent on this requirement (i.e. if this requirement is changed, they may also have to be changed)

9. **Is_dependent_on**
   This is a list of references to requirements on which this requirement depends. The *Is_dependent_on* relationship is therefore the inverse of *Dependants*.

10. **Model_links**
    This is a link to one or more system models which add detail to the requirement

11. **Comments**
    This is any other information which may be useful. In practice, it is almost impossible to define a schema which covers everything, and having a general description field is often very useful.

This schema does not allow for links between the requirements and other design or implementation information. If a single database is used to store all of the documents from a systems engineering process (designs, source code, etc.), then it makes sense to create dependency links between these by extending this schema. However, it is difficult and expensive to maintain project databases and they are only cost-effective for very large projects.

There are now many different database products available ranging from simple PC databases to very complex mainframe or server systems. There is no ideal database and the database used for requirements management should depend on the factors shown in Figure 5.4.

If you have to manage a very large number of requirements, you will need to use a powerful database management system such as ORACLE or INGRES. This might be organised as a database server on a workstation with access

Figure 5.4
Factors influencing the choice of a requirements database.

Factor	Description
The statement of requirements	Requirements may be expressed in a mixture of natural language, graphical models, mathematical expressions, etc. In some cases, additional information such as photographs may be stored as part of the requirements rationale. If there is a need to store more than just simple text, a database with multi-media capabilities may have to be used.
The number of requirements	The requirements for a small to medium sized system (up to 1000 requirements, say) can be managed using commercial PC databases. Larger systems usually need a database which is designed to manage a very large volume of data running on a specialised database server.
Teamwork, team distribution and computer support	If the requirements are developed by a distributed team of people, perhaps from different organisations, you need a database which provides for remote, multi-site access. If different types of computer are used, an Intranet-based solution which provides access to the requirements database through a WWW browsing system may be appropriate.
CASE tool use	CASE tools of different types may be used at other stages in the development process. If these use a database it clearly makes sense to use the same database for requirements management.
Existing database usage	If a database for software engineering support is already in use, this should be used for requirements management. If a database isn't used, the costs of acquiring and training staff to use a database for storing requirements must be considered.

through other client workstations or PCs. This is an expensive approach but the power of these systems allows for fast database manipulation. They usually have excellent report generation tools which can be used to create skeletal requirements documents from the requirements database. These databases can support many simultaneous users and provide good facilities for backup and recovery in the event of system failure. Commercial requirements management systems usually rely on such commercial databases for requirements storage.

5.3   Change management

Change management is concerned with the procedures, processes and standards which are used to manage changes to system requirements. Change management ensures that similar information is collected for each proposed change and that overall judgements are made about the costs and benefits of proposed changes. Without formal change management, it is impossible to ensure that proposed changes to the requirements support the fundamental business goals.

To ensure a consistent approach to change management, organisations may define a set of change management policies. These cover:

1. The change request process and the information required to process each change request.

2. The process used to analyse the impact and costs of change and the associated traceability information.

3. The membership of the body which formally considers change requests. It is important to have some 'independent' group who considers change requests as they can make an objective decision about the contribution of the change to the overall goals of the system and the cost-effectiveness of the change. In military projects, this is called the 'Change Request Board' or 'Change Control Board' but in other organisations a less formal group may be used.

4. The software support (if any) for the change control process.

We discuss change management processes in the following section and software support for change management in section 5.3.2.

5.3.1   Change management processes

The process of requirements change management consists of a set of activities for documenting, reporting, analysing, costing and implementing changes to

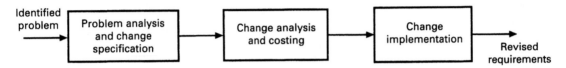

Figure 5.5
Stages in the
change manage-
ment process.

a set of system requirements. This is obviously comparable to other change management processes such as change management to delivered software.

The change management process can be thought of as a three-stage process as shown in Figure 5.5.

1. Some requirements problem is identified. This could come from an analysis of the requirements, new customer needs, or operational problems with the system. The requirements are analysed using problem information and requirements changes are proposed.

2. The proposed changes are analysed to see how many requirements (and, if necessary, system components) are affected by the change and roughly how much it would cost, in both time and money, to make the change.

3. The change is implemented. A set of amendments to the requirements document or a new document version is produced. This should, of course, be validated using whatever normal quality checking procedures are used.

The specific processes for problem analysis and change implementation are dependent on the type of change, the requirements affected and the type of requirements document. However, change analysis and costing is a more general process, as shown in Figure 5.6.

Figure 5.6
The change
analysis and
costing process.

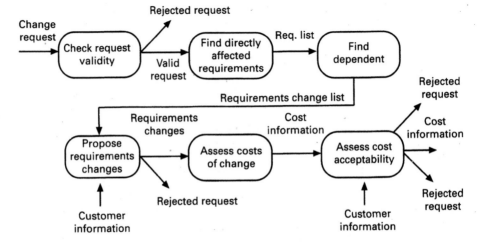

There are six basic activities in the change analysis process:

1. The change request is checked to see if it is valid. Sometimes, customers misunderstand the requirements and suggest unnecessary changes.

2. The requirements which are directly affected by the change are discovered.

3. Traceability information (see the following section) is used to find dependent requirements which may also be affected by the change.

4. The actual changes which must be made to the requirements are proposed. There may be consultation with customers at this stage to ensure that they are happy with these changes.

5. The costs of making the changes are estimated. This estimate should include both the effort required to make the change and the amount of calendar time needed. The availability of resources to implement the change must also be considered.

6. Negotiations with customers are held to check if the costs of the proposed changes are acceptable to them. At this stage, it may be necessary to go back to step 4 to propose alternative changes if the customer feels that the change proposal is too expensive. Alternatively, the customer may modify the change request so that the whole process has to be repeated.

The change request may be rejected at three stages in this process.

♦   If the change request is invalid: this normally arises if a customer has misunderstood something about the requirements and proposed a change which isn't necessary.

♦   If the change request results in consequential changes which are unacceptable to the user: for example, a change request to decrease the time required to process a transaction may mean that fewer concurrent transactions can be handled.

♦   If the cost of implementing the change is too high or takes too long.

During the change management process, information about the change and about the system is passed to and from a number of different people. To help keep track of what stage in the process has been reached and to formally document the change request, it is usual for a change request form to be defined. This form is progressively filled in as the change works it way through the process.

For example, say a librarian requests a change in the EDDIS library system which we have introduced elsewhere in the book. The following people might be involved in handling the change request form.

1. The initial proposer of the change and the person in the library responsible for liaison with the system developers. They fill in a description of the required change.

2. The person in the system developer responsible for liaison with the library. They check if the requested change is valid and fill in the appropriate fields in the change request form. Often, people request changes which have already been agreed or which are already in the system and these changes are rejected at this stage.

3. Requirements engineers who assess the technical feasibility of the change and make some assessment of its impact and costs.

4. System designers who assess the effects of the change on the system design and, again, assess its impact and costs. Both requirements engineers and system designers document their analysis on the change request form.

5. Managers from the library and the system developers who decide if it is cost-effective to accept the change proposal.

The organisation of a change request form depends on whatever detailed process is adopted in an organisation and the electronic support for the change management process. Essential fields which should be included in all change request forms are:

1. fields to document the result of each stage of the change analysis

2. date fields showing when the activity started and when it was passed to a later activity

3. fields showing who was responsible for carrying out each activity

4. an overall status field which may have values such as 'rejected', 'under consideration', 'accepted for immediate implementation', 'accepted for later implementation', etc.

5. a comments field where any other relevant information may be included

Obviously, where many requirements changes are proposed (a normal situation for large systems), there will be a large volume of change information produced. This should be recorded in a database and, if possible, changes should be directly linked to the requirements in the requirements database which are affected by the change. We discuss this briefly in the following section.

5.3.2   Tool support for change management

Change management involves handling large amounts of information and passing it between individuals in an organisation. It is often necessary to keep track of which changes have been proposed, which have been implemented, which are still under consideration, etc. The whole process can benefit enormously from effective tool support.

Support for requirements change management may be provided by specialised requirements management tools or by CASE tools designed to support software configuration management. The capabilities which these tools may provide are:

1. electronic change request forms which are filled in by different participants in the process

2. a database to store and manage these forms

3. a change model which may be instantiated so that people responsible for one stage of the process know who is responsible for the next process activity

4. electronic transfer of forms between people with different responsibilities and electronic mail notification when activities have been completed

5. in some cases, direct links to a requirements database. In some cases, this may support the maintenance of multiple versions of a requirement with change information indicating why new requirements versions have been derived. Only the most sophisticated tools provide this functionality.

The general problem with these tools is that they all have their own implicit model of the change process. Organisations which adopt these tools must conform to that model. Special-purpose tools are also fairly expensive and there may be difficulties when integrating these with other CASE tools used in an organisation. For these reasons, specialised change support tools are mostly used large organisations such as aerospace companies who are involved in very large projects.

General purpose tools such as word processors, spreadsheets, and electronic mail systems may be used to implement a more limited change management system. The status of all changes, for example, may be summarised in a spreadsheet with word processor files used to record change management information. The change management process should specify that change documentation is stored in a standard location and electronic mail messages are used to notify process participants whenever a stage in the activity is completed.

All information can be made available in an Intranet where all change information is accessed through a WWW browser. This type of system has the advantages that it is relatively simple to implement and uses already available software. However, it does not provide the fine-grain process control facilities of special-purpose tools.

Andriole (1996), in his practical book on requirements management, includes a very comprehensive list of tools for change management and more generally, requirements management tools. The book's web pages include a number of links to tool vendors who provide requirements management and change management tools.

5.4   Traceability

A critical part of the requirements change management process is the assessment of the impact of a change on the rest of the system. If the change is proposed while the requirements are being developed, you must assess how that change affects other requirements. If the change is proposed while the system implementation is underway, the impact assessment involves assessing how the change affects the requirements, the system design and its implementation. If the change is proposed after the system has gone into operation, there must also be an additional check to see how all stakeholders in the system might be affected by the change.

To carry out this kind of impact assessment, information about requirements dependencies, requirements rationale and the implementation of requirements should be maintained to supplement the information in the requirements document. This is usually called traceability information. Change impact assessments depend on this traceability information to find out which requirements are affected by a proposed change.

Davis (1993) has classified traceability information into four types.

1.   **Backward-from traceability**
     links requirements to their sources in other documents or people.

2.   **Forward-from traceability**
     links requirements to the design and implementation components.

3. **Backward-to traceability**

    links design and implementation components back to requirements.

4. **Forward-to traceability**

    links other documents (which may have preceded the requirements document) to relevant requirements.

Potentially, this covers a very large volume of information. In practice, it is impossibly expensive to collect and manage all types of traceability information. As we discuss in section 5.5.2, project managers should define traceability policies setting out what essential traceability information must be maintained.

Surprisingly, Davis does not mention what we consider to be the most important traceability information namely information which records the dependencies between the requirements themselves. However, if we extend Davis's definition of backward-from and forward-to traceability to allow links to the same document (the requirements document) as well as external documents then this is covered by his classification.

Davis's classifications are a useful way to understand the concept of traceability as the traceability information can be visualised as arrows going forwards and backwards from different documents. We illustrate this in Figure 5.7, which shows how a statement of requirements can include traceability links to and from a design specification and a business plan.

Figure 5.8 shows how these different types of traceability can be instantiated more concretely by links between specific information in the requirements document and other system documents.

In practice, the traceability information which is most commonly maintained during requirements management is requirements-requirements traceability and requirements-design traceability. However, Gotel and Finkelstein (1995) discuss the importance of tracing requirements back to their sources. As we discussed in Chapter 3, these sources might be people, other requirements, documents or standards. Finkelstein and Gotel have proposed a set of entities and relations (contribution structures) which can be used for maintaining this type of traceability.

Figure 5.7
Backwards and forwards traceability.

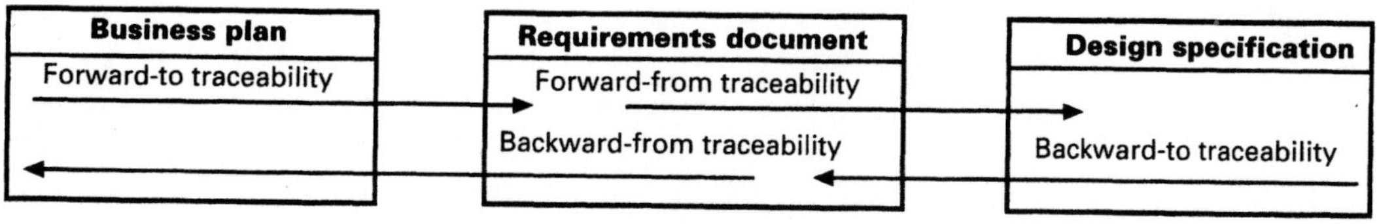

Figure 5.8
Types of
traceability.

Traceability type	Description
Requirements-sources traceability	Links the requirement and the people or documents which specified the requirement.
Requirements-rationale traceability	Links the requirement with a description of why that requirement has been specified. This can be a distillation of information from several sources.
Requirements-requirements traceability	Links requirements with other requirements which are, in some way, dependent on them. This should be a two-way link (dependants and is-dependent on).
Requirements-architecture traceability	Links requirements with the sub-systems where these requirements are implemented. This is particularly important where sub-systems are being developed by different sub-contractors.
Requirements-design traceability	Links requirements with specific hardware or software components in the system which are used to implement the requirement.
Requirements-interface traceability	Links requirements with the interfaces of external systems which are used in the provision of the requirements.

5.4.1   Traceability tables

Traceability tables show the relationships between requirements or between requirements and design components. Requirements are listed along the horizontal and vertical axes and relationships between requirements are marked in the table cells. A requirements database is not necessary, although recording traceability information in a database can make it much easier to navigate between dependent requirements. The database schema which we suggested in section 5.2 includes traceability links. These are the references to dependent requirements and to those requirements which depend on the current requirement.

Traceability tables for showing requirements dependencies should be defined with requirement numbers used to label the rows and columns of the table. In the simplest form of traceability table, you simply put some mark, such as an asterisk, in the table cell where there is some kind of dependency relationship between the requirements in the cell row and column. That is, if the requirement in row X (say) depends on the requirement in columns P, Q, and R, you should mark table cells (X, P), (X, Q), and (X, R). By reading down a column, you see all requirements which depend on a requirement; by reading across a row, you see all requirements which the requirement in that row depends on.

Figure 5.9
A simple
traceability
table.

Depends-on	R1	R2	R3	R4	R5	R6
R1			*	*		
R2					*	*
R3				*	*	
R4		*				
R5						*
R6						

A very simple example of a traceability table is shown in Figure 5.9 for a system with 6 requirements.

Each row in the table shows dependencies, so that R1 is dependent on R3 and R4, R2 is dependent on R5 and R6, etc. Therefore, if a change to R4 is proposed, you can see by reading down the R4 column that requirements R1 and R3 are dependent requirements. The impact on R1 and R3 of the proposed change to R4 can therefore be assessed.

If a relatively small number of requirements have to be managed (up to 250, say), traceability tables can be implemented using a spreadsheet. Traceability tables become more of a problem when there are hundreds or thousands of requirements as the tables become large and sparsely populated. Sometimes, dependencies between requirements are confined to requirements groups and separate traceability tables for these groups may be created. Dependencies across groups can be specified separately.

As the number of requirements grows and matrices become unmanageable, a simplified form of traceability table may be used where, along with each requirement description, one or more lists of the identifiers of related requirements are maintained. Traceability lists are simple lists of relationships which can be implemented as text or as simple tables. Figure 5.10 shows a traceability list for the dependencies shown in the Figure 5.9.

Traceability lists are more compact than traceability tables and do not become as unmanageable with large numbers of requirements. They are therefore less prone to error than traceability tables. The disadvantage of these lists compared to traceability tables is that there is no easy way to assess the inverse of a relationship. You can easily see that R1 is dependent on R3 and R4 but, given R4, you must look through the whole table to see which requirements depend on it. If you wish to maintain this 'backward-to' information, you need to construct another table showing these relationships.

Figure 5.10
A traceability
list.

Requirement	Depends-on
R1	R3, R4
R2	R5, R6
R3	R4, R5
R4	R2
R5	R6

5.4.2 Traceability policies

The fundamental problem with maintaining traceability information is the high cost of collecting, analysing and maintaining that information. There a high initial cost involved in assessing dependencies. Additional costs are incurred to update this information every time a requirements change is made. When projects are working to a tight time schedule, other work must sometimes take a higher priority. All too often, traceability information is not updated. The information becomes progressively less useful so there is little incentive to use it and keep it up to date. Within a relatively short time, it is discarded and change analysis is carried out informally.

To help those who are responsible for requirements management, it is helpful if an organisation maintains a set of traceability policies which set out the traceability information to be maintained. These should normally include the following:

1. The traceability information (as shown in Figure 5.8) which should be maintained.

2. The techniques, such as traceability matrices, which should be used for maintaining traceability.

3. A description of when the traceability information should be collected during the requirements engineering and system development processes. The roles of the people, such as the traceability manager, who are responsible for maintaining the traceability information should also be defined.

4. A description of how to handle and document policy exceptions, that is, when time constraints make it impossible to implement the normal traceability policy. There will always be occasions where changes to the requirements or the system have to be made without first assessing all change impacts and maintaining traceability information. The policy exceptions should define how these changes should be sanctioned.

5. The process used to ensure that the traceability information is updated after the change has been made. This should cover both normal and exceptional change processes.

Traceability policies usually have to be specialised for each project. This may involve leaving out some traceability information, deciding on exactly how traceability information should be represented, deciding on the responsibilities for traceability information collection, etc. Projects (and customers) all have different requirements and life cycles and the traceability policies for a simple information system designed for internal use may be completely different from those required for a critical system for a government customer. The factors which influence the specialisation of traceability policies are shown in Figure 5.11.

Whatever traceability policies are specified, it is very important that they should be realistic. Maintaining traceability information is tedious, time-consuming and labour-intensive. Very comprehensive traceability policies may be fine in principle but, if they cannot actually be implemented, they are useless. Lightweight policies which everyone in a project can commit to and use are far better than comprehensive but unimplementable traceability policies.

One way of managing traceability is to develop a traceability manual as a supplement to the requirements document. A traceability manual keeps together, in one place, all of the traceability information which is relevant to

Factor	Description
Number of requirements	The greater the number of requirements, the more the need for formal traceability policies. However, complete requirements-design traceability is impractical for large systems as there is too much information to maintain. If there are a very large number of requirements, you have to be realistic and limit the traceability information which is maintained.
Estimated system lifetime	More comprehensive traceability policies should be defined for systems which have a long lifetime.
Level of organisational maturity	Detailed traceability policies are most likely to be cost-effective in organisations which have a higher level of process maturity (see Chapter 2). Organisations at the basic maturity level should focus on simple requirements-requirements traceability.
Project team size and composition	With a small team, it may be possible to assess the impact of proposed changes without structured traceability information. With larger teams, however, you need more formal traceability policies. This is particularly true if members of the team work at different sites.
Type of system	Critical systems such as hard real-time control systems or safety-critical systems need more comprehensive traceability policies than non-critical systems.
Specific customer requirements	Some customers may specify that specific traceability information should be delivered as part of the system documentation.

Figure 5.11
Factors influencing traceability policy specialisation.

a project so project team members can (relatively) easily find the traceability information they need. Maintaining a traceability manual is particularly important for critical systems where it may be necessary to make a formal case for system safety or security. The manual is a formal record which may be used to show that components are independent or are unaffected by some particular change proposal.

Traceability information must be regularly updated if it is to remain useful. If the traceability manual is a paper document there will always be the possibility that requirements engineers are working with an out-of-date document. To avoid this possibility, the traceability manual should be implemented as a networked electronic document rather than as a paper document. When traceability information is required, the document is either consulted on-screen or the relevant sections of the document are printed. The move towards company-wide Intranets where information is accessed using Internet technology now makes the maintenance of a web-based traceability manual possible.

A traceability manual manager should have the responsibility of ensuring that the traceability manual is kept up-to-date. He or she should work with system developers to ensure that changes to the requirements/design, etc., have been incorporated in the manual and should review and update traceability policies. The manager should be responsible for following up deviations from traceability policies and ensuring that the necessary information is added to the traceability manual.

◆ **Key Points**

◆ Requirements change is inevitable as customers develop a better understanding of their real needs and as the political, organisational and technical environment in which a system is to be installed changes.

◆ Requirements which are concerned with the essence of a system are more likely to be stable than requirements which are more concerned with how the system is implemented in a particular environment. Types of volatile requirement include mutable requirements, emergent requirements, consequential requirements and compatibility requirements.

◆ Requirements management requires that each requirement should be uniquely identified. If a large number of requirements have to be managed, the requirements should be stored in a database and links between related requirements should be maintained.

♦ Change management policies should define the processes used for change management and the information which should be associated with each change request. They should also define who is responsible for doing what in the change management process.

♦ Some automated support for change management should be provided. This may come through specialised requirements management tools or by configuring existing tools such as spreadsheets and an electronic mail system to support the change management process.

♦ Traceability information records the dependencies between requirements and the sources of these requirements, dependencies between requirements and dependencies between the requirements and the system implementation. Traceability matrices may be used to record traceability information.

♦ Collecting and maintaining traceability information is expensive. To help control these costs, organisations should define a set of traceability policies which set out what information is to be collected and how it is to be maintained.

♦ **Exercises**

5.1 Suggest 5 reasons why the requirements for the EDDIS library system (see Chapter 10) might change.

5.2 Classify the following requirements from a library system as stable or volatile requirements:

EDDIS will be configurable so that it will comply with the requirements of all UK and (where relevant) international copyright legislation

EDDIS will support the management of ordering and supplying all types of documents, both digitised and non-digitised

Users will access EDDIS via standard web browsers such as Netscape and Internet Explorer

Users will log-in to EDDIS via accounts which will be created by the administrator. There will be two types of accounts: individual and group accounts. In general, individual accounts will have access to more services than group accounts

5.3 Using the requirements database schema shown in Figure 5.3, write a program in any suitable language which will create a requirements-requirements traceability matrix for a set of requirements which are maintained in the database.

5.4 Using the information from Section 5.3, design a change control form for specifying requirements changes and the consequent change analysis.

5.5 Using the change analysis process described in Figure 5.6, suggest how software which is commonly available on personal computers (word processor, spreadsheet, etc.) could be used to support this process.

5.6 Suggest how prototyping (see Chapter 3) may be used in the requirements change management process.

5.7 Explain why traceability matrices become difficult to manage when there are a large number of requirements for a system. Suggest how the use of viewpoints (see Chapter 7) may be used to help address this problem.

5.8 What are the advantages to an organisation of having a defined set of traceability policies rather than asking each project manager to specify the traceability information which should be maintained.

◆ References

Andriole, S. J. (1996). *Managing Systems Requirements: Methods, Tools and Cases.* New York: McGraw-Hill.

Brown, A. W., Earl, A. N., et al. (1992). *Software Engineering Environments.* London: McGraw-Hill.

Davis, A. M. (1993). *Software Requirements: Objects, Functions and States.* Englewood Cliffs, New Jersey: Prentice-Hall.

Gotel, O. C. Z. and Finkelstein, A. C. W. (1995). Contribution Structures. *Proc. RE'95,* York, UK, IEEE Press.

◆ Further reading

Considering the economic and practical importance of the topic, there is surprisingly little good background information available on requirements management. Many authors of requirements texts either don't mention it at all or only include a very brief note on the topic.

Traceability. J. D. Palmer. In *Software Requirements, 2nd edition.* ed. R. H. Thayer and M. Dorfman. IEEE Press, 1997. A very good introductory overview which covers the notion of traceability and its importance in the requirements engineering process.

PART TWO

Requirements Engineering Techniques

◆ **Summary**

The goals of the book are to introduce various techniques and methods for requirements elicitation and formulation and to explain 'how' these techniques may be applied during the requirements engineering process. Chapter 6 introduces structured techniques and methods. These include requirements techniques based on data-flow and object-oriented models and (briefly) techniques based on formal methods. Chapter 7 describes emerging viewpoint-oriented requirements engineering methods which support analysis of the system from multipline perspectives. Chapter 8 covers non-functional requirements, discusses why these are often critical for a system's success and suggests some techniques for modelling them. Chapter 9 develops some of the viewpoints work introduced in Chapter 7 to explain how this approach may be used in the specification of interactive systems. Lastly, Chapter 10 introduces a detailed case study and shows how a viewpoint-based technique was used to develop the system requirements.

6 Methods for Requirements Engineering

◆ **Summary**

The process of eliciting, structuring and formulating software requirements is normally guided by a requirements method. Requirements methods are systematic ways of producing system models. System models are based on computational concepts such as objects or functions rather than application domain concepts. They are therefore important bridges between the analysis and the design process. This chapter describes four commonly used system models and some methods based on these models. This chapter also describes two types of formal approaches and discusses the role of formal methods in requirements engineering.

◆

Requirements refer to the needs of the users. They include why the system is being developed, what the system is intended to accomplish, and what design constraints are to be observed. The process of formulating, structuring and modelling requirements may be guided by a requirements method which is a systematic approach to documenting and analysing system requirements. Associated with the method is usually a notation that provides a means for expressing the requirements. We believe that there are certain necessary properties that a requirements method should possess if it is to effectively address the difficult problem of establishing an adequate set of requirements for a software system. These properties are described below.

1. **Suitability for agreement with the end-use**
    This indicates the extent to which the notation is understandable (as opposed to writeable) by someone without formal training. One of the perceived problems with formally expressed specifications and their notations is that they cannot be easily understood by most people. Hence gaining understanding of the system may be quite difficult. One solution to this problem may be to integrate both formal and informal descriptions of the system requirements. This can be done by incorporating into the method a mechanism for cross-referencing to natural language requirements.

2. **The precision of definition of its notation**
    This indicates the extent to which requirements may be checked for consistency and correctness using the notation. Imprecise notations may lead to errors and misunderstanding. It should be possible to check requirements both internally and externally against a description of the real world.

3. **Assistance with formulating requirements**
    The process of understanding the system under analysis, the services required of it and its environment involves the capture, structuring, analysis and resolution of many ideas, perspectives and relationships at varying levels of detail. The requirements method intended to establish the system requirements must be guided by a problem analysis technique that takes all these viewpoints into account.

4. **Definition of the world outside**
    The requirements model is incomplete unless the environment with which the component interacts is modelled. If the environment is not well understood, it is unlikely that the requirements as specified will reflect the actual needs the component must fulfil.

5. **Scope for malleability**
    It must be recognised that requirements are built gradually over long periods of time and continue to evolve throughout the component's life cycle. The approach used and the resultant specification must be tolerant of temporary incompleteness and adaptable to changes in the nature of the needs being satisfied by the component. In essence, whatever the method or approach used to formulate requirements, it should be able to accommodate change without the need to rework the entire set of requirements.

6. **Scope for integrating other approaches**

    There is no one requirements approach (or modelling technique) that adequately articulates all the requirements of a system be it from the developers' or users' viewpoints. For example a data-flow model may not adequately represent the control requirements of the system and a formal language may not be able to express non-functional requirements adequately. It is important that a requirements method is able to support the incorporation of other modelling techniques in order that their complimentary strengths are brought to bear on the problem.

7. **Scope for communication**

    The requirements process is a human endeavour, so the requirements method or tool needs to be able to support the need for people to communicate their ideas and obtain feedback.

8. **Tool support**

    Although notations and methods can provide much conceptual help with the process of defining requirements, it is their incorporation into or support by tools which make the biggest contribution to improving our ability to manage complexity on large projects, System development generates a large amount of information that must be analysed. A tool imposes consistency and efficiency on the requirements process (Dorfman and Thayer, 1990).

It is worth noting that there is no ideal requirement method; few methods possess all the attributes listed here. A number of methods attempt to overcome this deficiency by using a variety of modelling techniques to formulate system requirements. The system model can be enriched by modelling different aspects of it using modelling techniques that capture and describe those aspects best.

1. **Data-flow models**

    Data flow diagrams may be used to show how data is processed at different stages in the system.

2. **Compositional models**

    Entity-relationship diagrams may be used to show how some entities are composed of other entities.

3. **Classification models**

    Object/inheritance diagrams may be used to show how entities have common attributes.

4. **Stimulus-response models**
    State transition diagrams may be used to show how the system reacts to internal and external events.

5. **Process models**
    Process models may be used to show the principal activities and deliverables involved in carrying out some process.

6.1 Data-flow modelling

The data-flow model is based on the notion that systems can be modelled as a visualisation of the data interaction that the overall system or part of it has with other activities, whether internal or external to the system. Data-flow approaches use data-flow diagrams (DFDs) to graphically represent the external entities, processes, data-flow, and data stores. Interconnections between graphical entities are used to show the progressive transformation of data. Figure 6.1 shows the data-flow diagram notation, first proposed by Tom DeMarco (DeMarco, 1979). Variants of the notation have been proposed by others (Ross and Schoman, 1977; Gane and Sarson, 1979; Orr, 1981). A DFD is composed of data on the move, shown as a named arrow; transformations of data into other data, shown as named bubbles; sources and destinations of data, shown as rectangles called terminators; and data in static storage (i.e. data store), shown as two parallel lines. Transformations form the basis for further functional decomposition.

There is little uniformity in industry concerning the DFD notation. The notation shown in Figure 6.1 was advanced by DeMarco; Gane and Sarson use rounded rectangles for bubbles, shadowed rectangles for sources and destinations, and squared-off C's for data stores; Orr uses rectangles for bubbles, ellipses for sources and destinations, and ellipses for data stores.

The first data-flow diagram derived by the analyst represents the 'target' system at its context level. The example in Figure 6.2 represents a simplified context level data-flow diagram for a library system intended to automate the issue of library items. The aim of the context level data-flow diagram, in data-flow analysis, is to view the system as an unexplored 'black box', and to direct the focus of the analysis on the type of the data-flows that enter the system from the source and those that travel from the system to their destination.

Figure 6.1
Data-flow
diagram
notation.

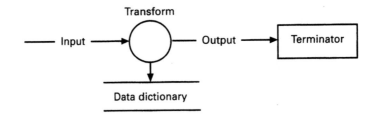

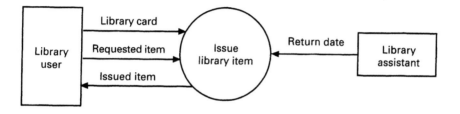

Figure 6.2
The context-level data-flow diagram for Issue library item.

The creation of the context level data-flow diagram also permits the developer to sketch the boundaries of the target system, so that the client and developer can agree on the scope of the system to be developed.

The next level (level 1) of the data-flow diagram for the library system is constructed by decomposing the top-level system bubble into sub-functions. Figure 6.3 shows the next level of decomposition of the library system. Each function in Figure 6.3 represents a potential sub-system through further decomposition.

6.1.1 Structured analysis

The data-flow approach is typified by the structured analysis method (SA). The structured analysis method has undergone several 'refinements' since its introduction in the late 1970s, but its underlying principles have remained the

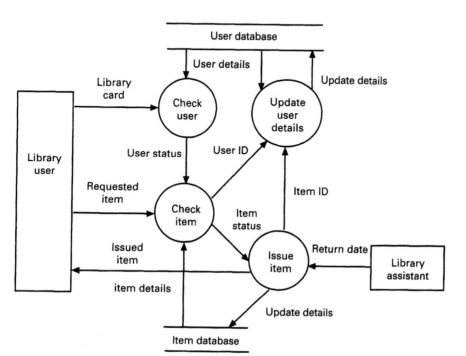

Figure 6.3
Level 1 of the Data-flow diagram for the Issue library item.

same. Two major strategies dominate structured analysis. The 'old' method popularised by DeMarco and Gane and Sarson, and the 'modern' approach by McMenamin and Yourdon (McMenamin and Palmer, 1984; Yourdon, 1990). The next section describes each of these strategies

6.1.2 DeMarco's approach

DeMarco advocates a top-down approach in which the analyst maps the current physical system onto the current logical data-flow model. The DeMarco approach can be summarised in four steps:

1. analysis of current physical system
2. derivation of logical model
3. derivation of proposed logical model
4. implementation of new physical system

The objective of the first step is to establish the details of the current physical system, then to abstract from those details the logical data-flow model. The derivation of the proposed logical model involves modifying the logical model to incorporate logical requirements. The implementation of the proposed model can be considered as arriving at a new physical system design.

6.1.3 Modern structured analysis

The modern approach first appeared in the literature in 1984 as the work of MacMenamin and Palmer. MacMenamin expanded on DeMarco's work and made considerable progress in elucidating the difference between user's real needs (called essential requirements) and those requirements that represent the external behaviour satisfying those needs. Structured analysis has further been modernised by Yourdon (1990) to integrate several ideas advanced in earlier approaches and to incorporate CASE tools.

Up and until the mid-1980s structured analysis had focused on information systems applications and did not provide an adequate notation to address the control and behavioural aspects of real-time system engineering problems. Ward and Mellor (Ward 1985) and later Hartley and Pirbhai (1987) introduced real-time extensions into structured analysis. These extensions resulted in a more robust analysis method that could be applied effectively to engineering problems.

Other well known structured analysis approaches include: Structured Analysis and Design Technique (SADT) developed by Ross (1977), Structured Requirements Definition (SRD) developed by Orr (1981) and Structured Systems Analysis and Design Methodology (SSADM) (Eva, 1994; Skidmore et al., 1992). A common criticism levelled at data-flow diagrams is their weakness in describing complex interfaces. DFDs are not an efficient way to describe sub-systems with complex interfaces, as a separate diagram is required for each possible input data item. The overall picture of the interface can only be gained by integrating these models. Nevertheless methods based on the data-flow approach have been successfully used to specify large complex systems.

6.2 Semantic data models

An important aspect of system modelling is to define the logical form of the data processed by the system. One way of doing this is to use the relational model suggested by Codd and Date (Codd, 1979; Date, 1990). In the relational model, data is specified as a set of tables, with some columns being used as common keys. This model allows relationships to be defined without considering the physical organisation of the database.

There are two main disadvantages associated with the relational model (Sommerville, 1996).

1. **Implicit data typing**
   It does not allow for the definition of a type associated with relations. Types may need to be inferred from the relation names.

2. **Inadequate modelling of relations**
   Important logical relations (such as PART-OF and IS-A) between data items are represented implicitly, through shared values in the table. The relations cannot be named or given attributes.

To allow for a better abstract model of the system to be produced, an alternative approach should include information about the semantics of the data. Approaches to semantic data modelling include the entity-relationship model proposed by Chen (1976), the SDM proposed by Hammer and McLeod (1989), and Codd's own extension of the relational model, RM/T (Codd, 1979). All these approaches identify the entities in a database, their attributes and explicit relationships between them.

Like most modelling notations, semantic data models are described using graphical notations for ease of understanding. A number of these notations are supported by commercial CASE tools. Figure 6.4 shows the common notation for semantic data models. The ERM notation comprises the following components.

♦ **Entity**
  A distinct object or activity about which the organisation wishes to store information. Examples include customers, orders and products. Each entity has a unique identifier.

- **Attribute**

  Every entity in an ERM is defined by its list of attributes. An attribute describes some aspect of the entity to which it belongs. For example, a customer entity might have attributes like account number, name, address, phone number and so on.

- **Relationship**

  A meaningful association between entities. A relationship has three properties: cardinality or degree, optionality and dependency (defined later).

- **Cardinality or degree**

  In a typical orders database a customer might have multiple orders in a file (that is, a customer can be associated with one or more orders) but any particular order can be linked to only one customer (that is, each order can be associated with only one customer). Relationships may be one-to-one (1:1), one-to-many (1:n), many-to-one (n:1) or many-to-many (n:m).

- **Optionality**

  Using the same example as above, a customer record might be stored in the database, but have no orders currently on file (that is, a customer can be associated with zero or more orders). An order, however, must always be associated with a particular customer. Thus, in this relationship a customer entity is said to be mandatory (orders cannot exist without an associated customer) and the orders entity is optional (customers may exist without associated orders).

Hull and King (1987) have described a number of extensions to the basic ERM. The extensions have involved adding sub and super-types to the basic entity and relation primitives. Types may have sub-types through a special relation

Figure 6.4
Notation for semantic data models.

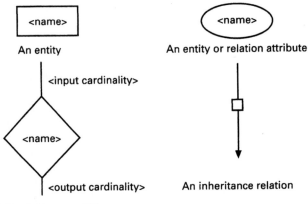

called inheritance. Types may inherit the attributes of their super-types. In addition, sub-types may have private attributes.

Data models are often used to supplement the information provided on data-flow diagrams. As an example, consider how a simple software requirement may be represented. Using the extension of Chen's entity-relation model (ERM) as described by Hull and King we can represent the requirement as shown in Figure 6.5.

A typical software requirement has a number of important components. These include the requirement identifier, its source, its description (in natural language), its type, its priority (or weighting) and the requirement specification. In addition to these obvious components, the requirement may have other attributes, that may themselves have attributes. The requirement change history is good example of this. It is common for requirement to evolve through many changes in its lifetime. Each requirement change has a number of attributes that uniquely identify the change, provide a description of the change, its rationale, author and impact (see Chapter 5). Significant changes in a requirement may result in the creation of new versions of the requirement, as illustrated in Figure 6.5.

6.3 Object-oriented approaches

Until a few years ago the only system models for requirements definition were based on one form of the process orientation or another. The information model (entity relationship model popularised by Chen (1976) in the 1980s is

Figure 6.5
Semantic data model of a software requirement.

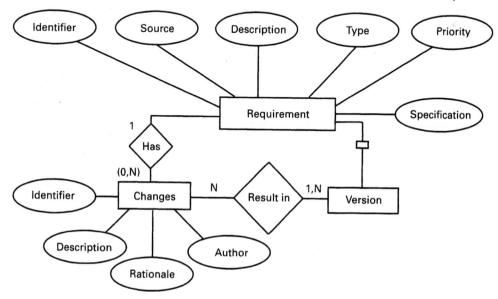

the closest precursor to the object-oriented model. The entity relationship model is based on refining hierarchies of sub-types and associative objects, but although this approach closely mirrors the object-oriented model, it is lacking in the key object-oriented concept of data encapsulation.

The first published material on object-oriented analysis was by Shlaer and Mellor (1988). Since then, several requirements methods based on object orientation have been proposed, including, Colbert (1989), Coad and Yourdon (1989), Wirfs-Brock et al. (1990), Rumbaugh et al. (1991), Jacobson et al. (1992) and Martin and Odell (1992). These notations are semantically similar and any of them could be used for model description.

At the heart of the object-oriented model is the notion of an object. An object is an entity defined by a set of common attributes, and operations associated with it. Objects are major actors, agents and servers in the problem space of the system, and can be identified by carefully analysing the domain. Objects can be found among the devices that the system interacts with (for example, sensors), other systems that interface with the system under study, organisational units (departments, divisions, etc.), things that must be remembered over time (for example, details about events occurring in the systems environment), physical locations or sites, and specific roles played by humans (clerks, doctors, pilots, etc.).

Basic to the idea of an object are concepts of encapsulation, class and inheritance. An object encapsulates data (the attribute values that define the object), operations or services (the actions that are applied to modify its attributes), other objects (composite objects), constants and other related information. The concept of classing allows objects within a collection to share common attributes, as needed. This framework is collectively referred to as inheritance.

The object-oriented paradigm promotes a number of related software engineering benefits over traditional requirements approaches such as data-flow. These include modularity, abstraction information hiding and reusability. Objects are inherently modular due to their incorporation of data and methods. Objects support component abstraction through the decomposition of object classes. Decomposition takes place until distinct class instances can be specified, modelled and implemented. Information hiding is supported through data and method encapsulation. Data and operations specific to an object are hidden from other objects, reducing the likelihood of inappropriate interactions among operations and data elements. Reusability is achieved by allowing software to be built out of components (classes) that already exist, and by allowing modified classes to be created using inheritance (this enables the reuse of methods and data structures of high-level classes).

The differences between the object-oriented model and the traditional data-flow approach are also accentuated when we look at the software development process. In the traditional approach, the conceptual models used for requirements analysis differ from those used for design and implementation. Software developers use data-flow diagrams for analysis, structure charts for design and programmers use the constructs of procedural languages like PASCAL, C and COBOL to implement the design. In object-oriented development the same model is used consistently from analysis to implementation, making the transition from analysis to design to implementation a more natural process (i.e. no 'conceptual walls').

6.3.1 Object-oriented concepts

The fundamental concepts in object-oriented modelling include:

- objects and classes
- methods
- messages
- encapsulation
- inheritance

Object: many definitions for an object have been proposed, most of which are quite similar. In this book we define an object as something real or abstract about which we store data and those operations that manipulate the data. Examples of these include an invoice, an account, a sensor, a software design, a car and an organisation. It is possible for an object to be composite, that is, composed of other objects. Every object is defined by its list of attributes (or data). An attribute describes some aspect of the object to which it belongs. For example, a customer entity might have attributes like account number, name, address, phone number and so on.

Class: this is an implementation of an object type. For example, the object type Bank Customer refers to a class of bank customers. A class refers to objects that share common attributes and operations. An object is an instance of a class. For example, if John Smith is a bank customer, then bank customer is the class and John Smith is an instance of the bank customer.

Operations: operations are used to read and manipulate the data of an object. The operations in an object type reference only the data structures of that object type. To access the data structures of another object, they must send messages to that object.

Method: methods specify the way in which operations are encoded in software. Each object has an associated set of methods (procedures or operations) which may be 'called' from outside of the object and which act on the object attributes.

Encapsulation: the packaging together of data and operations that manipulate the data is known as encapsulation. An object conceals the details of its internal implementation from the users of the object's data. Users understand which operations may be requested from of the object but do not know the details of how the operation is performed. Encapsulation prevents the unauthorised access of an object's data.

Inheritance: in the decomposition of classes into objects, objects at a lower level in the hierarchy by definition inherit the operations and attributes of their parent(s). They are also able to incorporate data and/or operations specific to themselves. In cases where an object inherits data from more than one parent, the process is called multiple inheritance.

Figure 6.6 illustrates general object-oriented concepts. Objects communicate by sending messages to each other. When an object receives a message it causes an operation to be invoked. The operation performs the appropriate method and may optionally return a response. The message comprises the name of receiver object, the operation to be invoked and an optional set of parameters. Figure 6.7 illustrates how messages are passed between objects.

6.3.2 Object modelling: an example

Consider the partial requirements for a simple university library system which is intended to provide its users with the ability to automate the process of acquiring, cataloguing, browsing and loaning library items. Library items comprise published and recorded material. It is intended that the system will be administered by a member of the library staff, whose primary role will be to maintain the library item and library user databases. Library users are required to register with the system administrator before they can borrow library items. Library items are to checked in and out by library staff. Library users are drawn from three primary groups; students, members of staff and

Figure 6.6
An illustration of object-oriented concepts.

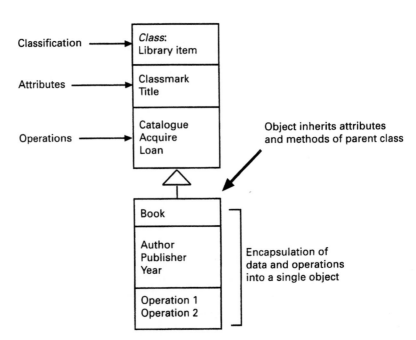

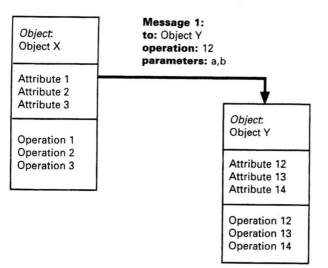

Figure 6.7
Message passing
between
objects.

external users. All library users have as part of their registration a name, a library number, an address and an account. In addition, students must provide details of their degree programme and admission numbers. The staff are required to provide staff numbers in addition to the basic registration details. External users must also provide details of their employer.

In this section we will briefly illustrate how an object-oriented approach can be used to model this simple library system. Most methods based on the object-oriented model share certain common analysis steps. These are:

1. identify core objects
2. construct the object structures defining the associations between object classes.
3. define the attributes associated with each object
4. determine the relevant operations for each object
5. define the messages that may be passed between objects
6. refine the object model

We do not have space here to perform a detailed object-oriented analysis of the library system, instead we will highlight the main issues associated with each step. The object notation shown in Figure 6.8 will be adopted for the analysis. The top part of the box contains the class name, the middle part the attributes and the lower part the operations.

The first step in object-oriented analysis involves identifying relevant problem domain objects. From the partial requirements above, we identify the several classes of objects. These include library users, library items, user account, library assistant and system administrator. Library items comprise published items such as books, journals and magazines, and recorded items such as software and listening tapes. Library users include students, members

Figure 6.8
Object notation.

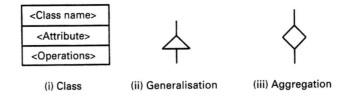

(i) Class   (ii) Generalisation   (iii) Aggregation

of the university staff and external users. We can distil these classes into the four classes shown in Figure 6.9.

The second step identifies the relationships between the various classes. We can identify the following relationships from the partial requirements.

(i)   A library user **borrows** a library item.
(ii)   A library item **is** recorded or published.
(iii)   The system administrator **registers** the library user.
(iv)   Library users **are** students, staff and external users.
(v)   The system administrator **catalogues** the library items.
(vi)   The library assistant **issues** the library items.

Figure 6.10 shows the basic object model of the library system illustrating class attributes and relationships.

Apart from the library user attribute account, the attributes shown are all atomic, i.e. they do not have additional internal components. The account attribute keeps track of the borrowed items and their due dates.

Figures 6.11 and 6.12 illustrate the additional development of the library user and library item classes to show the inheritance relationships. In the library item class, we have identified two new classes of book and journal to exemplify the the notion of inheritance further.

Step 3 involves identifying the attributes for each object. Attributes can be revealed by the analysis of the system requirements. For example, it is a requirement that all library users must be registered before they can use the library. This means that we need to keep registration data about library users (e.g., name, address, account). Library users may also be provided with an account to keep track of the items loaned to them (see Figure 6.10).

A Library item has the attributes; title, description and classmark. The library item has two subclasses: published item and recorded item. The two subclasses inherit the attributes and operations of the Library item class, in addition to defining their own. Subclasses only show local attributes and local operations, inherited attributes and operations are not repeated in the

Figure 6.9
Initial classes for library system.

Library user	Library item	Library staff	Account

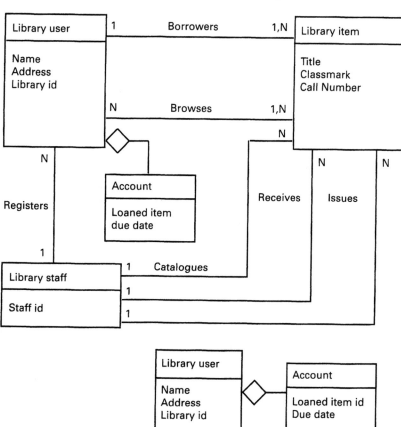

Figure 6.10
Object model
library system.

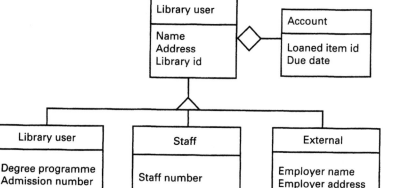

Figure 6.11
Inheritance
relationship for
library user.

subclasses (see Figure 6.11). The library user class has name, address and library id as the general attributes. Specific attributes are contained within the respective instances (see Figure 6.12).

Step 4 is intended to describe operations to be performed on the objects. A number of operations are implicit from the object structure. These include operations for accessing and modifying the attribute values. These operations are assumed and we need not show them explicitly in the model. One way of identifying operations is by modelling the messages that may be passed between the objects. An object is requested to perform one of its operations by sending it a message telling the object what to do. The receiver responds

Figure 6.12
Inheritance
relationship for
library item.

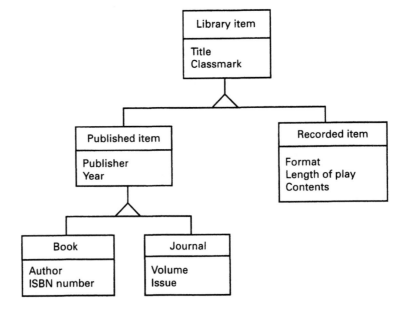

to the message by identifying the operation that implements the named message, executing this operation, and then returning control to the caller. This can done by simulating the object interactions.

Figure 6.13 shows messages that may be exchanged between three objects; library user, library item and library staff. The library user makes use of issue and return operations implemented in the library item, and the library operator makes use of the library item's acquire, catalogue and dispose operations. The library operator can also send register and query messages to the library user object. These are generalised messages which can be developed into detailed messages with further refinement.

The object operations are shown in Figure 6.14–6.16. Implicit operations associated with accessing and modifying attributes are not shown.

Rumbaugh et al. (1991) describes an additional approach to identifying operations. We do not have the space here to describe the process in detail,

Figure 6.13
Message passing
between
objects.

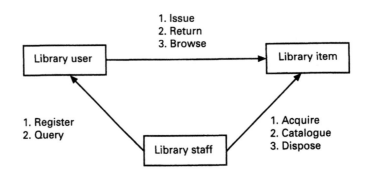

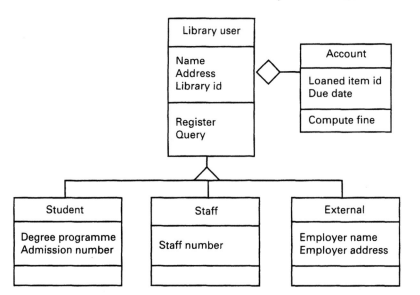

Figure 6.14
Operations for
library user.

readers are referred to Rumbaugh's book on object modelling. Briefly, operations are identified by modelling event scenarios for the different functions provided by the system. The events are then traced to objects that react to them. Typical scenarios model the interactions between the users and the system. Events representing the user interaction are shown arriving at the system interface, and the system responses leaving it. Figure 6.17 show a typical event scenario for library item loan. Normal event sequences are shown as continuous arrows and exceptions as broken arrows. Events are also number to show their sequence.

The library loan function is initiated by the user requesting a library item. The library assistant scans the user registration into the system for verification. The system responds by accepting the user registration or rejecting it (see event 3). If the system accepts the registration, the library assistant verifies that the item can be loaned to the particular user. If the system accepts the request, the item is loaned.

In the next section we will briefly describe four object-oriented methods; namely the Shlaer–Mellor method, the object-oriented analysis (OOA), the object modelling technique (OMT) and the Jacobson method. We will highlight the similarities and the differences between the methods. Other methods

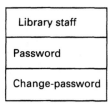

Figure 6.15
Operations for
library staff.

Figure 6.16
Operations for
library item.

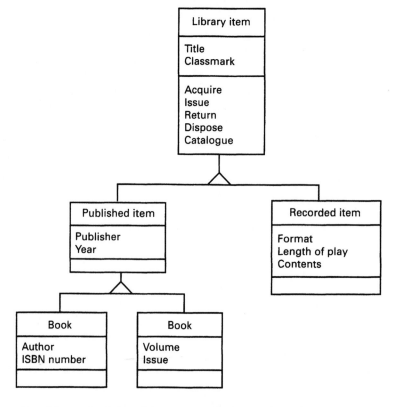

such as Booch's method for object-oriented design (Booch, 1994) may also be used in the requirements engineering process. At the time of writing, efforts are underway to integrate several object-oriented methods to create a tailorable universal method, and these are likely to come to fruition in the next few years. The first stage in this, a set of modelling notations (UML), has been published (Fowler and Scott, 1997).

Figure 16.17
Event scenario
for library item
loan.

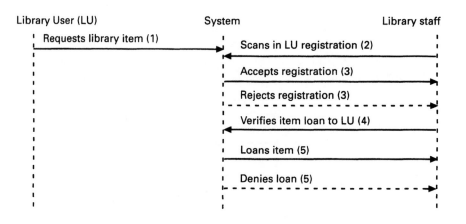

6.3.3   Shlaer–Mellor

The Shlaer–Mellor (Shlaer and Mellor, 1988) method is intended to cover the requirements analysis and design phases of the software development process. The first step in the method is entity (object) identification. The method provides general guidelines for identifying relevant problem domain entities. Relevant entities may include tangible things, roles, incidents, inter-actions and specifications. The second step associates the identified objects with their attributes, and the third step involves establishing the relationships between entities. A state transition model is used to model the object states and to verify the interactions between the state models and object .

The Shlaer–Mellor approach is more representative of information model-ling than of object modelling. The approach does not account for several fundamental object-oriented concepts. Specifically, the method and notation provides no way of expressing such concepts as, messages, methods and procedure encapsulation. The Shlaer–Mellor approach nevertheless provides the specifier with a starting point for object identification.

6.3.4   Object-oriented analysis

The object-oriented analysis method (OOA) was developed by Coad and Yourdon (1989). The OOA method is spread across three layers. The first layer, known as the subject layer, is intended to simplify the user's under-standing of the problem domain in order to identify relevant problem domain objects. The second layer, called the attributes layer, is concerned with iden-tifying attributes associated with the problem domain objects, and the third layer, the services layer, identifies object operations. OOA defines an object as an encapsulation of something in the problem domain, reflecting the capa-bilities of a system to keep information about it, interact with it or both. This is further defined to mean an encapsulation of an object's attributes and its exclusive services. A class is defined as a description of one or more objects with a uniform set of attributes and services, including a description of how to create a new instance of the class. An operation is defined to be a service; a specific behaviour that an object is responsible for exhibiting.

The first step in OOA is concerned with object identification. OOA provides guidelines similar to the Shlaer–Mellor approach for object identification. Objects include tangible things, roles, structures and so on. Two types of structure are identified, classification and assembly. As objects are identified in the problem domain, several structures may appear and the model may become complicated and cluttered. To simplify the understanding of the objects underlying these structures, the structures are viewed abstractly as subjects. Each subject corres-ponds to a macroscopic level of aggregation of objects and their associations.

The second step involves defining the attributes associated with the objects, and the last step is specifying the services performed by each object.

Accordingly, OOA identifies three types of services: occurrence, calculate and monitor. Occurrence services are related to creation, deletion and modification of instances of objects. Calculate services are used when an object requires the calculated result from another object. Each 'calculate' service is explicitly placed in the model. Monitor services are needed if an object is to continually monitor a process for a condition or event.

6.3.5 Object-oriented modelling technique

The object-oriented modelling technique (OMT) was developed by Rumbaugh and his colleagues (Rumbaugh et al., 1991). It is intended to cover object-oriented analysis and object-oriented design. OMT defines an object as a concept, abstraction or thing with crisp boundaries and meaning for the problem at hand. Classes are viewed as a group of objects with similar properties (attributes), common behaviour (typified by operations), common relationships to other objects and common semantics. The notion of a meta-class as a class describing other classes is introduced.

The method defines a sub-system as a major component of the system organised around some coherent theme, and uses this to divide the system into partitions and layers. A partition is a sub-system that provides a particular service. A partition may itself be constructed from lower level systems. A layer is a sub-system that provides multiple services, all of which are the same level of abstraction, built on subsystems at a lower level of abstraction.

OMT is intended to cover not only the requirements analysis phase of software development, but also to provide a transition to design. The technique is enriched by the incorporation of other modelling techniques. OMT includes functional modelling as part of the system modelling. Object operations are augmented with data-flow diagrams to capture the semantics of the operations. Scenarios are used to capture user interaction and an extended state transition model is used to model object behaviour. The state model is based on an extension of the work of Harel on Statecharts (Harel et al., 1988). The state notation distinguishes between activities and actions, and allows for the abstraction of states. The activity with the state forms the basis for further decomposition. OMT allows two types of concurrency to be supported inside the object. In one case an object is seen as an aggregate of component objects where parallelism is induced by the relative autonomy of the components, and in another, an object harbours multiple (semi) independent states.

6.3.6 The Jacobson method

The Jacobson method was developed at Objective Systems as part of a large project for the Swedish telephone company Ericsson (Jacobson et al., 1992). Jacobson defines an object as an entity characterised by a number of operations (behaviour) and a state which remembers the effects of the operations.

He describes a class as representing a template for several objects and describes how these objects are structured internally. Objects of the same class have the same definition both for their operations and their information structure. The notion of a meta-class is not included in the method.

Jacobson describes a way of constructing objects through partition hierarchies and the use of aggregates. Partition hierarchies can be used to construct objects from other objects through the use of consists-of relationships. Aggregation is the opposite of partition and can be used to show the union of several objects. The grouping of Man, Woman and Child can, for example, be represented by the aggregate object Family.

The Jacobson method describes two models to cover the requirements definition phase; the requirements and the analysis models. The requirements model is intended to capture user requirements by specifying all the functionality of the system should perform, in close collaboration with the user. The analysis model forms the basis for the system's structure. In the analysis model, all the logical objects to be included in the system and their relationships, are specified.

The requirements model consists of use case, interface descriptions and problem domain models. The use case model uses actors and use cases, to aid in defining what exists outside the system (actors) and what should be performed by the system (use cases). Actors interact with the system. They represent everything that needs to exchange information with the system. An actor is differentiated from a user, who is the actual person who uses the system, whereas an actor represents the role that the user can play. Actors are regarded as classes and users as instances of actors. The sequence of transactions performed when the user interacts with the system is referred to as a use case. Each use case is a specific way of using the system and every execution of the use case may be viewed as an instance of the use case. We have already covered use cases or scenarios for requirements elicitation in Chapter 3.

Use cases are supported by interfaces of the use cases. These are intended to simulate what the users will see when executing a use case. The domain object model of the system consists of problem domain objects and serves as a support for the development of the requirements model. Each use case is partitioned into three object types: entity, interface and control. Functionality specified in the use cases is then allocated to the different objects. The aim here is that each use case will be offered objects in the analysis model. In practice, however, it is difficult to perform allocation as it is difficult to draw precise borders between functionalities in the system. In many instances, developers are forced to make many trade-offs in relation to splitting functionality between objects. Figure 6.18 shows a typical use case scenario for the library system.

The analysis model is built by specifying objects in the information space. The information space represents the three dimensions of the information held in the system, information, behaviour and presentation. The method identifies

Figure 6.18
Typical use case
scenario for a
library system.

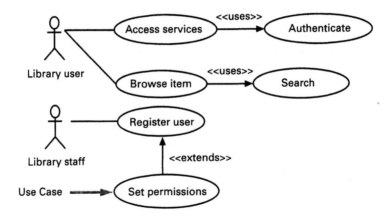

three object types to capture these information dimensions: entity objects, interface objects and control objects. The entity object type models information in the system that should be held for a long time. This object also contains the behaviour naturally associated with this information. An example of an entity object is a person with his associated data and behaviour. The control object models functionality that is not naturally tied to any other object. A typical behaviour of the control object may be to calculate taxes using several factors.

6.4 Formal methods

Requirements specification techniques can be categorised on a formality spectrum. Structured methods (e.g. structured analysis and object-oriented analysis) with their use of text, diagrams, tables and simple notation fall at the informal and semi-formal end of the spectrum (Pressman, 1992). At the formal end of the spectrum, mathematically formal syntax and semantics are used to specify system function and behaviour.

The use of formal methods should be seen as a way of achieving a high degree of confidence that a system will conform to its specification. There can never be an absolute guarantee of correctness, because the system will be embedded in an informal world, where correctness is difficult to achieve. Formal methods have little directly to offer to the problems of managing software projects, although the benefit gained from gaining a clear understanding of the task at an early stage should not be underestimated.

A formal specification language is composed of three primary components.

◆ *Syntax* that defines the specific notation with which the specification is represented. The syntactic domain of a formal specification is often based on a syntax that is derived from standard set theory notation and predicate calculus (Wiltala, 1987).

◆ *Semantics* that help to define a 'universe of objects' (Wing, 1990) that will be used to describe the system. The semantic domain of a specification indicates how the language represents system requirements.

◆ *Relations* which define the rules that indicate which objects properly satisfy the specification.

Formal methods for requirements specifications are slowly emerging from academic research labs and are now being applied in industrial software development. This is particularly true in the case of systems where safety or security is critical (Spivey, 1989; Sommerville, 1996). However a widespread general acceptance of formal methods amongst software developers is still some way off (Greenspan, 1991; Davis, 1992). This can be attributed to several factors, including:

◆ difficulty by system procurer (or users) and, indeed, some software developers in understanding the notations

◆ difficulty in formalising certain aspects of requirements, for example, the specification of user interfaces

◆ software management is conservative and unwilling to adopt new techniques whose payoff is not obvious.

The number of formal specification languages in use today can be broadly divided into two categories:

1. those that use model-based notations such as Z (Spivey, 1989) and the Vienna Development Method (VDM) (Jones, 1990)

2. those based on process algebras such as Communicating Sequential Processes (CSP) (Hoare, 1985; Moore, 1990), CCS (Milner, 1989), and LOTOS (Bjorner, 1987).

There is little doubt that formal specification methods such as Z and VDM offer some advantages over informal methods. Because they are based on mathematical formalism it is possible to verify the correctness, incompleteness and inconsistency checking of the specification. In addition, formal specification removes ambiguity and encourages greater rigour in the early stages of software engineering.

However formal methods suffer from several problems which inhibit their practical application.

◆ Formal methods focus primarily on function and data; behavioural aspects of a problem are more difficult to represent.

♦ Some requirements (e.g. human engineering issues) are highly subjective and can only be determined through prototyping.

♦ The use of formal methods in requirement engineering increases confidence that given requirements actually correspond to the users' desires. However, formal methods do not address the problem of how the requirements are constructed in the first place.

♦ There is a lack of adequate tool support (Davis, 1992; Sommerville, 1996). Although some tools have been developed to automate certain elements of the specification and verification process for Z, VDM, CSP and Larch, these are not widely used.

Greenspan (1991) concludes that many of the obstacles to success in requirements engineering are not amenable to formal methods. Even if some aspects of the problems could be formalised, it may not be worth doing, because the amount of knowledge needed may be too great, for example, in user interface specification. However, research on formal methods for specifying and reasoning about systems and their requirements have had and will continue to have great value for their role in increasing our understanding of system development.

6.4.1 Model-based formal methods

Model-based formal specification relies on the construction of a mathematical model of the system state and possible operations on that state. This model must be created using well-defined mathematical entities such as sets, functions and relations. The operations are defined by specifying how the state is affected by the operation.

There are a number of well-developed notations for model-based specification. Frequently used approaches include VDM and Z but other techniques, such as the B method (Abrial, 1996) have also been used in industry. The mathematical notation used in Z is based on conventional set theory and predicate calculus with some minor extensions which provide the expressive power to allow the specifier to deal with many structures encountered during the development process. A specification in Z is presented as a collection of schemas, where a schema introduces some specification entities and sets out relationships between them. A Z schema comprises three main parts: the schema name, schema declarations and schema predicates. The schema declarations set out the names and types of entities introduced in the schema. The schema predicate sets out the relationships between the entities in the declaration by defining a predicate over the declaration entities. A schema has the general form shown in Figure 6.19.

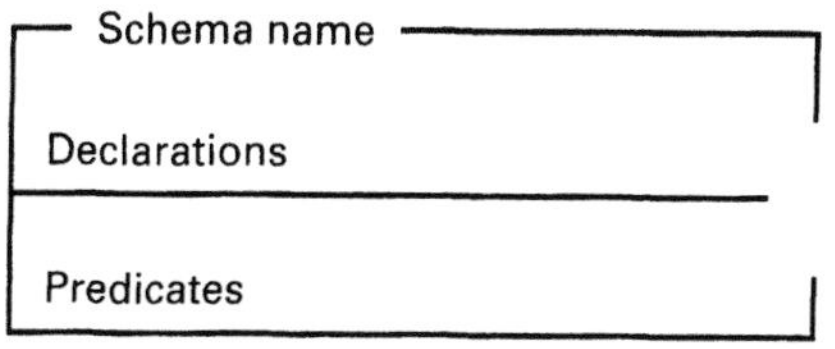

Figure 6.19
Z schema.

The variable declarations are of the form identifier:type, and the predicates give properties of and relationships between the variables. A schema may be used to describe either a state or an operation. To describe a state, the declared variables form the components of the state and the predicates give the invariant properties of the state. For an operation, the declarations consist of the initial state components, the final components, the inputs and the outputs of the operation. For an operation, the predicate part describes the relation between the inputs, outputs, and initial and final states.

The Vienna Development Method (VDM) is a model-based formal specification method based on the set theoretic approach. VDM was developed by Bjorner and Jones (1978), originally as a mechanism for accurately defining the structure and semantics of programming languages but has also been used for specifying sequential systems.

The main steps in VDM can be summarised thus:

1.   list the state variables of the system

2.   define the state invariant; this invariant must be verified at every operation of the VDM state description

3.   list the operations.

The specification of operations, done in terms of pre- and postconditions, establishes the link between the initial and final configurations of the state variable.

6.4.2   Z schema for library example

To illustrate schemas in Z, consider the library system described in section 6.1. The state space of the lending library can be defined using the schema of Figure 6.20.

In the schema declaration, we have declared two names: stock and onLoan. Stock is the set of books held by the library. The notation $\mathbb{P}$ S means Powerset S. That is, the type of stock is defined as the set of sets of books. onLoan refers to the set of books that have been lent out. Each member of the set is mapped to a known borrower. The predicate **dom** onLoan $\subseteq$ stock denotes that the books on loan are a subset of existing stock. The general term **dom** R represents the

Figure 6.20
Schema for
Library.

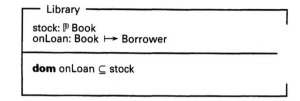

subset of a source set involved in relation R. We will now define three operations on Library: Borrow, New and Return.

The schema in Figure 6.21 shows the Borrow operation. The notation $\triangle$ Library, known as the delta schema, indicates that the Borrow operation causes a state change to occur in Library. The state of a schema S after some operation has been carried out is indicated with S'. The Borrow operation takes two inputs, reader and book. Z uses a ? to denote inputs (for example, reader ?) to an operation and ! to denote outputs. The predicates on the operation indicate that the following required book must be a member of the set of books in stock and not a member of the books on loan. The value of onLoan is updated after the operation to include the borrowed book. The value of stock remains unchanged after the operation.

The schemas for New and Return operations are shown in Figure 6.22. The operation New adds a new book the current stock and Return returns a book which has been on loan, to the library.

In the operation New, the predicate indicates that the value of stock is updated to include the new addition (stock'= stock $\cup$ {book?}). The set of books on loan is unaffected by the operation. In the operation Return the stock remains unchanged but the set of books on loan is updated.

Figure 6.21
Schema for
Borrow
operation.

```
┌─ Borrow ──────────────────────────────┐
│
│  ΔLibrary
│  book?: Book
│  reader?: Borrower
├───────────────────────────────────────
│  book: ∈ stock
│  book? ∉ dom onLoan
│  onLoan' = onLoan ∪ {(book?, reader?)}
│  stock' = stock
└────────────────────────────────────┘
```

```
┌─ New ──────────────────────────────────────────────┐
│ ΔLibrary                                            │
│ book?:Book                                          │
│ ───────────────────────────────────────────────    │
│ stock' = stock ∪ {book?}                            │
│ onLoan' = onLoan                                    │
└─────────────────────────────────────────────────────┘
```

```
┌─ Return ───────────────────────────────────────────┐
│ ΔLibrary                                            │
│ book?:Book                                          │
│ ───────────────────────────────────────────────    │
│ book? ∈ dom onLoan                                  │
│ dom onLoan' = dom onLoan ⊕ book?                    │
│ stock' = stock                                      │
└─────────────────────────────────────────────────────┘
```

Figure 6.22
Schema for New and Return operations.

◆ Key Points

◆ There is no such thing as an ideal requirements method. Few methods, if any, possess all the necessary attributes of a requirements method.

◆ The system model can be considerably enriched by modelling different aspects of it using modelling techniques that capture and describe those aspects best.

◆ The data-flow model is based on the notion that systems can be modelled as a set of interacting functions. A data-flow diagram is composed of a set of inputs, a transforming process and a set of outputs.

◆ The object-oriented approach is based on the notion that systems can be modelled as a set of interacting objects. Objects communicate by passing messages. Fundamental concepts in object-oriented modelling are; objects and classes, methods, messages, encapsulation and inheritance.

◆ Formal methods are based on mathematical principles and are intended to achieve a high degree of confidence that a system will conform to its specifications. There can never be an absolute guarantee of correctness, because the system will be embedded in an informal world, where correctness is difficult to achieve.

◆ Exercises

6.1 Describe the necessary properties of an ideal requirements method. Explain one way to address this lack of 'perfection' in requirements methods.

6.2 Explain the fundamental concepts behind of data-flow modelling; illustrate your answer with an example. What is a common criticism of data-flow diagrams?

6.3 Modify the simple library example given in section 6.1 to incorporate the following additional functionality:

    (i)   processing of returned items

    (ii)   imposing fines on users who return borrowed items late; the fine is to be computed as a function of the total number of 'late days' multiplied by a fixed charge

    (iii) allowing users to search for library items.

6.4 Consider a simple auto-teller machine (cash-point). The machine accepts customer requests and dispenses cash, displays and prints out mini statements, and provides the bank manager with a daily transaction report. Users interact with the ATM through a video display unit and a keypad. An ATM user must have a valid cash-card and Personal Identification Number (PIN) before he or she can access the services of the ATM. Cash withdrawals must be less than or equal to the user's balance. Apart from providing services to its users, the ATM is also required to update the customer account database each time there is a cash withdrawal. The bank manager uses a staff PIN to access the system for transaction reports.

Construct a two-level DFD of the ATM showing the services that are provided.

6.5 Describe the fundamental concepts in object-oriented modelling. Illustrate your answers with examples.

6.7 Identify possible objects for the ATM system described in question 6.4. and classes. Construct an object model of the ATM system.

6.8 Explain the three primary components of a formal specification language. What are the advantages of formal methods over informal methods? Explain why formal methods are not widely used in industrial software development.

◆ References

Abrial, J. (1996). *The B book*. Cambridge University Press.

Bjorner, D. and Jones, C. (1978). *The Vienna Development Method*. New York: Springer-Verlag.

Bjorner, D. (1987). 'On the use of formal methods in software development'. *9th IEEE International Conference on Software Engineering*, Washington, DC.

Booch G. (1994). *Object-oriented Design with Applications*. Redwood City, California: Benjamin Cummins.

Chen P. (1976). Entity-relationship Approach to Data Modelling. *ACM Transactions on Database Systems*, **1**(1): 9–36.

Chung, L. Mylopoulos, J., and Nixon, B. (1992). Representing and Using Nonfunctional Requirements – A Process-oriented Approach. *IEEE Transactions on software engineering*, **8**(6): 483–497.

Coad, P. and Yourdon, E. (1989). *OOA-Object-Oriented Analysis*. Englewood Cliffs New Jersey: Prentice-Hall.

Codd, E. F. (1979). Extending the database relational model to capture more meaning. *ACM Transactions on Database Systems*, **4**(4): 397–434.

Colbert, E. (1989). The Object-oriented Software Development Method: A Practical Approach to Object-oriented Development'. *TRI-Ada'89 – Ada Technology in Context: Application, Development and Deployment*.

Date, C. J. (1990). *An introduction to database systems*. Reading MA: Addison-Wesley.

Davis, A. (1992). *Software Requirements: Objects, Functions and States*. Englewood Cliffs, New Jersey: Prentice-Hall.

DeMarco, T. (1979). *Structured Analysis and System Specification*. Englewood Cliffs, New Jersey: Prentice-Hall.

Dorfman, M., and Thayer, R. H. (1990). *Requirements Definition, Standards, Guidelines, and Examples on System and Software Requirements Engineering*. Los Alamitos: IEEE Computer Society Press.

Eva, M. (1994). *SSADM Version 4: A User's Guide*. London: McGraw-Hill.

Fowler, M., and Scott, K. (1997). *UML Distilled: Applying the Standard Object Modelling Language*. Reading, Massachusetts: Addison-Wesley.

Gane, C., and Sarson, T. (1979). *Structured Systems Analysis: Tools and Techniques*. Englewood Cliffs, New Jersey: Prentice-Hall.

Greenspan, S. (1991). The Scruffy Side of Requirements Engineering. *3rd European Software Engineering Conference*, Milan, Italy.

Hammer, M., and McLeod, D. (1989). Database Description with SDM: A Semantic Database Model. *ACM Transactions on Database Systems*, **6**(3).

Harel, D., Lachover, D., Naamad, A., Pnueli, A., Politi, M., Sherman, R., and Shtultrauring, A. (1988). STATEMATE: A Working Environment for the Development of Complex Reactive Systems. *10th IEEE International Conference on Software Engineering*, 396–406, Washington, DC: IEEE Press.

D. Hartley and I. Pirbhai (1987). *Strategies for real-time systems specifications*. New York: Dorset House.

Hoare, C. A. R. (1985). *Communicating Sequential Processes*. London: Prentice-Hall.

Hull, R. and King, R. (1987). Semantic Database Modelling: Survey, Applications, and Research Issues. *ACM Computing Surveys*, **19**(3).

Jacobson, I., Christerson, M., Jonsson, P., and Gunnar, O. (1992). *Object-oriented Software Engineering: A Use Case Driven Approach*. Addison-Wesley.

Jones, C. B. (1990). *Systematic Software Development Using VDM*. Prentice-Hall.

Martin, J., and Odell, J. J. (1992). *Object-oriented Analysis and Design*. Englewood Clifff, New Jersey: Prentice-Hall.

McMenamin, S., and Palmer, J. (1984). *Essential Systems Analysis*. Englewood Cliffs, New Jersey: Prentice-Hall.

Milner, R. (1989). *Communication and Concurrency*. London, Englewood Cliffs, New Jersey: Prentice-Hall.

Moore, A. P. (1990). The specification and verified decomposition of system requirements using CSP. *IEEE Transactions on Software Engineering*, **16**(9): 932–48.

Orr, K. (1981). *Structured Requirements Definition*. Topeka, Kansas: Ken Orr and Associates.

Pressman, R. (1992). *Software Engineering: A Practitioner's Approach*. McGraw-Hill.

Ross, D. (1985). 'Applications and Extensions of SADT. *IEEE Computer*, **18**(4): 25–34.

Ross, D., and Schoman, K. E. (1977). 'Structutred analysis for requirements definition', *IEEE transactions on software engineering*, **3**(1): 6–15.

Rumbaugh, J., Blaha, M., Premerlani, W., Eddy, F., and Lorensen, W. (1991). *Object-oriented Modelling and Design*. Prentice-Hall.

Shlaer, S., and Mellor, S. (1988). *Object-oriented Systems Analysis*. Englewood Cliffs , New Jersey: Prentice-Hall.

Skidmore, S., Farmer, R., and Mills, G. (1992). *SSADM Version 4*. Machester, NCC: Blackwell.

Sommerville, I. (1996). *Software Engineering*. Wokingham: Addison-Wesley.

Spivey, J. M. (1989). *The Z Notation: A Reference Manual*. Prentice-Hall.

Ward, P., and Mellor, S. (1985). *Structured development for real-time systems*. Englewood Cliffs, New Jersey: Prentice-Hall.

Wiltala, S. A. (1987). *Discrete Mathematics: A Unified Approach*. McGraw-Hill.

Wing, J. M. (1990). A specifier's introduction to formal methods. *IEEE Computer*, **23**(9): 8–24.

Wirfs-Brock, R., Wilkerson, B., and Wiener, L. (1990). *Designing Object-oriented Software*. Englewood Cliffs, New Jersey: Prentice-Hall.

Yourdon, E. N. (1990). *Modern Structured Analysis*. Prentice-Hall.

◆ Further reading

Object-oriented experiences and future trends (*Comm. ACM*, **38(10)**, October 1995). This journal discusses a number of important issues associated with adopting an object-oriented environment for development. The journal also discusses the future trends of the technology, and provides some real life case studies.

Bouzeghoub, M., Gardarin, G., and Valduriez, P. (1997). *Object Technology: Concepts and Methods*, Thomson, 1997. This book provides a general discussion of object-oriented concepts, and a detailed comparative study of various object-oriented techniques and languages.

Formal Methods (*IEEE Computer*, **29(4)**, April 1996). This journal provides an illuminating discussion on the viability of formal methods in industrial practice. The discussions are provided in a point/counterpoint format, by some well known names in computing.

7 Viewpoint-oriented Requirements Methods

◆ **Contents**

◆ **Summary**

Viewpoints are an explicit mechanism which takes into account the different system and problem perspectives of different stakeholders. Implicit viewpoints were first introduced in the SADT method and were made explicit in the CORE method. We briefly describe the notion of viewpoint in both these methods and introduce two more modern approaches to viewpoint-oriented requirements engineering. These are VOSE, where a viewpoint is a template for describing a system model in a particular representation, and VORD, where a viewpoint represents a receiver of system services. Finally, we describe a viewpoint-based technique for requirements validation. The example of a library system is used to illustrate each of these approaches.

◆

To understand the requirements for a system, we must understand the services the system provides, the application domain of the system, non-functional constraints on the system and its development process, the environment where the system is to be installed and organisational issues affecting the system's operation. Consequently, the requirements engineering process involves the capture, analysis and resolution of many ideas, perspectives and relationships at varying levels of detail. Requirements methods based on rigid structuring schemes do not have an expressive framework to elicit and structure the diverse requirements knowledge which is required. To address this problem, a number of methods have evolved based on the notion of viewpoints.

A viewpoint is a collection of information about a system or a related problem, environment or domain which is collected from a particular perspective. These perspectives can include end-users of the system, other systems, engineers involved in the development of the system, any system stakeholders, etc. The information in each viewpoint is incomplete so the overall requirements are derived by integrating the information from each viewpoint. As it is normal for viewpoints to have differing requirements, this normally involves some conflict resolution process to remove inconsistencies between the different viewpoint specifications.

For example, consider the requirements for a system to be installed on a train which will automatically bring the train to a halt when it wrongly goes through a danger signal. Some examples of viewpoints for this system and the requirements they encapsulate might be as follows.

1. **Driver**
   Requirements from the train driver on the system. As this is an automatic system, these will mostly be non-functional requirements concerned with usability.

2. **Trackside equipment**
   Requirements from trackside equipment which must interface with the system to be installed.

3. **Existing on-board systems**
   Compatibility requirements coming from other on-board control systems.

4. **Safety engineer**
   Safety requirements for the system from the railway safety engineer.

5. **Braking characteristics**
   Requirements which are derived from the braking characteristics of a train.

The advantage of viewpoint-oriented approaches is that they explicitly recognise the diversity of sources of requirements and provide a mechanism for organising and structuring this diverse information. Using viewpoints means that it is less likely that important system information will be left out of the requirements, and it provides a means for requirements sources or stakeholders to identify and check their contribution to the requirements. We therefore believe that viewpoint-oriented approaches are the most effective technique for supporting requirements engineering.

This chapter describes four requirements methods that have adopted viewpoint-oriented schemes for formulating and managing requirements. Although the viewpoint-oriented methods described here differ considerably in scope, they provide a means of representing and managing the viewpoints that arise during system development and a framework or techniques for viewpoint integration/resolution. The objective of all viewpoint-oriented methods is to strike a balance between preservation of multiple perspectives during system development and the demands for consistency.

The different approaches that we provide each have their own strengths and weaknesses. There is no **best** method of requirements engineering and any of the methods described here may be appropriate in different circumstances. Of the viewpoint-oriented methods we describe, one method (SADT) has been widely used for many years, another (CORE) has been used in the European aerospace industry but has not made a significant impact outside that domain, and the final two methods (VOSE and VORD) are more modern methods which are still at the stage of experimental use. VORD is also described in detail in Chapter 9 where we discuss the use of viewpoints in interactive system specification.

7.1   Structured Analysis and Design Technique (SADT)

The Structured Analysis and Design Technique (SADT) was developed in the late 1970s by Ross (1985) and is based on a data-flow model that views the system as a set of interacting activities. SADT takes its acronym from the box and arrow diagramming of structured analysis (SA) and a design technique (DT). SADT has been used successfully in specifying a wide variety of products, especially complex large-scale projects.

The notation consists of a rectangle representing some system activity and a set of four arrows, each with a different semantic meaning. Figure 7.1 shows the SADT notation. The arrow at the right represents data output and the arrow at the top represents control information or data to facilitate the process. SADT integrates requirements analysis and design and incorporates this in its notation. The arrow at the bottom of the box represents the mechanism or algorithm by which the process is to take place. Here we are only concerned with the aspects of the notation that deal with requirements analysis and specification.

SADT decomposes the problem into a set of hierarchical diagrams, each one composed of a set of boxes and arrows. Each lower level is documented separately and represents the refinement to the previous level. The most

Figure 7.1
SADT notation.

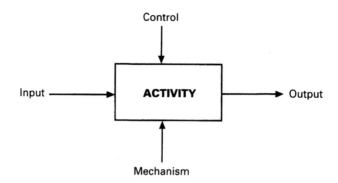

abstract level is called the context diagram. A rectangular box representing the systems's activity together with a set of inputs and outputs constitutes the starting point for functional decomposition.

7.1.1 SADT Viewpoints

SADT does not have an explicit definition of viewpoints; instead viewpoints are an intuitive extension of its modelling technique. SADT viewpoints are sources and sinks of data. Figure 7.2 shows the first level of the issue item function, of the library system, with three possible viewpoints, the library user, issue clerk and item database viewpoint. The library user viewpoint represents the source and destination of the unchecked and checked library item, the issue clerk checks the item and stamps it with a return date. The library item database represents the source of information about the library item as well as the destination of update information.

The control information sets out the conditions under which the inputs coming from the environment are transformed into the outputs shown on the right. The control information associated with these processes is shown at the top of the box. We have shown at least two pre-conditions that must be satisfied for the library item to be issued. The library user must, for example, be a valid member of the library and not be a loan defaulter. It is also important that the requested item is available for issue. The control information is

Figure 7.2
Activity diagram for library system.

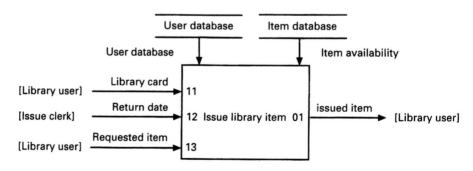

associated with two viewpoints. The user validation information can be associated with the 'user database viewpoint' and the item availability with the 'item database viewpoint'.

The next level of decomposition is shown in Figure 7.3; the input, control and output data from the context level diagram is mapped onto the inputs, control and outputs at the detailed level. The repetitive decomposition goes on until there is sufficient detail for design to proceed.

SADT has an intuitive rather than an explicit notion of viewpoint. That is, there is no stage in the method concerned with viewpoint definition and viewpoints only appear at the context level. SADT does not extend the analysis of its viewpoints beyond considering them as data sinks and sources.

7.2 Controlled Requirements Expression (CORE)

Controlled Requirements Expression (CORE) was developed for British Aerospace in the late 1970s by system designers (Mullery, 1979). Like SADT CORE is based on functional decomposition, but unlike SADT CORE is explicitly based on viewpoints. CORE has been extensively used in the European aerospace industry. Some notable projects include the Experimental Aircraft Programme (EAP) in the mid-1980s in which CORE was used for system and software definition, and more recently the European Fighter Aircraft (EFA) for which CORE was chosen as the standard requirement analysis method

CORE is one of few requirements methods that explicitly adopts a viewpoint approach to formulating requirements. CORE defines its viewpoints at two levels. The first level comprises all entities that interact with or affect the intended system in some way. These viewpoints are referred to as defining viewpoints. At this level, CORE provides guidelines for identifying functional and non-functional viewpoints. The second level distinguishes between defining and bounding viewpoints. Defining viewpoints are sub-processes of

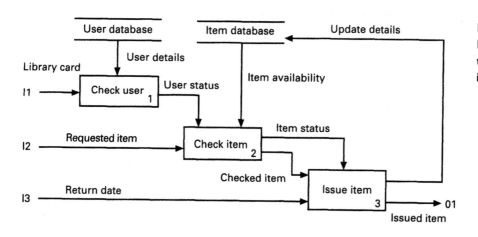

Figure 7.3
Refinement of
the issue library
item function.

the system, viewed in a top-down manner, and bounding viewpoints are entities that interact indirectly with the intended system.

The CORE method consists of six iterative steps:

1. viewpoint identification
2. viewpoint structuring
3. tabular collection
4. data structuring
5. single viewpoint modelling
6. combined viewpoint modelling
7. constraint analysis

Figure 7.4
Initial list of viewpoints.

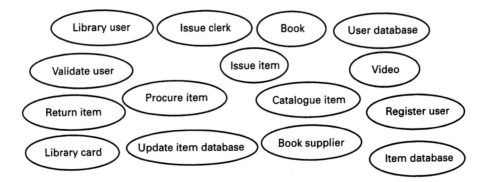

The first step involves identifying possible viewpoints. Figure 7.4 shows a possible list of initial viewpoints. From this list, defining and bounding viewpoints are identified. There are no hard and fast rules for identifying relevant viewpoints. Rather, CORE suggests a session of 'brainstorming' comparisons of users, buyers and specifiers of the system.

Figure 7.5
Bounding and defining viewpoints.

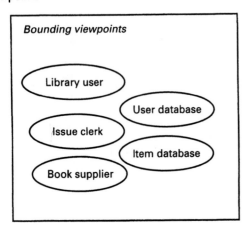

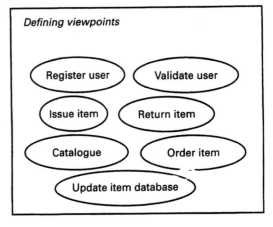

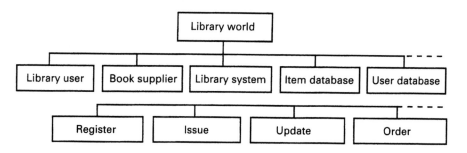

Figure 7.6
Viewpoint
structuring for
library system.

The last stage in viewpoint identification involves pruning the identified viewpoints into a set of bounding and defining viewpoints as shown in Figure 7.5. Each bubble represents the most abstract form of the viewpoint.

Viewpoint structuring provides a framework for requirements capture and analysis. It involves iteratively decomposing the 'target system' into a hierarchy of functional sub-systems, essentially performing a top-down decomposition. Structurally bounding viewpoints are placed at the same level as the target system. Each functional subsystem constitutes a viewpoint. Figure 7.6 shows part of the viewpoint structure of the library system.

Step 3 in CORE is tabular collection. Tabular collection is a mechanism for gathering information about a viewpoint. Each viewpoint is considered in turn with respect to the action it performs, data used for these actions, the output data derived, the source of the data and the destination of the data. Tabular collections serve the purpose of exposing omissions and conflicts in the information flow across viewpoints. As viewpoints must be the sources and destinations of inputs and outputs, the tabular collection across viewpoints must be consistent. Figure 7.7 shows part of the tabular collection for the Library system

The data structuring step involves decomposing data items into constituent parts and creating a data dictionary. Steps 5 and 6 involve modelling viewpoint actions using action diagrams. An action diagram is similar in notation to an SADT diagram, and is used to specify the processing actions associated with a tabular collection diagram (see Figure 7.3). The final step in CORE involves performing constraint analysis on the system as a whole.

Perhaps the main shortcoming of CORE is its poorly defined notion of a viewpoint. Because a CORE viewpoint can be any entity that interacts with

Figure 7.7
Tabular
collection
example.

Source	Input	Action	Output	Destination
Library user	Requested item	Check item	Issued item	Library user
			Error message	Issue clerk
Library user	Library card	Validate user	Loan default message	Issue clerk

the proposed system it is difficult to say what is and what is not a valid viewpoint. This problem is further complicated by having defining and bounding viewpoints. Bounding viewpoints are supposed be 'external' entities that exchange information with the system, while defining viewpoints are sub-processes of the 'target system'. CORE addresses this problem by proving some guidelines on identifying 'reasonable' viewpoints.

The analysis in CORE is concentrated on what are really internal perspectives – defining viewpoints. Bounding viewpoints which represent the system's interaction with its environment are not analysed beyond being seen as sinks and sources of data. In addition, because of the underlying structure of the CORE viewpoint model, it is difficult to model processes using different representations.

7.3   Viewpoint-oriented System Engineering (VOSE)

Unlike the other viewpoint-oriented techniques described here, Viewpoint-oriented System Engineering is a framework for integrating development methods. The approach is intended to address the entire system development cycle, hence the name. VOSE was developed at Imperial College, London in the early 1990s and is well documented in the literature (Finkelstein, et al. 1992; Nuseibeh et al.). The underlying philosophy of the framework is that software development involves the participation of many experts, in various aspects of software development and the application area. Each participant may have responsibilities and concerns which may change and shift as the software develops and evolves.

To capture and manage these varying perspectives, the approach advocates the use of viewpoints. VOSE uses the notion of viewpoints to partition and distribute the activities and knowledge of the participants. Viewpoints capture the role and responsibility of a participant at a particular stage of the software development process. Viewpoints are identified by the role of the participant, domain-relevant to his or her interest and the knowledge about the domain of application. This knowledge is encapsulated in viewpoint and represented using a single appropriate representative scheme called a style. A VOSE viewpoint (written ViewPoint in VOSE) can be thought of as a template describing a style or representative scheme in which the viewpoint expresses what it sees; the domain it sees, a specification, work plan that defines the conditions under which the specification can be changed and a work record. Figure 7.8 shows the slots of a standard ViewPoint template.

VOSE viewpoints can be organised into configurations, which are collections of related viewpoints. A configuration for a hypothetical problem domain may consist of templates with different styles, 'viewing' the same partition of the problem domain, or templates with the same style 'viewing'

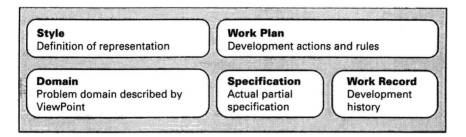

Figure 7.8
Slots of a
ViewPoint
template in
VOSE.

different partitions of the problem domain. The final system is a combination of the configurations with all the conflicts resolved. In the case of templates with the same style 'viewing' different partitions, conflict resolution involves ensuring that there is consistency in the information flow between the different partitions. However in the case where configurations consist of different templates with different styles, 'viewing' the same domain, styles must be chosen carefully to ensure that they have a high degree of correspondence.

Consider the case of a library item presented by the user at the issue desk for borrowing, returning or reserving. We can model this 'library world' by partitioning it into the domains of the issue desk and the library user. In the next section we use a data-flow and a state transition scheme to model the library item from the point of view of each domain.

Data flow model (issue desk domain). The library item undergoes certain processing at the issue desk. The activities are represented by the check, issue and release processes as shown in Figure 7.9. The check process accepts as input the presented item and processes it for issuing, removal or reserve. The issue process accepts as input the checked item and provides as output an issued item. The release process, releases items from the reserve.

State transition model (issue desk domain). It is also possible to model the various states of the library item as seen from the domain of the issue desk Figure 7.10. shows the states and the events that cause the transitions.

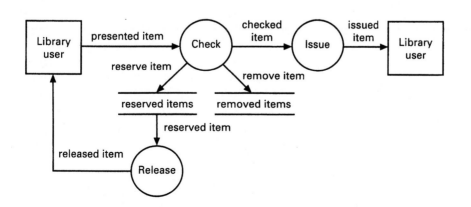

Figure 7.9
Data-flow
process from
the domain of
the issue desk.

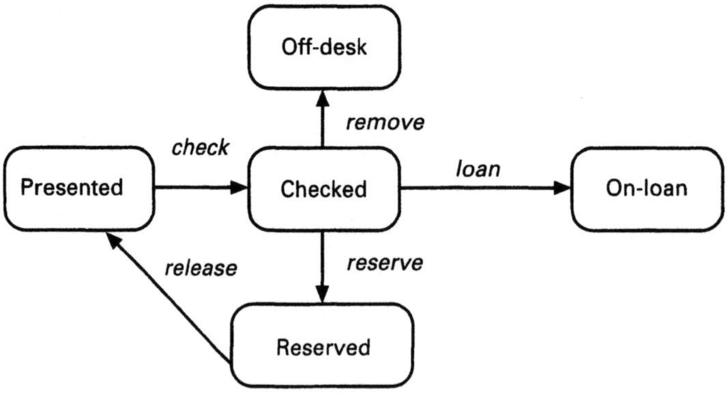

Figure 7.10
State transition
diagram showing
the states seen
by the issue
desk.

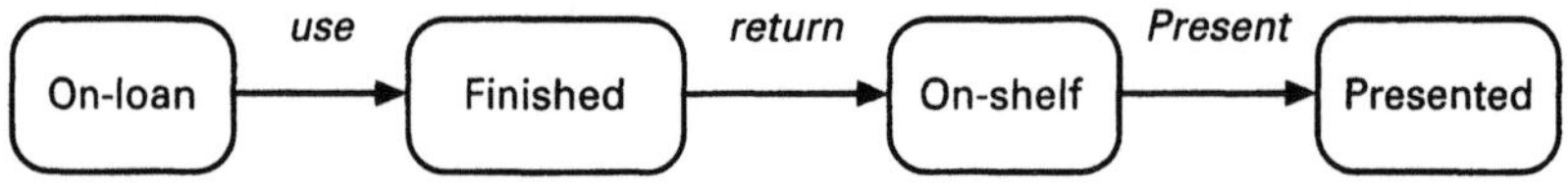

Figure 7.11
State transition
diagram showing
the states seen
by the library
user.

This is a very simple state transition diagram and we have not shown the preconditions and actions that would normally accompany the events.

State transition model (library user domain). Similarly, we can model the states of the library item as seen from the domain of the library user. The library user sees four states of the item: the on-loan, finished, on-shelf, and presented. Figure 7.11 shows four states of the issue desk. The user borrows a library item, reads the item, and returns the item.

For each of the two representation schemes, the development rules and actions are described in the work plan slot of the ViewPoint template. The work performed to arrive at the three representations shown is recorded in the work record slot of the viewpoint template.

7.3.1 Mapping configurations and resolving conflicts

We have illustrated how two partitions of the library domain can be represented using different representation schemes. The next step is to ensure that consistency is maintained between different representations of the domains. Figure 7.12 shows the mappings between the different configurations and how conflicts need to be resolved. The requirements analyst must check that the representations of the system are consistent by examining the entities and relations in each representation and mapping one onto the other. Inconsistency in a system model may be a result of genuine requirements conflicts which must be resolved or may be a consequence of mistakes or omissions in the requirements.

In the case of templates with the same style viewing different domains (e.g. data-flow diagrams), it is a simple matter to ensure that there is consistency in the information flow between the different partitions. Conflicts

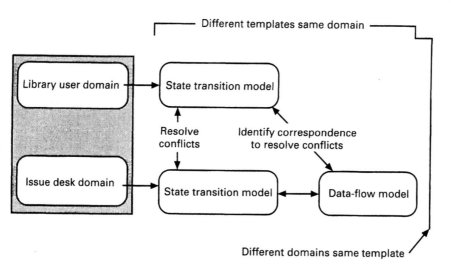

Figure 7.12 Representation of consistency checking.

between similar templates are resolved by checking for the loss of continuity between the respective models. For example, in the state transition model, the present state seen by the issue desk maps onto the state seen by the library user. Similarly on-loan maps onto on-loan. Off-desk maps onto on-shelf. Although this is not essential, these may be renamed to indicate that they are the same thing.

Where different styles are used to view the same domain, the correspondences between different representation schemes need to be identified to facilitate consistency checking. For this reason it is important that representative schemes are selected, whose correspondence can be established. The possible correspondence between state transition models and data flow models is shown in Figures 7.13 and 7.14. Therefore, inputs and outputs in a

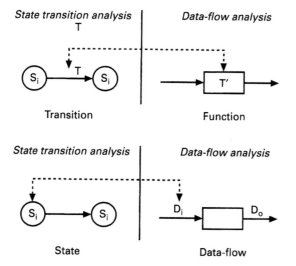

Figure 7.13 Possible correspondence between a state transition and a function.

Figure 7.14 Possible correspondence between a state and data.

Figure 7.15
Example of
correspondence
between
different
representation
schemes.

Mapping different templates, same domains	
Issue desk DFD	**Issue desk ST**
check	check
issue	loan
release	release

Figure 7.16
Example of
correspondence
between similar
representation
schemes.

Mapping different domains, same templates	
Issue desk ST	**Library user ST**
presented	presented
on-loan	on-loan

data-flow diagram map onto states in a state transition model and functions map onto transitions.

Having identified the correspondence between the schemes, it is possible to trace data items to states and functions to transitions. An example is of this mapping is given in Figure 7.15 and 7.16. Figure 7.15 show the mapping between the issue desk data-flow diagram (DFD) and the issue desk state transition diagram.

Figure 7.16 shows the points of continuity between the two different domains using similar representation schemes. The library user's on-loan and presented states map onto similar states on and issue desk domain. The on-loan and presented states, constitute the common states seen by both domains.

7.4 Viewpoint-oriented Requirements Definition (VORD)

Viewpoint-oriented Requirements Definition method (VORD) is primarily intended for specifying interactive systems, but can also be used to specify other classes of system (Kotonya and Sommerville, 1996). VORD is based on viewpoints that focus on user issues and organisational concerns. The model adopted for viewpoints is service-oriented, where viewpoints are analogous to clients in a client-server system. The system delivers services to viewpoints and the viewpoints pass control information and associated parameters to the system. Viewpoints map to classes of end-users of a system or with other systems interfaced to it. The viewpoints that make up the core model are known as direct viewpoints. In recognition of the fact that not all requirements are derived from people or systems which interact with the system being specified, viewpoints concerned with the system's influence on the application domain are also considered. These are indirect viewpoints.

Direct and indirect viewpoints are defined as follows:

1. **Direct viewpoints**

   These correspond directly to clients in that they receive services from the system and send control information and data to the system. Direct viewpoints are either system operators/users or other sub-systems which are interfaced to the system being analysed.

2. **Indirect viewpoints**

   Indirect viewpoints have an 'interest' in some or all the services that are delivered by the system but do not interact directly with it. Indirect viewpoints may generate requirements which constrain the services delivered to direct viewpoints.

Indirect viewpoints may range from engineering viewpoints (i.e. those concerned with the system design and implementation) through organisational viewpoints (those concerned with the system's influence on the organisation) to external viewpoints (those concerned with the system's influence on the outside environment). Therefore, if we take a simple example of a library system, some viewpoints might be:

1. a systems planning viewpoint which is concerned with future delivery of library services (indirect)

2. library user viewpoint which is concerned with accessing the system services through the internet (direct)

3. a trade-union viewpoint which is concerned with the effects of system introduction on staffing levels and library staff duties (indirect).

We have used the VORD method to specify an interactive system in Chapter 9, so a detailed description of the method will be provided in that chapter.

7.5 Viewpoint-oriented requirements validation

Leite and Freeman (1991) describe an approach based on viewpoints that can be used for early requirements validation. The objective of the approach is identify and classify problems related to completeness and correctness. The approach is built around three main concepts: a viewpoint, a perspective and a view. A viewpoint is defined as a standing or mental position used by an individual when examining a universe of discourse (the overall context in which the software will be developed, including all the sources of information and people involved). A perspective is defined as a set of facts observed and modelled according to a particular aspect of reality. A view is defined as an integration of these perspectives.

A viewpoint language (VWPL), is used to represent the viewpoints. The method involves at least two analysts (viewpoints) using VWPL to express their perception of the universe of discourse. In order to construct a view, an analyst describes the problem using three perspectives: data, process and actor perspectives. The analysts also use the is-a and part-of hierarchies to improve their own view. The perspectives and hierarchies are analysed and a 'list of discrepancies' and a 'types of discrepancies' produced. The next step is to integrate the perspectives into a view. This view is expressed in the process perspective together with the hierarchies. After two views are available it is possible to compare the different viewpoints for correctness and completeness. Figure 7.17 shows the diagrammatic processes involved in the method; the circles represent processes and the unshaded boxes the inputs and outputs to the processes.

Figure 7.17
Viewpoint-based requirements validation.

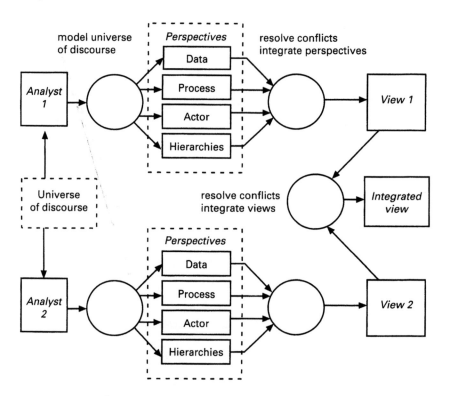

♦ **Key Points**

♦ Requirements engineering involves the capture, analysis and resolution of many ideas, perspectives and relationships at varying levels of detail. To address this problem a number of methods have evolved based on the notion of viewpoints.

♦ A viewpoint is a collection of information about a system or related problem, environment or domain which is collective from a particular perspective.

♦ Structured analysis techniques do not have explicitly defined viewpoints, instead viewpoints are an intuitive extension of the modelling technique. Data sinks and data sources constitute viewpoints in these approaches.

♦ CORE has two types of viewpoints: defining and bounding viewpoints. Defining viewpoints are sub-processes of the system and bounding viewpoints are entities that interact with the intended system

♦ A VOSE viewpoint is a template describing style or representative scheme in which the viewpoint expresses what it sees, the domain it sees, a specification, a work plan and a work record.

♦ **Exercises**

7.1 Using an example, explain how the notion of viewpoints can aid in understanding a system's requirements.

7.2 Briefly describe the different notions of viewpoints which are used in requirements engineering.

7.3 Use the SADT approach to identify potential data sources and sinks in an airline ticket reservation system.

7.4 Use the CORE method to identify bounding and defining viewpoints in a university student records system.

7.5 A video library intends to develop a interactive web-based video-on-demand system for its customers. The service will allow its members to select and play video recordings of their choice via the internet. Identify the potential viewpoints of the system and their likely concerns and requirements.

7.6 Using the example given in 7.4 as a software engineering group project, explain how you would use VOSE to organise the team and tasks.

◆ References

Ross, D. (1985). Applications and extensions of SADT. *IEEE Computer*, **18**(4): 25–34.

Mullery, G. (1979). A method for controlled requirements specifications. *4th international conference on software engineering*, 126–135, Munich, Germany, IEEE Computer Society Press.

Finkelstein, A., Kramer, J., Nuseibeh, B., and Goedicke, M. (1992). Viewpoints: A framework for integrating multiple perspectives in systems development. *International Journal of Software Engineering and Knowledge Engineering*, **2**(10): 31–58.

Kotonya, G., and Sommerville, I. (1996). Requirements Engineering with viewpoints. *Software Engineering*, **1**(11): 5–18.

Leite, J. C. P., and Freeman, P. A. (1991). Requirements validation through viewpoint resolution. *Transactions of Software Engineering*, **12**(12): 1253–1269.

Nuscibeh, B., Kramer, J., and Finkelstein, A. (1994). A framework for expressing the relationships between multiple view in requirements specification. *Transactions of Software Engineering*, **20**(10): 760–773.

◆ Further reading

Viewpoints for requirements definition (G. Kotonya and I. Sommerville, Software engineering journal, 7(6), 375–387, 1992). This paper provides a detailed survey of viewpoint-based approaches.

8 Non-functional Requirements

◆ **Summary**

Non-functional requirements are requirements which are not specifically concerned with the functionality of a system. They place restrictions on the product being developed and the development process, and they specify external constraints that the product must meet. Non-functional requirements include safety, security, usability, reliability and performance requirements. In this chapter we discuss different types of non-functional requirements including product requirement, process requirements and external requirements. We describe a process for deriving the non-functional requirements on a system and then focus specifically on different types of requirement for critical systems. In the final section we introduce a requirements engineering process for safety-related systems which leads to the derivation of critical non-functional requirements.

◆

Non-functional requirements define the overall qualities or attributes of the resulting system. They place restrictions on how the user requirements are to be met. The user may place constraints on the software related to interfaces, quality, resources and timescales. Because they are restrictions or constraints on system services, non-functional requirements are often of critical importance, and functional requirements may need to be sacrificed to meet these non-functional constraints.

Certain non-functional requirements may constrain the development process rather than the product. They include requirements on development standards, methods and implementation languages to be followed. Customers generally impose these constraints to achieve good product quality and to maintain compatibility with methods used for system design and implementation. Other non-functional requirements may not be directly associated with the product or development process, but arise from external constraints outside the enterprise. These include legal, economic and interoperability constraints.

Although it is often helpful to distinguish requirements which specify a system's functionality from 'non-functional' requirements, it is important to understand that there is not a clear distinction between functional and non-functional requirements. Whether or not a requirement is expressed as a functional or a non-functional requirement may depend on the level of detail to be included in the requirements document or the degree of trust which exists between a system customer and a system developer. To illustrate this, consider a requirement for system security: the system shall ensure that data is protected from unauthorised access.

Conventionally, this would be considered as a non-functional requirement because it does not specify specific system functionality which must be provided. However, it could have been specified in slightly more detail as follows: the system shall include a user authorisation procedure in which users must identify themselves using a login name and password. Only users who are authorised in this way may access the system data.

In this form, the requirement looks rather more like a functional requirement as it specifies a function (user login) which must be incorporated in the system. In fact, this illustrates a very common situation where an abstract non-functional requirement is decomposed into more detailed functional sub-system requirements.

Non-functional software requirements are often determined by the nature of the larger system in which the software is embedded (Loucopulos and Karakostas, 1995). For example, the non-functional software requirements for embedded systems such as process-control, air traffic control and patient monitoring cannot be considered in isolation. In this type of system, the larger system imposes constraints on the embedded components. These may include performance requirements such as fast response times, reliability requirements such as constant availability and safety-related constraints. Overall system needs may also affect other types of non-functional requirements such as portability and modifiability (Davis, 1992).

8.1 Classification of non-functional requirements

Non-functional requirements can be defined as restrictions or constraints placed on a system service (Sommerville, 1996). The 'IEEE-Std 830 – 1993' lists

13 non-functional requirements (including quality requirements) to be included in the 'Specific Requirements Section' of the Software Requirements Document. These non-functional requirements are shown in Figure 8.1 (requirements 3.2 to 3.14).

Different ways of classifying non-functional requirements have been proposed. One of the earliest classifications was proposed by Boehm (1976). It referred to qualities that a software must exhibit. A similar approach was proposed by Deutsch and Willis (1988). Davis (1992) classifies them as 'non-behavioural requirements'. Recently more general classifications encompassing all aspects of system engineering have been proposed.

Sommerville stresses that non-functional requirements arise because users need to achieve certain goals. These may be brought about by budget constraints, organisational policies, need for interoperability with other software and hardware, the need for certain development process to be followed, and external factors such as safety and security regulations. He classifies non-functional requirements into product, process and external requirements. Figure 8.2 shows a classification structure for some non-functional requirements based on these categories. In practice, there is not necessarily a clear distinction between these categories and some requirements could easily be classified under more than one heading. We shall see examples of these in the following sections.

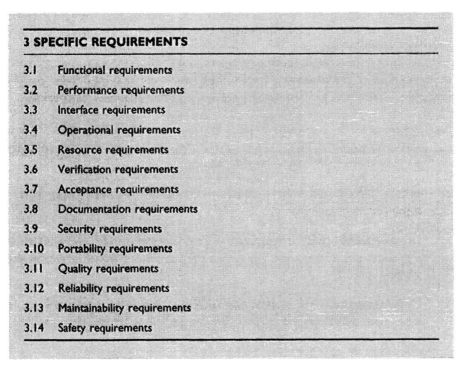

3 SPECIFIC REQUIREMENTS

3.1	Functional requirements
3.2	Performance requirements
3.3	Interface requirements
3.4	Operational requirements
3.5	Resource requirements
3.6	Verification requirements
3.7	Acceptance requirements
3.8	Documentation requirements
3.9	Security requirements
3.10	Portability requirements
3.11	Quality requirements
3.12	Reliability requirements
3.13	Maintainability requirements
3.14	Safety requirements

Figure 8.1
Non-functional requirements in 'IEEE Std-830-1993'.

Figure 8.2
Classification of
non-functional
requirements.

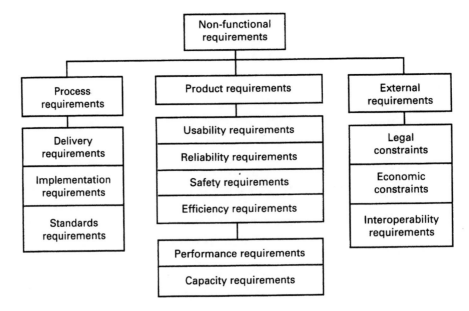

8.1.1   Product requirements

Product requirements are requirements which specify the desired characteristics that a system or subsystem must possess. Some, such as performance
and capacity, can be formulated precisely and thus easily quantified, while
others, such as usability, are more difficult to quantify and consequently are
often stated informally.

Most product requirements are concerned with the specifying constraints on
the behaviour of the executing system. They limit the freedom of the system
designers. Therefore, the following product requirements may be specified.

1.   System service X shall have an availability of 999/1000 or 99%. This is
     a reliability requirement which means that out of every 1000 requests
     for this service, 999 must be satisfied.

2.   System Y shall process a minimum of 8 transactions per second. This is
     a performance requirement.

3.   The executable code of System Z shall be limited to 512 Kbytes. This is
     a space requirement which specifies the maximum memory size of the
     system.

4.   The request for the user's PIN shall be issued within 5 seconds of the card
     being entered in the card reader. This is a performance requirement.

As well as these requirements which constrain the system's behaviour, there may be product requirements which relate to the source code of the system. For example:

1. the system shall be developed for PC and Macintosh platforms; this is a portability requirement which affects the way in which the system may be designed

2. the system must encrypt all external communications using the RSA algorithm; this is a security requirement which specifies that a specific algorithm must be used in the product

3. System X shall be implemented using Release 5 of Library Y; this can be considered to be a product requirement as it means that certain design solutions may be impossible, however, it could also be an external requirement as it may be imposed because of external organisational decisions which have been made.

It is often the case that product requirements are mutually conflicting. For example, a requirement for a certain level of performance may be contradicted by reliability and security requirements which rely on processor capacity to carry out dynamic system checking. A requirement on the space utilisation of the system may be contradicted by another requirement which specifies that a standard compiler which does not generate compact code must be used.

The process of arriving at a trade-off in these conflicts depends on the level of importance attached to the requirement and the consequence of the change on the other requirements and the wider system goals. In addition to these specific requirements, there are high-level organisational and other global requirements against which all requirements must be analysed. Detailed conflict resolution and management is a topic of ongoing research and is outside the scope of this book. Interested readers are referred to the work of Nuseibeh and Easterbrook for more information on this topic (Easterbrook and Nuseibeh, 1996).

8.1.2 Process requirements

Process requirements are constraints placed upon the development process of the system. They may be included because the customer for a system wishes to influence this process. Process requirements include requirements on development standards and methods which must be followed, CASE tools which should be used and the management reports which must be provided. Therefore, examples of process requirements might be that:

1.   the development process to be used must be explicitly defined and must be conformant with ISO 9000 standards

2.   the system must be developed using the XYZ suite of CASE tools

3.   management reports setting out the effort expended on each identified system component must be produced every two weeks

4.   a disaster recovery plan for the system development must be specified.

Process requirements are typically included when large organisations with existing standards and practices and qualified technical staff are procuring systems. They may vary in detail from very specific instructions on the process which must be followed (e.g. the US Defence Department's 2167A process standard for software engineering) to more general requirements such as that above which specifies that the process must be ISO 9000 conformant.

Process requirements can place real constraints on the design of a system. For example, an organisation may specify that a specific set of CASE tools must be used for system development because it has experience with these tools. If these tools do not support object-oriented development (say), this means that the system architecture cannot be object-oriented.

8.1.3   External requirements

External requirements are requirements which may be placed on both the product and the process and which are derived from the environment in which the system is developed. These requirements therefore may be based on application domain information, organisational considerations, the need for the system to work with other systems, health and safety or data protection regulations or even basic natural laws such as the laws of physics.

Some examples of external requirements which are placed on a system might therefore be as follows.

1.   *Student record system*   The format of the student record data available through the national Student Record System (SREC) is defined using the content description notation shown in Figure 8.3.

The record data sequence is defined using the content description notation as follows:

Admission_No + Name + Address + University + Course

The individual data items are defined thus:

Data construct	Notation	Meaning
	=	Is composed of
Sequence	+	And
Selection	[	]	Either-or
Repetition	$^m\{\ \}^n$	iterations of enclosed component. Minimum number of repetitions is m and maximum is n
	( )	Optional data
	* *	Delimits comments

Figure 8.3 Content description notation for data record.

Admission_No = Year + Personal_Number
Year = $^4\{Digit\}^4$
Personal_Number = $^5\{Digit\}^5$
Digit = 0|1|..|9
Name = Surname + (Middlename) + Firstname
Surname = $^1\{Letter\}^{15}$ + (Hyphen) + $^1\{Letter\}^{15}$
Middlename = $\{Letter\}^{10}$
Firstname = $^1\{Letter\}^{15}$
Letter =
A|B|C|D|E|F|G|H|I|J|K|L|M|N|O|P|Q|R|S|T|U|V|X|Y|Z
Hyphen = -
Address = $^1\{Char\}^{140}$
Char = Digit|Letter|-| |,
University = $^1\{Letter\}^{20}$
Course = $^1\{Letter\}^{20}$

2. *Medical data system* The organisation's data protection officer must certify that all data is maintained according to data protection legislation before the system is put into operation.

3. *Train protection system* The time required to bring the train to a complete halt is computed using the following function:

The deceleration of the train shall be taken as:

$\lambda_{train} = \lambda_{control} + \lambda_{gradient}$
where:

$\lambda_{gradient}$ = 9.81 ms^{-2} * compensated gradient / alpha and where the values of *9.81 ms^{-2}/ alpha* are known for the different types of train.

Figure 8.4
Example of train
deceleration.

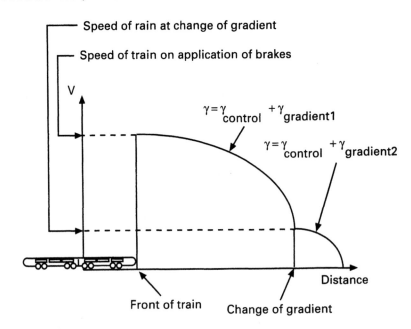

$\lambda_{control}$ is initialised at 0.8 ms^{-2}, this value being parametrised in order to remain adjustable. Figure 8.4 illustrates an example of the train's deceleration by using the parabolas derived from the above formula where there is a change in gradient before the (predicted) stopping point of the train.

The first of the above requirements is a requirement from an external system. The second comes from the need for the system to conform to data protection legislation and the third comes from the application domain and is a specification of the physical braking characteristics of a train.

External requirements rarely have the form 'the system shall ...' or 'the system shall not ...'. Rather, they are descriptions of the system's environment which must be taken into account. For this reason, it is often very difficult to include external requirements in a structured system model.

8.2 Deriving non-functional requirements

Non-functional requirements are not adequately covered by most requirements engineering methods. Existing RE methods are usually based on functional analysis or object-oriented analysis and are inherently limited as far as non-functional requirements are concerned (Chung et al., 1992; Dobson, 1991; Kotonya and Sommerville, 1993).

The reason why these methods do not support non-functional requirements is that it is very difficult to do so. They are diverse and must usually be expressed in domain-specific ways. A number of important issues contribute to the problem of expressing non-functional requirements.

1. Certain constraints, for example response time to failure, are related to the design solution that is unknown at the requirements stage.

2. Other constraints, especially those associated with human engineering issues, are highly subjective and can only be determined through complex empirical evaluations.

3. Non-functional requirements tend to be related to one or more functional requirements. Expressing functional and non-functional requirements separately makes it difficult to see the correspondence between them, whereas stating them together may make it difficult to separate functional and non-functional considerations.

4. Non-functional requirements tend to conflict and contradict each other (with the consequence that the design solution is the result of trade-offs).

5. There are no rules and guidelines for determining when non-functional requirements are optimally met. Every 'solution' might provoke a proposal for a more refined solution and so on.

Chung has proposed a goal-oriented model method in which accuracy requirements are treated as potentially conflicting goals. Dobson has suggested developing logical models of non-functional requirements whose meaning derives from the organisational environment of computer system. Kotonya (Kotonya and Sommerville, 1996) has suggested a viewpoint-based framework that integrates functional and non-functional requirements. The main issue underlying all these proposals is the importance of translating general objectives or goals into statements that refer to measurable properties of the systems.

The process of formulating software requirements involves the elicitation of requirements from the system stakeholders. As we have discussed in Chapter 3, stakeholders often don't have a clear idea of what they really want from a system. Their 'requirements' may be expressed in a vague way and they may have a number of 'concerns' which are important to them but which are difficult to articulate as system requirements.

These concerns correspond to high-level strategic objectives for the system and are typically non-functional. They may correspond to critical business objectives (such as standardisation) or may reflect essential system characteristics such as security. Other examples of concerns which might be associated with a system include safety, performance, functionality, maintainability. If the system is to be successful, these concerns must be met. Concerns must therefore be considered at every stage of requirements elicitation, and satisfying the concerns may have to take priority over other functional requirements.

Meeting a concern may necessitate the formulation of a number of functional requirements but they will also act to constrain other requirements. Loucopoulos (Loucopoulos and Karakostas, 1995) illustrates how vaguely defined user concerns may be related to non-functional requirements (Figure 8.5).

Concerns are also a way of expressing critical 'holistic' requirements which apply to the system as a whole rather than to any specific sub-set of its services or functionality. Sommerville (1996) describes how the concerns may be broken down into sub-concerns and finally into specific questions which act as a check list to ensure that specific requirements do not conflict with global priorities. To be effective, the number of concerns should be small (typically 6 or fewer) and rigorously scrutinised to eliminate all but the most overriding, system-wide, high-level goals and constraints.

To illustrate this approach, Figure 8.6 shows the decomposition of safety and compatibility concerns for a train protection system. This system automatically halts the train if it goes through a danger signal or if it exceeds the safe speed for a track segment. In this system, there are two principal concerns, namely safety and compatibility. Safety is a concern because failure of the system could lead to a railway accident, and compatibility is a concern because the system must be installed in an environment where other control systems are already used.

Figure 8.5
Relationships between user needs and non-functional requirements.

User's need	User's concern	Non-functional requirement
Function	1. Ease of use	1. Usability
	2. Unauthorised access	2. Security
	3. Likelihood of failure	3. Reliability
Performance	1. Resource utilisation	1. Efficiency
	2. Performance verification	2. Verifiability
	3. Ease of interfacing	3. Interoperability
Change	1. Ease of repair	1. Maintainability
	2. Ease of change	2. Flexibility
	3. Ease of transport	3. Portability
	4. Ease of expansion	4. Expandability

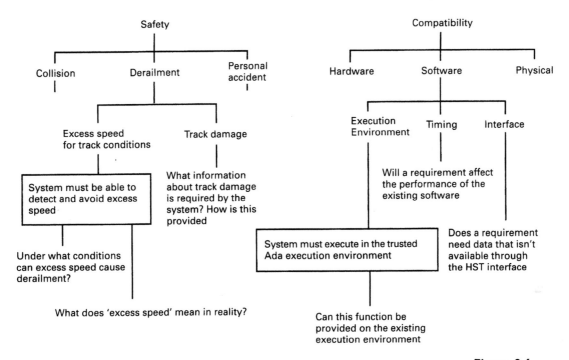

Figure 8.6
Concern
decomposition.

The concerns may lead directly to system requirements (shown in boxes in Figure 8.6) or to questions which must be answered during the requirements engineering process.

Loucopulos and Karakostas (1995) proposed a comparable approach to deriving non-functional requirements. Their approach, based on an enterprise model, involves relating non-functional requirements to the goals of the enterprise. The process begins with the statement of an enterprise goal followed by successive decomposition of the goal into sub-goals and subsequently non-functional requirements. This process is followed by successively examining the requirements until a measurable statement can be defined. One advantage of the approach is that it provides a means of tracing non-functional requirements to originally stated, vague expressions in the enterprise domain.

This approach is illustrated using a requirement drawn from the air traffic domain (Figure 8.7). The abstract goal that the system should visualise air traffic scenarios in real time motivates a system requirement that it should perform in real time. This motivates two non-functional requirements that are mainly concerned with performance and capacity, which in turn motivates quantitative non-functional requirements. For example, the non-functional requirement that 'radar data should be displayed in real time' motivates the more detailed non-functional requirement 'aircraft position should be displayed in less than 0.165 of the radar sweep period'. Further analysis of the non-functional requirements results in successively more specific requirement statements represented as the leaves of the diagram shown in Figure 8.7.

Although it is very important to understand that customers and other stakeholders may have vague goals which cannot be expressed precisely, these should not be confused with more specific non-functional requirements. All too often, vague and imprecise 'requirements' are included in a requirements document and cause problems both for system designers and for customers when the system does not meet their expectations.

Sommerville and others (Sommerville 1996; Deutsch and Willis, 1988) contend that this problem can only be overcome by ensuring that non-functional requirements satisfy two attributes: they must be objective and they must be testable. A non-functional requirement is objective if it does not express a wish, a goal or a personal opinion, and is testable if there is some process by which the requirement can be tested. Examples of measurable properties are given in Figure 8.8.

However, although deterministic specification of non-functional requirements is the ideal, it is not always possible, as we discuss in the following section.

Figure 8.7
Relationship between enterprise and system goals.

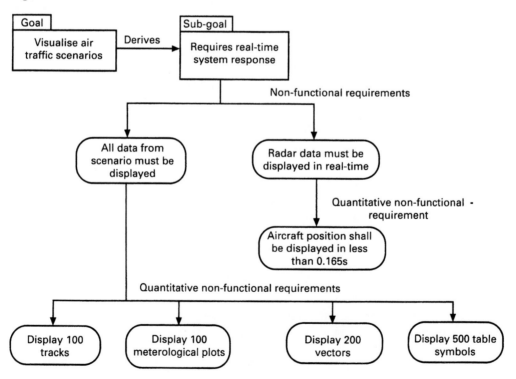

Property	Metric
Performance	1. Processed transactions per second
	2. Response time to user input
Reliability	1. Rate of occurrence of failure
	2. Mean time to failure
Availability	Probability of failure on demand
Size	Kbytes
Usability	1. Time taken to learn 80% of the facilities
	2. Number of errors made by users in a given time period
Robustness	Time to restart after system failure
Portability	Number of target systems

Figure 8.8
Examples of measurable metrics for non-functional requirements.

8.3 Requirements for critical systems

Critical systems are systems whose 'failure' causes significant economic, physical or human damage to organisations or people. There are three principal types of critical system.

1. **Business critical systems**
   where a failure of the system causes significant economic damage to a business. An example of such a system is an airline reservation system.

2. **Mission critical systems**
   where the failure of the system means that some mission cannot be accomplished. An example of such a system is a control system on a spacecraft.

3. **Safety critical systems**
   where a failure of a system endangers human life or causes significant environmental damage. An example of such a system is a control system for a radiation therapy machine.

A failure of a critical system may result from a failure to meet a functional requirement but, more often, it results from a failure of the system to satisfy some non-functional constraint on its operation. The principal non-functional constraints which are relevant to critical systems are:

1. reliability
2. performance
3. security
4. usability
5. safety

It is important to understand that these non-functional requirements are requirements on the system as a whole and not just on the software. They are usually expressed in a fairly general way and must then be decomposed into more specific requirements for the different parts of the system. As we discussed in the introduction, a non-functional system requirement may lead to specific functional requirements for the software or other sub-systems.

Conflicts between system requirements are common and during the requirements engineering process these conflicts should be explicitly identified and negotiated. These conflicts are not necessarily a result of errors in the process. They arise because the different types of system requirement naturally pull the system in different directions.

1. System performance is enhanced if the amount of redundant code in the system is reduced to a minimum. However, adding redundancy to the software in the form of additional checks may detect errors before they result in system failure. Therefore, redundancy decreases performance but increases reliability.

2. System security is increased if procedures exist for validating that the issuer of a system command is authorised. However, these procedures may involve additional operator inputs and hence may decrease the usability of the system.

3. A system may have a fail-safe position, i.e. a state that is known to be safe and which should be entered in the event of a system failure. If a very conservative approach is taken, the fail-safe state may be entered when there is any possibility (no matter how remote) of system failure. However, when in this state, the system is unlikely to be available for use so the overall availability of the system is reduced. Therefore, the need for safety contradicts the requirement for system availability.

There is no simple and easy way to resolve these tensions. In each case, some compromise must be reached which satisfies the majority of system stakeholders.

8.3.1 Reliability

Reliability requirements are constraints on the run-time behaviour of the system. They can be considered under two separate headings.

♦ Availability – is the system available for service when requested by end-users?

♦ Failure rate – how often does the system fail to deliver the service expected by end-users?

These are obviously related and in some cases end-users of a system will not make any distinction between them. As far as they are concerned, the system is not giving them the service that they want. In other cases, however, they must be treated separately. For example, in a telephone switching system most customers would prefer the system to be unavailable than system failures to occur where they were connected to and charged for a connection to the wrong person.

Reliability requirements can often be expressed quantitatively. Availability may be specified in terms of the time when the system is unavailable for service (e.g. 3 minutes in 24 hours) and the acceptable failure rate may be specified in terms of the rate of occurrence of failures in a given time period (ROCOF) or the mean time between system failures (MTTF).

8.3.2 Performance

Performance requirements constrain the speed of operation of a system. Various different types of performance requirement may be specified.

♦ Response requirements which specify the acceptable response of the system to end-user input: for example, it might be specified that the system should respond to a user request for service within 2 seconds.

♦ Throughput requirements which specify the amount of data which must be processed in a given time: for example, it might be specified that the system must process at least 10 transactions per second.

♦ Timing requirements which specify how quickly the system must collect input from sensors before it is overwritten by the next input value, or which specify how quickly outputs must be produced for processing by other systems: for example, it might be specified that the system must poll sensors at least 6 times per second.

In some cases, the RAM required for an executing software system might also be considered as a performance requirement on the system, as it relates to the system's run-time behaviour and as it also affects the speed of system operation. Like reliability requirements, performance requirements should be specified quantitatively wherever possible.

8.3.3 Security

Security requirements are included in a system to ensure that unauthorised access to the system and its data is not allowed and to ensure the integrity of the system from accidental or malicious damage. As systems become distributed and connected to external networks, security requirements are becoming more and more important.

Examples of security requirements are as follows.

1. The access permissions for system data may only be changed by the system's data administrator.

2. All system data must be backed up every 24 hours and the backup copies stored in a secure location which is not in the same building as the system.

3. All external communications between the system's data server and clients must be encrypted.

Security is an essential prerequisite for safety, as it is impossible to be confident that a system is safe unless you can be confident that the system and its data cannot be tampered with. Consequently, all safety-related systems should also have associated security requirements. Like safety requirements, security requirements cannot usually be expressed in a quantitative way and may be written as 'shall not' requirements which constrain the solution space of the system.

8.3.4 Usability

Usability requirements are concerned with specifying the user interface and end-user interactions with the system. It is generally accepted that well structured user manuals, informative error messages, help facilities and consistent interfaces enhance usability (Fenton, 1991). Experience has shown that detailed user interface specification in terms of screen designs does not work well as user interfaces are best developed using an process of evolutionary prototyping. However, this process may be constrained by higher level usability requirements. Gilb (1988) describes measurable attributes of usability (in each case the actual measure has to be decided by the 'user' according the particular type of product).

Entry requirements: measured in terms of years of experience with class of applications (in the case of, for example, a word-processing system), or simply age in the case of, for example, a junior school tutoring system.

Learning requirements: denotes the time needed to learn the facilities of the system. This could be measured, for example, in terms of speed of learning the, say hours of training required before independent use is possible.

Handling requirements: denotes the error rate of the end-users of the system. This could be measured in terms of the errors made when working at normal speed.

Likeability: denotes 'niceness' to use. The most direct to measure user satisfaction is to survey actual users and record the proportion who 'like to work with the product'.

These types of usability requirement may be specified quantitatively although, inevitably, for many types of system this will be fairly arbitrary. Newman and Lamming (1995) discuss how such quantitative usability requirements may be derived. In other cases, usability requirements are less concrete and may be concerned with achieving consistency across a number of different systems. For example, a possible usability requirement might be: the forms used in the system's user interface shall, wherever possible, be consistent with the forms used in System XYZ.

It is probably impossible to be more definite than this in the requirements specification as system design decisions affect which forms will be used. It cannot be decided in advance when compatibility is required.

The COQUAMO approach provides an automated support facility for setting and measuring usability. The system provides a set of 'templates' which must be filled in. A completed template for usability is shown in Figure 8.9.

Classification	General quality – application dependent
Level required	High
Associated qualities	
synonyms	learnability, operability, user friendliness
related concepts	understandability
Definition 1	ease with which users can learn to use system
Explosion 1.1	average time for specific classes of user to achieve level of competence with system
Measurement unites	days
measuring tool/data source	survey forms and results of survey
Measurement conditions	new graduate intake
	number required for test is 20
Worst case	8
Planned level	4
Best case	2
Current level	10
Justification	improvement specifically requested by XYZ
Consequence of failure	cost

Figure 8.9
COQUAMO usability template.

8.3.5 Safety

There is no consensus in the system's engineering community about what is meant by the term 'safety requirement'. Safety requirements are sometimes considered to be all requirements (functional and non-functional) on safety-related systems, sometimes the sub-set of these requirements which are directly related to ensuring safe operation and sometimes requirements on protection systems which are designed to protect against accident. The specific usage of the term often depends on the culture and practice of the organisation in which it is used.

We do not find any of these definitions particularly satisfactory. The definition which we prefer is an informal one: safety requirements are the 'shall not' requirements which exclude unsafe situations from the possible solution space of the system.

This means that the safety requirements constrain the freedom of designers in such a way that they will not introduce potentially unsafe system characteristics. Therefore, examples of safety requirements might be:

◆ the system shall not permit operation unless the operator guard is in place

◆ the system shall not allow the sedative dose delivered to the patient to be greater than the maximum value which is determined by the patient's physician

◆ the system shall not operate if the external temperature is below 4 degrees Celsius.

Safety requirements may not actually define the functionality of a system but, rather, describe unacceptable or undesirable system behaviour. These requirements may lead to more specific functional or non-functional requirements. Because of their nature, it is not usually possible to specify safety requirements in a quantitative way.

8.4 Requirements engineering for safety-related systems

The incorporation of computer-based control systems into a wide range of industrial and domestic products means that the associated software systems are safety-related. A software system failure can compromise the overall safety of the system and thus may harm system operators, the environment where the system is installed, customers of the organisation using the system and the general public.

Safety is not just dependent on a set of 'safety' requirements; it also requires that other types of non-functional requirement should be defined taking safe operation into account. For example:

1. if a system is unreliable, it may fail unpredictably and thus be unavailable to provide safety-related functions when required

2. if a system is insecure, accidental or malicious damage may occur which makes safe operation impossible

3. if a system fails to perform as required, critical safety-related deadlines may be missed

4. if a system user interface is difficult to learn and use, operator errors may occur which compromise the overall safety of the system.

In this section, therefore, we discuss the derivation of requirements for safety-related systems as these may encompass all the types of critical, non-functional requirement discussed in the previous section.

To ensure that proper account is taken of the need for safe system operation, the requirements engineering process for safety-related systems should incorporate a specific safety-analysis activity. System safety analysis is concerned with ensuring and certifying that a delivered system does not pose an unacceptable danger to its end-users or to the environment in which the system is installed. The widely accepted model of the system critical systems life cycle (BCS and IEE 1989) as shown in Figure 8.9, identifies two stages in the safety analysis process.

1. **Safety requirements discovery**
    The establishment of global safety requirements or constraints which the system must satisfy. This involves hazard identification and analysis, risk assessment and the formulation of system safety requirements. This stage may be carried out in some generic way (e.g. for all aircraft) and the generic requirements are then instantiated for a specific system.

2. **Safety validation**
    The analysis of the system requirements against these global safety constraints to ensure that these requirements either individually or in conjunction do not contradict the identified safety constraints. This process continues, of course, through the design and implementation of the system.

As part of the process of safety analysis, there are various activities such as hazard identification and analysis which require inputs and lateral thinking

Figure 8.10
The safety-
critical systems
life-cycle.

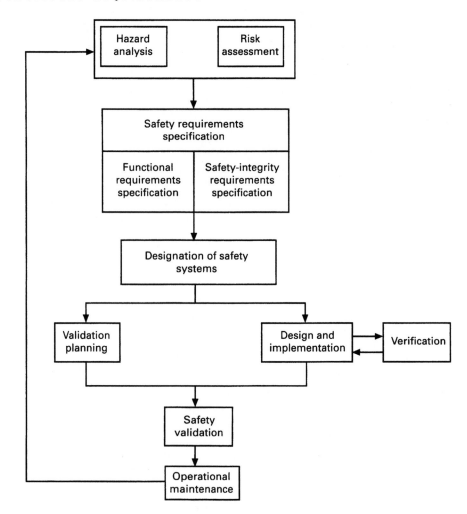

from different groups of people. In essence, these groups represent different viewpoints and it may be useful to formalise this process using the notion of viewpoints (described in Chapter 7). In this case, rather than a set of system requirements, the outcome of the process is a set of hazards which may arise. This example focuses on safety validation rather than on initial safety requirements formulation.

Various methods such as fault-tree analysis and Petri net analysis (Leveson and Harvey, 1983; Leveson, 1986) have been developed for safety validation. The technique proposed here involves integrating these methods with an appropriate requirements method and providing integrated tool support for requirements and safety analysis.

We illustrate the derivation of requirements for a safety-critical system here through the example of a simple guillotine system for cutting paper. The guillotine consists of a cutting table where the paper is positioned and a vertical blade which drops to trim the paper. The operation of the guillotine is controlled by embedded software that interfaces with the blade controller motor and a sensor which detects the completion of the cutting operation. Various other sensors are included in the system to ensure its safe operation.

The guillotine is operated a single operator under the supervision of an operations manager. The paper cutting operation is initiated by the operator pressing a start button and interrupted by the operator pressing a stop button. When the guillotine detects the 'cutting done' signal, the controller automatically resets the blade to its starting position and waits for a new 'start' signal, when new paper is positioned on the table before restarting the cutting operation.

The starting point for specifying the system is a set of abstract organisational needs and constraints. The organisation buying the system requires that it should operate safely and reliably without causing injury to its operator. Safety in the organisation is the responsibility of a Safety Officer. He or she requires the system manufacturer to take a systematic approach to safety issues. These include:

1. identifying hazards, risks and risk criteria

2. identifying the necessary risk reduction to meet the risk criteria

3. defining the overall safety requirements specification for the safeguards necessary to achieve the required risk reduction.

The requirements process, shown in Figure 8.11, may be extended to incorporate an explicit safety analysis activity whose results are used to modify (where necessary) suggested system requirements. The safety analysis process is based on requirements information drawn from the requirements elicitation and documentation process. A set of abstract safety requirements serves as a reference model for identifying initial safety considerations or concerns relating to each requirement source or viewpoint. An operator using the guillotine, for example, has obvious safety concerns relating to the operation of the paper guillotine. The output from the safety analysis process is a set of suggestions and improvements that are fed back into the main requirements process.

It is important to remember that the integration of requirements formulation and safety analysis is an iterative process. The output from any one stage may be fed back to its preceding stage for review and improvement. The output from the safety analysis, for example, informs the requirements definition process, the result of which acts as the input to the safety analysis process.

Figure 8.11
The process of
integrating safety
analysis and
requirements
formulation.

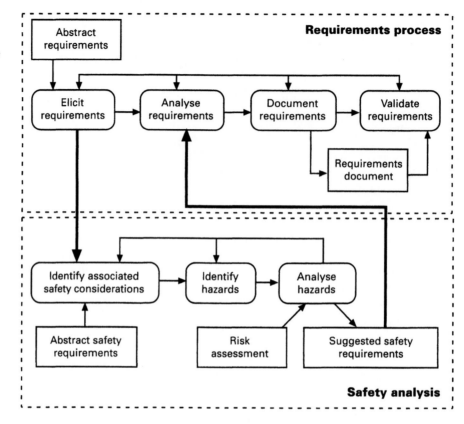

The safety analysis process includes:

1.   the identification of safety considerations
2.   hazard identification
3.   hazard analysis
4.   risk analysis and derivation of safety requirements

The hazard analysis and risk assessment stages can use any appropriate hazard and risk analysis techniques and are not tied to particular techniques. It is possible for example to use fault-trees for hazard analysis and a risk analysis scheme based on the severity and probabilities of the accidents. Let us consider the operational hazard of the guillotine crushing the operator's hand. The fault-tree analysis for the hazard 'guillotine crushes operator's hand' is shown in Figure 8.12. Fault tree analysis builds a graphical model of the sequential and concurrent combinations of events that can lead to a hazardous event or system state. Fault tree analysis uses Boolean logic to describe the combinations of events and states that constitute a hazardous state.

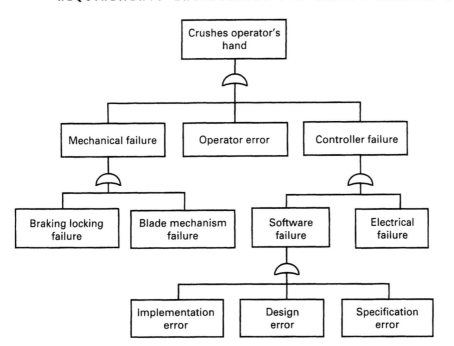

Each leaf event may have an associated 'severity' and a plan of action to minimise its occurrence. The proposed risk reduction strategies for each event are propagated to the top-level hazard so that a collective strategy is available as input to the requirements analysis process. Suggested changes form the basis for further decisions. In the case of safety analysis they can be used to derive more safety requirements.

There are three types of requirement which may be derived from such a hazard analysis:

1. *avoidance requirements*, which ensure that the hazard cannot occur

2. *prevention requirements*, which ensure that, if the hazard occurs, it does not result in an accident causing damage to people or the system's environment

3. *protection requirements*, which ensure that, if an accident occurs, the scale of the damage is limited.

Let us now consider possible requirements for the guillotine system based on the different types of hazard identified namely mechanical failure, operator error and controller failure.

Mechanical failure may result from mistakes made during system maintenance or from physical failure of the mechanical components involved in the system. Examples of software system requirements which may result from potential mechanical problems with the system might be as follows.

1. The system must maintain a maintenance log and, on system start-up, must check if system maintenance is due. If a scheduled maintenance session has not been carried out within 2 days of the required date, the software should disable operation of the system.

2. The guillotine blade must be fitted with a twin locking system and both locks must be monitored by the controller software. If a failure in either lock is detected, the software should disable operation of the system and should alert the operator to this failure.

Obviously, these requirements lead to other requirements, such as requirements for specifying when maintenance is carried out and requirements which describe how lock failure may be detected.

Operator error may result in an accident if the machine operator accidentally starts the system while his or her hand is in the path of the guillotine blade. This is an example of where a usability requirement can be used to ensure that hazards are avoided.

1. The operation of the system must require two switches which are physically separated by at least 30 cm to be pushed simultaneously.

2. The control system must monitor each switch and, if either or both switches are closed for more than 0.25 seconds, system operation must be disabled.

The first of these requirements means that operators must use both hands to operate the machine, so ensuring that they can't have one hand in the paper pathway. The second requirement supports this as it ensures that the operator can't tape down one of the switches and also will cause the system to be disabled if either or both switches fail in the 'on' position.

Controller system failure can result in an accident if it results in the machine being activated unexpectedly. System requirements which can reduce the probability of controller system failure resulting in an accident include the following:

1. the software control system must be formally specified in Z and the consistency of the specification must be demonstrated using mathematical arguments

2. the integrity of the system data area must be checked by the control system twice per second; if inconsistencies in the data are detected, system operation should be disabled.

The requirement to formally specify the control system is a process requirement which is specified because formal specification and checking increases the probability that specification errors will be detected. The second requirement above is really a security requirement which specifies that the system data areas must be checked. If these have been corrupted either by control system failure or for some other reason, then there is a potential for system error and operation should be disabled.

◆ Key Points

◆ Non-functional requirements define the overall qualities or attributes of the resulting system. They place restrictions on how the user requirements are best met.

◆ Non-functional requirements may be classified into three main types: product, process and external requirements.

◆ Product requirements specify the desired characteristics that the system or subsystem must posses, process requirements are constraints placed on the development process and external requirements are requirements which are derived from the environment in which the system is developed.

◆ Non-functional requirements tend to conflict and interact with other system requirements and functional requirements may have to be sacrificed in order to meet the non-functional constraints.

◆ The principal non-functional constraints which are relevant to critical systems are reliability, performance, security, usability and safety.

◆ Exercises

8.1 What are non-functional requirements? Explain the differences between process, product and external requirements. Give an example of each.

8.2 Giving examples explain how process requirements can influence other functional and non-functional system requirements.

8.3 Consider a university system whose main goal is to allow potential students to apply for admission remotely. Use this goal to derive possible sub-goals and non-functional requirements for the system (see Figure 8.5).

8.4 Explain how the following non-functional requirements may conflict; security vs. flexibility, security vs. performance, usability vs. efficiency, maintainability vs. efficiency. Illustrate your answers with examples.

8.5 A bank intends to develop a system to allow its customers to access their account information via the internet. The system will also allow customers to transfer funds between their accounts. Identify non-functional requirements that may need to considered before such a system is built. Explain the reason and importance of each identified non-functional requirement.

8.6 Suggest security requirements that might apply to a student information system used in a University department.

8.7 Explain why safety and security requirements are particularly difficult to validate.

8.8 Suggest how fault-trees (see Figure 8.10) might be used to help derive security requirements for a system.

8.9 Using reliability requirements in an example, explain why it is often difficult to associate non-functional requirements with specific functional system requirements.

8.10 Suggest appropriate usability requirements for the EDDIS Library system (see Chapter 10).

◆ References

Boehm, B. (1976). Software engineering. *IEEE Transactions on Computers*, **25**(12): 1226–1241.

Chung, L. Mylopoulos, J., and Nixon, B., (1992). Representing and using nonfunctional requirements – A process-oriented approach. *IEEE Transactions on Software Engineering*, **8**(6): 483–497.

Davis, A. (1992). *Software Requirements: Objects, Functions and States*. Prentice-Hall.

Deutsch, M. S., and Willis, R. R. (1988). *Software Quality Engineering*. Englewood Cliffs, New Jersey: Prentice-Hall.

Dobson, J. (1991). A methodology for analysing human computer-related issues in secure systems. *International Conference on Computer Security and Integrity in our Changing World*, 151–170, Espoo, Finland.

Easterbrook, S., and Nuseibeh, B. (1996). Using viewpoints for inconsistency management. *Software Engineering Journal*, **11**(1): 31–43.

Fenton, N. E. (1991). *Software Metrics: A Rigorous Approach*. Chapman & Hall.

Gilb, T. (1988). *Principles of Software Engineering Management*. Addison-Wesley.

Kotonya, G., and Sommerville, I. (1993). A framework for integrating functional and non-functional requirements. *International Workshop on Systems Engineering for Real Time Applications*, 148–153, Cirencester, UK.

Kotonya, G., and Sommerville, I. (1996). Requirements Engineering with viewpoints. *Software Engineering*, **1**(11): 5–18.

Loucopulos, P., and Karakostas, V. (1995). *Systems Requirements Engineering*. McGraw-Hill.

Leveson, N. G. (1986). Software safety – why, what, and how. *Computing Surveys*, **18**(2): 125–163.

Leveson, N. G., and Harvey, P. R. (1983). Analyzing software safety. *IEEE Transactions on Software Engineering*, **9**(5): 569–579.

Newman, W., and Lamming, M. (1995). *Interactive System Design*. Addison-Wesley.

Sommerville, I. (1996). *Software Engineering*. Addison-Wesley.

◆ Further reading

Software requirements: Objects, functions and states (A.M. Davis, 2nd Edition, Prentice-Hall, 1993) This book has a good section on specifying non-behavioural (non-functional) requirements.

Non-functional requirements in the software development process (V. Sivess, *Software Quality*, **5**(4), 285–294, 1995). This paper describes an approach for modelling non-functional requirements that uses Milner's Calculus of Communicating Systems, with agents representing roles and documents in the development environment.

G. Kotonya and I. Sommerville (1997). Integrating safety analysis with requirements engineering. *Asia-Pacific Software Engineering Conference and International Computer Science Conference*, 259–271, Hong Kong, China. IEEE Computer Society Press.

Software quality: theory and management (A.C. Gillies, Thomson, 1992) This book describes the concept of quality and the way in which it can be applied to software. with descriptions of the techniques employed in software quality assurance.

9 Interactive System Specification

◆ **Summary**

Interactive systems are systems that involve a significant degree of user interaction. Formulating the requirements for such systems poses a number of problems. Because of their interactive nature, consideration must be given to formulating their 'external requirements'. In this chapter we introduce the properties of interactive systems and illustrate them through the specification of a simplified automated teller machine example. A viewpoint-based requirements method (VORD) intended to specify interactive systems is used to specify the ATM requirements.

◆

Interactive systems can be defined as the class of systems whose operations involve a significant degree of interaction with users. The mode of interaction may take a number of forms, each involving the interchange of information between the system and the user. Common media for interaction include; the keyboard, voice, video, touch screens, the mouse, and others. The process of formulating the software requirements for interactive systems must take into account the important issues associated with formulating the requirements of such systems. A number of these issues are discussed below.

User interface: the ability to model and represent user interface requirements is important for interactive systems because of the central role of end-user interaction.

User classes: interactive systems have varied classes of users with potentially conflicting requirements and expectations. It is important that the approach used to model the intended system is able to expose these potentially conflicting requirements.

Other systems: interactive systems may interface with other systems in their environment. The requirements generated by the existing system(s) may constrain the development of the intended system and must be considered along with the intended system's requirements.

Indirect system concerns: these are not directly concerned with user interaction, but are related to the issue of system design and implementation, the influence of the system on the organisation and the system's influence on the environment. These issues are important and must be addressed as they often have great influence within the organisation.

Quality of service: the closeness of the system to the end-user lends special significance to the quality of the services delivered. Issues such as the reliability of the services delivered by the system, the system performance, format of service and others must be taken into account when formulating the system requirements.

The requirements method intended to specify interactive systems must support the formulation of these 'external' system issues if it is to be effective. In the next section we will use a simple example to illustrate these issues.

9.1 VORD – viewpoints for interactive system specification

The automated teller machine (ATM) is an good example of an interactive system, as it embodies all the attributes discussed earlier. We will use the example of an ATM to illustrate the process of formulating the requirements of an interactive system. We will use the VORD method, briefly introduced in Chapter 7, to formulate the requirements for the ATM. The requirements methods discussed in Chapter 6 focus on constructing internal system models and are not well suited to modelling the external system issues discussed earlier. VORD has been primarily developed to support the specification of interactive systems and focuses on the external entities that interact with the system or affect its development. VORD represents the system requirements as services delivered by the system to viewpoints (external entities).

Consider a simplified ATM which contains an embedded software system to drive the machine hardware and to communicate with the bank's customer database. The system accepts customer requests and produces cash and account information, and provides for limited message passing and funds transfer. The ATM is also required to make provisions for major classes of customers, namely customers whose accounts are with the bank which owns the ATM (home customers) and customers from other banks who have access to the ATM (foreign customers).

All ATM users are issued with a cash-card and a personal identification number (PIN) that they must use to access the ATM services. Home customers receive all the services provided by the ATM. Foreign customers can only receive a subset of the ATM services. Apart from providing services to its users, the ATM is also required to update the customer account database each time there is a cash withdrawal or funds transfer.

All the services provided by the ATM are subject to certain conditions, which can be considered at different levels. The top level sets out conditions necessary for accessing the services. These include a valid ATM cash-card and correct personal identification number (PIN). The next level is concerned with service requests and is subject to the availability of particular services. Beyond this level, all services provided by the ATM are subject to specific conditions set out for their provision.

9.2 Requirements definition

In this section we describe how VORD can be used to specify the ATM. We shall illustrate the requirements definition process by developing the example through the steps of the method. VORD is based on three main iterative steps, namely:

1. viewpoint identification and structuring
2. viewpoint documentation
3. viewpoint requirements analysis and specification

Figure 9.1 shows the iterative VORD process model. The processes are shown as round edged boxes and products as square edged boxes. Each product can be viewed as the checkpoint for a review process. The first step in VORD is concerned with identifying relevant viewpoints in the problem domain and structuring them. The starting point for viewpoint identification are abstract statements organisational needs and abstract viewpoint classes.

The second step is concerned with documenting the viewpoints identified in step 1. Viewpoint documentation consists of documenting:

◆ viewpoint, identifier, label and description

◆ viewpoint type that traces the viewpoint to a direct or indirect viewpoint

◆ viewpoint attributes that characterise the viewpoint in the application domain

Figure 9.1
VORD process
model.

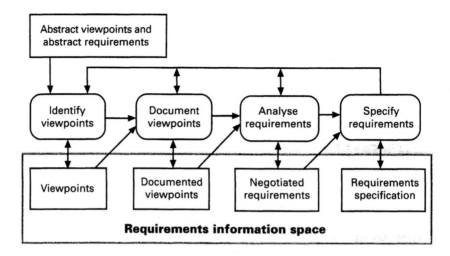

- viewpoint requirements; these include a set of required services, control requirements and non-functional requirements

- event scenarios that describe the interaction between the viewpoint and the intended system

- viewpoint history that describes the evolution of viewpoint requirements.

The third step is concerned with identifying errors and conflicts and resolving them. The end result is a requirements specification document.

The graphical notation used to represent viewpoints is shown in Figure 9.2. Viewpoints are represented by rectangular boxes. The viewpoint identifier is shown in the top left hand corner of the box and the viewpoint label in the lower half of the box. The viewpoint type or trace is shown in the top right half of the box. Viewpoint attributes, discussed in section 9.2.3, are shown by a vertical line dropping from the left side of the box. A viewpoint may also

Figure 9.2
Viewpoint
notation.

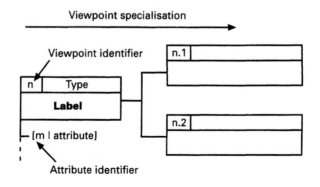

have one or more specialised types. A viewpoint specialisation shares certain services and attributes with its parent viewpoint but may receive additional services or impose its own constraints on inherited services.

9.2.1 Identifying ATM viewpoints

All structured methods must address the basic difficulty of identifying relevant problem domain entities for the system being specified or designed. The majority of methods provide little or no active guidance for this, and rely on the method user's judgement and experience in identifying these entities. However, VORD provides the analyst with some help in the critical step of viewpoint identification.

The process of understanding the system under analysis, its environment, requirements and constraints under which it must operate places a lot of reliance on the 'system authorities'. These are people or documents with an interest or specialist knowledge of the application domain. They include system end-users, system procurers, system engineers and documentation of existing system(s).

We have generalised these 'system authorities' into a set of viewpoint classes, which can be used as a starting point for finding viewpoints specific to the problem domain. Figure 9.3 shows part of the tree diagram of the abstract viewpoint classes. Normally indirect viewpoints will be decomposed to greater depth than shown here depending on the problem domain.

The root of the tree represents the general notion of a viewpoint. Information can be inherited by viewpoint sub-classes, and so global requirements are represented in the more abstract classes and inherited by sub-classes. In the direct viewpoint class, the system viewpoint represents the

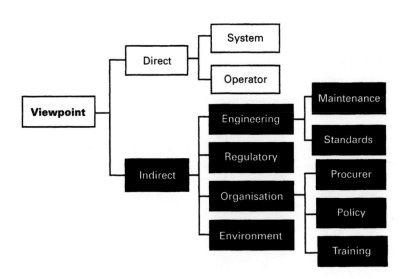

Figure 9.3
Abstract viewpoint classes.

abstract class of systems that may interact directly with the proposed system. These include shared databases and other sub-systems. The operator class represents the abstract class of people who will interact with the system directly.

Under the indirect viewpoint class, the organisation viewpoint represents the requirements and policy of the organisation which is purchasing the system, the regulatory viewpoint represents legal and regulatory requirements affecting the system development, the engineering viewpoint represents the engineering requirements for the system, and the environment viewpoint represents the environment issues affecting the system development.

It is important to stress that this class hierarchy is not generic. Each organisation must establish its own hierarchy of viewpoint classes based on the needs and the application domain of the systems which it develops.

The method of viewpoint identification which we propose involves a number of stages.

1. Prune the abstract viewpoint class hierarchy shown in Figure 9.3, to eliminate viewpoint classes which are not relevant for the specific system being specified. In the ATM example, let us assume that there is no external certification authority and no environmental effects. We therefore do not need to look for viewpoints under these headings.

2. Consider the system stakeholders, i.e. those people who will be affected by the introduction of the system. If these stakeholders fall into classes which are not part of the organisational class hierarchy, add these classes to it.

3. Using a model of the system architecture, identify system viewpoints, i.e. viewpoints representing other systems. This model may either be derived from the existing system models or may have to be developed as part of the RE process. In the example of the ATM we can identify two main sub-systems, the customer database and card issuer database. We note that architectural models of systems almost always exist because new systems must be integrated with existing organisational systems.

4. Identify system operators who use the system on a regular basis, who use the system on an occasional basis and who request others to use the system for them. All of these are potential viewpoints. We can identify three instances of direct viewpoint in this example, namely the bank customer (regular), ATM operator (occasional), the bank manager (occasional).

5. For each indirect viewpoint class which has been identified, consider the roles of the principal individual who might be associated with that class. For example, under the viewpoint class 'organisation', we might

be interested in the roles of 'regulations officer', 'maintenance manager', 'operations manager', etc. There are often viewpoints associated with these roles. In the ATM example, there are many possible indirect viewpoints but we will confine our analysis to a security officer and the organisational policy, represented by the bank viewpoint.

Based on this approach, the viewpoints which might be considered when developing an ATM specification are shown in Figure 9.4. Home customer and Foreign customer viewpoints are specialisations of the Customer viewpoint and inherit its requirements and attributes. Likewise the Bank manager, Bank teller and ATM operator viewpoints are specialisations of Bank staff. The Card issuer viewpoint represents the database of the organisation responsible for issuing the magnetic cards used with the ATM. The Customer database viewpoint is an external database that holds details of the customer accounts.

9.2.2 Documenting viewpoint requirements

Viewpoint requirements are made up of a set of services (functional requirements), non-functional requirements and control requirements. Control requirements describe the sequence of events involved in the interchange of information between a direct viewpoint and the intended system. Constraints describe how a viewpoint's requirements are affected by its own non-functional requirements and those generated by other viewpoints.

We do not have the space to look at the detailed requirements of each viewpoint here. However, Figures 9.5–9.7 show examples of initial requirements

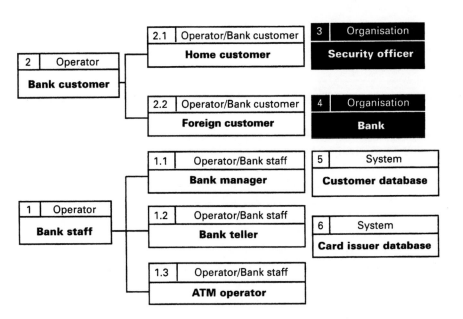

Figure 9.4
ATM
viewpoints.

Figure 9.5
Viewpoint
requirements
from the bank
staff viewpoints.

Viewpoint		Requirement			
Identifier	Label	Description		Type	Source VP
1	Bank staff	1.1	Provide access to administrative services based on valid staff PIN and the access permissions set out for the bank staff	sv	4
1.1	Bank manager	1.1.1	Provide transaction reports to bank manager.	sv	1.1
		1.1.2	The bank manager requires transaction reports to be provided on a daily basis	nf	1.1
1.2	Bank teller	1.2.1	Provide for cancellation of cash card in the event of lose or cancellation of card by bank.	sv	4
		1.2.2	Provide for card cancellation to be effected in no more than 3 minutes from request.	nf	4
1.3	ATM operator	1.3.1	Provide for system startup and shutdown based operator on valid staff PIN from ATM operator	sv	4
		1.3.2	Provide a facility for paging operator when funds are low in ATM	sv	4
		1.3.3	Failure rate of the paging service should not exceed 1 in 1000 attempts	nf	4

which might apply an auto-teller system. The requirement type refers to either a service (sv) or a non-functional requirement (nf). The ATM operator, card issuer database and customer database viewpoints are mainly concerned with providing control information to the proposed system. The ATM operator is concerned with stocking the ATM with funds and starting and stopping its operation. He or she needs to be alerted whenever the cash dispenser is low on funds. The customer database stores the customer account information which is used by the system to process transactions.

Because viewpoints are structured as class hierarchies, the requirements documented in the general classes, are inherited by the specialised classes. Specialised classes reserve the option to define specific requirements. For

Viewpoint		Requirement			
Identifier	Label	Description		Type	Source VP
2	Bank customer	2.1	Provide access to ATM services based on valid cash-card, valid PIN and access permissions set out for the bank customer	sv	4
		2.2	Provide for withdrawal of cash by bank customers	sv	4
		2.3	Cash withdrawal service should be available 999/1000 requests	nf	2
		2.4	Cash withdrawal service should have a response time of no more than 1 minute	nf	2
		2.5	At least 50% of the currency notes in the ATM should be 5 and 10 dollar bills.	nf	2
2.1	Home customer	2.1.1	Provide for funds transfer	sv	4
		2.1.2	Provide home customers with the facility to obtain a printout of their last five transactions	sv	4
		2.1.3	Provide for balance enquiry	sv	4
2.2	Foreign customer				

Figure 9.6
Initial requirements from the customer viewpoint.

example, viewpoints may place differing constraints on the same service. It is important that all these varied perceptions are documented at this stage and resolved at the analysis stage.

To facilitate requirements traceability and management, viewpoints and requirements are related through an identification scheme. A viewpoint has an identification number 'm', where 'm' refers to the relative position of the viewpoint in a hierarchy. For example, '1' refers to the parent viewpoint for the viewpoints 1.1 and 1.2. Requirement identifiers are structured so that the requirements can be traced to the viewpoints associated with them. Each requirement identifier has the format; **m**.n, where the bold part '**m**' denotes the viewpoint associated with the requirement and 'n' the requirement number.

A requirement that extends or describes the quality of another requirement within the same viewpoint is identified by extending the numbering of

Figure 9.7
Other viewpoint
requirements.

Viewpoint		Requirement			
Identifier	Label	Description		Type	Source VP
3	Security officer	3.1	All system security risks shall be identified, analysed and minimised according to the ALARP (as low as is reasonably possible) principle.	nf	3
		3.2	Standard encryption algorithms shall be used.	nf	3
		3.3	System shall print paper record of all transactions	nf	3
4	Bank	4.1	Complete system maintenance shall be done once every month.	nf	4
		4.2	Cash withdrawal service should be available in 90% of requests for the service.	nf	4
		4.3	Cash withdrawal should have a response time of no more than 2 minutes from the time of request	nf	4
		4.4	System shall be operational in 6 months	nf	4
		4.5	System should accommodate all current currency bills	nf	4
5	Customer database				
6	Card issuer database				

the 'parent' requirement. To maintain consistency, VORD uses the same identification scheme on other viewpoint components, such as attributes and event scenarios.

Viewpoint services can also be generalised into general service types for ease of identification and understanding. We suggest a classification scheme based on the service functionality and the receiving viewpoints. Based on this classification, services with similar functionality are grouped under a single label and identifier. The identifier refers to the parent viewpoint and uses a '0' to denote the general type. The identifier can then be used whenever an issue affects a general service type.

We have classified the ATM services into two general types: customer and administrative services. Customer services include all the services provided to the bank customers, and administrative services include all the 'administrative' services provided to the bank staff by the system. We can associate each of these two groups of services with special identifiers as shown in Figure 9.8. The bold part of the identifier refers to the parent viewpoint and the '0' indicates a general service type, and '1', the requirement number. A general service type must refer to at least two services.

9.2.3 Documenting viewpoint attributes

Viewpoint attributes represent values that characterise the viewpoint in the problem domain. They are things 'contained' or 'owned' by the viewpoint; for example, a customer viewpoint in a banking environment may have a customer account as an attribute. Attributes are important because they encapsulate data values.

Viewpoint attributes are represented graphically as shown in Figure 9.9. The attribute identifier and label are enclosed in square brackets and appears

Figure 9.8
Grouping similar services.

General Type		Service	
Ref.	Label	Reference	Description
1.0.1	Administrative services	1.1	Provide access to administrative services based on valid staff PIN and the access permissions set out for the bank staff
		1.2.1	Provide for cancellation of cash card in the event of lose or cancellation of card by bank
		1.3.1	allow for system startup and shutdown based on valid staff PIN from ATM operator
2.0.1	Customer services	2.1	Provide access to ATM services based on valid cash-card, valid PIN and access permissions set out for the bank customer
		2.2	Provide for withdrawal of cash by bank customers
		2.1.1	Provide home customers with the facility to transfer funds
		2.1.2	Provide home customers with the facility to obtain a printout of their last five transactions
		2.1.3	Provide for balance enquiry by bank customers

on a vertical line dropping from the left-hand side of a viewpoint. To refer to a specific viewpoint attribute, the attribute identifier must be preceded by the viewpoint identifier. For example, the complete reference for the account attribute of the Bank customer viewpoint is; '**2**.2'; where the bold part represents the viewpoint identifier and the non-bold part the attribute identifier.

The Bank Staff viewpoint has a staff-PIN to facilitate access to ATM, in addition the ATM operator has a pager and keeps some emergency funds for the ATM. The Bank Customer viewpoint has a cash-card and PIN to facilitate access to the ATM services. The customer database holds customer accounts and PINs. The card issuer database holds the details of the cash-cards.

9.2.4 Prioritising requirements

The most obvious way to prioritise requirements is to base priorities on the relative importance of the requirements with respect to the viewpoint. However, this fails to take into account the resources needed to deliver the requirement and the risk associated with the requirement. A better technique must take these two factors into account. Whatever technique is used, it must

Figure 9.9
Graphical representation of viewpoint attributes.

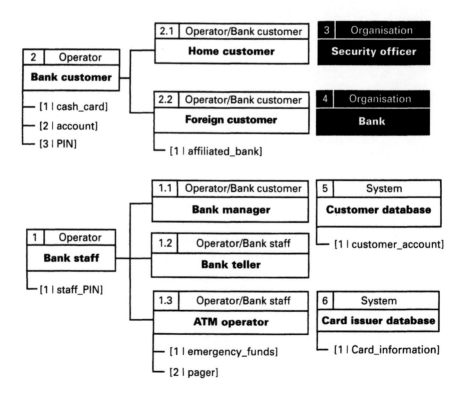

be testable and flexible enough to allow for the weightings to be tailored to the application.

VORD includes a simple weighting scheme that organises weightings around importance, resources and risk. Each requirement is weighted as high (H), medium (M) or low (L) in relation to estimates of the three factors. We have weighted the three factors on a scale of 1 to 3, but this may vary from application to application. Figure 9.10 shows the weightings and the factors.

The priority of a requirement is computed by adding the weightings on the three factors. An essential requirement has a priority of 9 and a minor requirement 3. It is important that each weighting is accompanied by a rationale. This is important not only for the future maintenance of the system, but can also be useful in informing a process where requirements need to be traded-off as result of conflicting options, and to support an incremental development process. Figure 9.11 shows a section the ATM requirements with each of the three factors weighted.

As we mentioned earlier, it is important that the rationale for the weightings is documented. Figure 9.12 shows such a rationale in relation to the cash withdrawal service.

9.2.5 Requirements and constraints

In Chapter 6 we described how non-functional requirements translate to constraints on system services and other requirements. Figure 9.13 shows the list of constraints distilled from the non-functional requirements in section 9.2.2 and how they affect various services. The table also provides an indication of the coverage of the constraints; for example, global constraints are associated with customer and administrative services. Specific constraints are shown with respect to each affected service. The coverage of the constraints provides an important input to the analysis process.

As the documentation demonstrates, VORD provides the user with a framework for formulating very detailed requirements, yet maintains a clear separation of concerns. This is important in exposing conflicting requirements

Weighting Factor	High(H)	Medium(M)	Low(L)
Importance	3	2	1
Resources required	1	2	3
Risk involved	1	2	3

Figure 9.10
Priority scheme for requirements.

Requirement		Weighting			
Ref	Description	Importance	Resources	Risk	Priority
2.1	Provide access to ATM services based on valid cash-card, valid PIN and access permissions set out for the bank customer	H	L	L	9
2.3	Cash withdrawal service should be available 999/1000 requests	M	H	M	5
2.4	Cash withdrawal service should have a response time of no more than 1 minute	M	H	M	5
2.5	At least 50% of the currency notes in the ATM should be 5 and 10 dollar bills.	M	L	L	8
2.1.3	Provide for balance enquiry by bank customers	M	M	L	7
3.1	All system security risks must explicitly identified, analysed and minimised according to the ALARP principle.	H	H	L	7
4.1	Complete system maintenance must be done once every month	H	H	M	6
4.2	Cash withdrawal service should be available in 90% of requests for the service	H	H	L	7
4.3	Cash withdrawal should have a response time of no more than 2 minutes from the time of request	H	H	L	7
4.4	System must be operational in 6 months	M	H	H	4

Figure 9.11
Priorities on
requirements.

and assessing the impact of requirement change. Consider the example of the cash withdrawal service. This service is intended for both the home and foreign customer, but the rationale for the services and the constraints may differ. In the case of the home customer, the rationale may be based on a marketing strategy and in the case of the foreign customer on an arrangement reached with other banks. As far as the bank is concerned, there may be a stronger case for maintaining the constraints associated with cash withdrawal for the home customer than the foreign customer.

At the viewpoint level, attributes characterise direct viewpoints and provide a means of structuring them. At the system level, attributes translate to input parameters that are consumed by events that effect control through the system. They can therefore be seen as translating to control information for the system. How this is modelled will be discussed in section 9.2.6 where we describe the ATM behaviour. Here we are only interested in seeing how non-functional requirements affect control information. Like other require-

Viewpoint Requirement			
Identifier	Description	Weighting	Rationale
2.2	Provide for withdrawal of cash by bank customers	Importance H	This is the most important ATM requirement reflecting ATM functionality
		Resources M	Hardware and software support available
		Risk L	The risk involved is low as the domain is well understood, the technology is available. Previous implementation knowledge can be reused to inform the requirements

ments, attributes are also affected by constraints generated through non-functional requirements. Constraints on control information can be traced to the non-functional requirements that generate them via the constraint identifiers which match those of the non-functional requirements. Figure 9.14 shows the constraints on viewpoint attributes.

Figure 9.12 Rationale for priorities.

9.2.6   Modelling ATM behaviour

The provision of a viewpoint service can be viewed as the culmination of a series of events arising from the viewpoint layer, and filtering through levels of control to system entities that are ultimately responsible for the its provision. VORD uses event scenarios to model this dynamic system behaviour. Briefly, an event scenario is defined as a sequence of events together with exceptions which may arise during the interchange of information between a viewpoint and the intended system.

Viewpoint events are a reflection of control requirements as perceived by the user. Normally the provision of a service involves the participation of many viewpoints, each bringing its control influences to bear on the service. It is important in documenting a viewpoint service to identify other viewpoints affecting or participating in the provision of a service. This provides a means of tracing the impact of changes in the requirements.

VORD uses the extended state transition notation shown on Figure 9.15 to model event scenarios.

We will illustrate how event scenarios can be used to model system behaviour by describing event scenarios associated with:

(i)   start-up and shut-down service
(ii)   service access service
(iii)   cash withdrawal and funds transfer service

Viewpoint Service		
Identifier	**Description**	**Constraint**
1.0.1	Administrative services	3.1 All security risks must explicitly be identified, analysed and minimised according to the ALARP principle
		4.1 Complete system maintenance to be done once every month
		4.4 System must be operational in 6 months
2.0.1	Customer services	3.1 All security risks must explicitly be identified, analysed and minimised according to the ALARP principle
		3.2 Standard Bank encryption algorithm must be used
		4.1 Complete system maintenance to be done once every month
		4.4 System must be operational in 6 months
1.1.1	Transaction reports	1.1.2 Transaction reports must be provided on a daily basis
1.2.1	Suspend card use	1.2.2 Service should have a response time of no more than 3 minutes
1.3.2	Operator paging when funds are low in ATM	1.3.3 Failure rate of the paging service should not exceed 1 in 1000 attempts
2.2	Cash withdrawal	2.3 Cash withdrawal service should be available 999/1000 requests
		2.4 Cash withdrawal service should have a response time of no more than 1 minute
		2.5 At least 50% of the currency notes in the ATM should be 5 and 10 dollar bills
		4.2 Cash withdrawal service should be available 9/10 requests for the service
		4.3 Cash withdrawal should have a response time of no more than 2 minutes
		4.5 System should accommodate all currency bills

Figure 9.13
Constraints on
ATM services.

9.2.6.1 Start-up and shut-down service

Administrators of systems need to be able to start and shut them down as the need arises. The services provided by the systems to facilitate this operation are collectively known as start-up and shut-down services. The system start-up service is concerned with starting up the system and setting up the environment parameters that provide the ordinary user with access to the system's services. The shut-down service is concerned with shutting down the system in a controlled manner without the loss of information. A typical start-up sequence

	Viewpoint Attribute		
Identifier	Description	Constraint	
1.1	staff_PIN	3.2	standard bank encryption algorithms must be used
2.1	cash_card	3.2	standard bank encryption algorithms must be used
2.3	PIN	3.2	standard bank encryption algorithms must be used
1.3.1	emergency_funds	2.5	At least 50% of the currency should be in 5 and 10 dollar bills.
5.1	customer_account		
6.1	Card_information		

Figure 9.14
Constraints on
viewpoint
attributes.

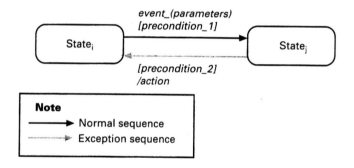

Figure 9.15
Notation for
event scenarios.

involves the operator logging onto the system and initiating a start-up sequence. The start-up sequence may involve the system performing some self-diagnostics.

In the case of the ATM, the operator starts the system by logging in with a staff PIN. The system verifies the PIN and proceeds to perform a self-test. If a system error is encountered during a self-test this is reported in the system status report. The staff PIN verification process involves the system checking the entered staff PIN against a set of valid staff PINs. An invalid staff PIN causes an exception condition to occur and an error message is displayed. If the PIN verification is okay, the system goes into a wait state until a start-up command is issued. When the command is issued, the system goes into a ready state, displaying a welcome message and available services. The ATM operator can perform a complete shut-down of the system by entering a shut-down command from his service menu. This initiates a controlled shut-down sequence to ensure that no data or information is lost inadvertently.

It is also possible for the ATM operators to shut-down only certain services. Figure 9.16 shows the event scenario of the start-up and shut-down services of the ATM. The ready state forms the common point for accessing all other ATM services; this is dealt with next.

9.2.6.2 Service access service
Before the user can access an ATM service, the system needs to be in the ready state shown by the grey rectangle in Figure 9.16. When the system is in the ready state, it sets out the preconditions necessary for accessing the ATM services. These conditions include a valid cash-card and correct PIN. These conditions must be satisfied before the system can go into the service state. In the service state, the system displays the available services (see Figure 9.17).

9.2.6.3 Cash withdrawal and funds transfer services
We do not have the space to model all the services of ATM here. However, we shall model the cash withdrawal and funds transfer services. These services affect the bank customer and the ATM operator. The bank customer is concerned that the cash withdrawal service is provided quickly and reliably, and the cash transfer service securely. The ATM operator is concerned that the ATM should never be without funds. The operator needs to be alerted whenever the cash in the dispenser falls below an acceptable minimum.

Figure 9.18 shows the event scenario associated with the cash withdrawal service from the customer viewpoint. When the customer selects the cash

Figure 9.16
Event scenario for ATM start-up and shut-down services.

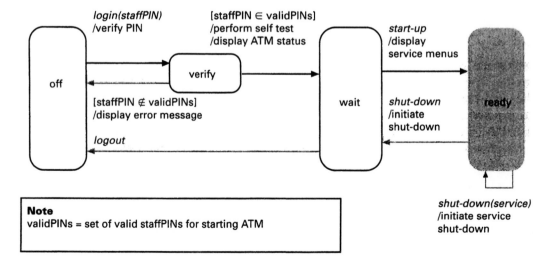

login(staffPIN)
/verify PIN

[staffPIN ∈ validPINs]
/perform self test
/display ATM status

start-up
/display
service menus

off   verify   wait

[staffPIN ∉ validPINs]
/display error message

logout

shut-down
/initiate
shut-down

ready

shut-down(service)
/initiate service
shut-down

Note
validPINs = set of valid staffPINs for starting ATM

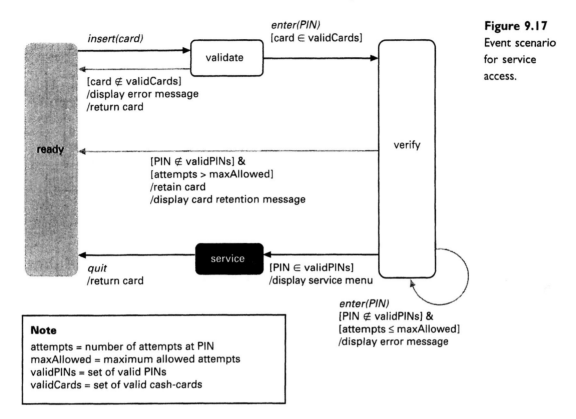

Figure 9.17
Event scenario
for service
access.

insert(card)

validate

enter(PIN)
[card ∈ validCards]

[card ∉ validCards]
/display error message
/return card

ready

verify

[PIN ∉ validPINs] &
[attempts > maxAllowed]
/retain card
/display card retention message

service

quit
/return card

[PIN ∈ validPINs]
/display service menu

enter(PIN)
[PIN ∉ validPINs] &
[attempts ≤ maxAllowed]
/display error message

Note
attempts = number of attempts at PIN
maxAllowed = maximum allowed attempts
validPINs = set of valid PINs
validCards = set of valid cash-cards

option on the main service menu, the system goes into the cash mode state. In the cash mode state, the system can be in one of two states: FundsLow or adequateFunds. The system is in the FundsLow state if the funds in the ATM fall below a preset minimum. The system pages the operator when the funds in the ATM fall below this minimum. The customer is able to perform cash withdrawals when the system is in either state. However, the cash withdrawals may not exceed the customer balance or the funds in the ATM.

We will assume that the target account for the funds transfer service is the ATM account. Once the system is in the service ready state, the customer must satisfy two preconditions before the service can be accessed. Firstly the service must be available, and secondly the customer must be a home customer. The funds transfer service is only available to home customers. In the transfer state, a list of the customer's existing accounts and their balances is displayed. The customer can select the source account from this list together with required amount. The transfer is accomplished if the amount requested for transfer is less or equal to the balance in the source account (Figure 9.19).

Figure 9.18
Event scenario
for cash
withdrawal.

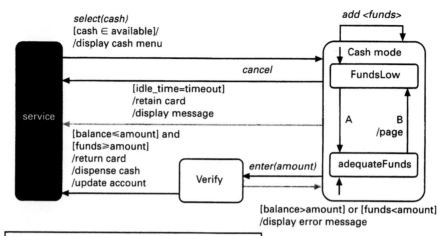

Note

cash	= cash service
funds	= funds in ATM
balance	= funds available in customer account
available	= set of available services
idle_time	= system idle time
timeout	= maximum allowed idle time
A = [funds	≥ minimum]
B = [funds	< minimum]

Figure 9.19
Event scenario
for funds
transfer service.

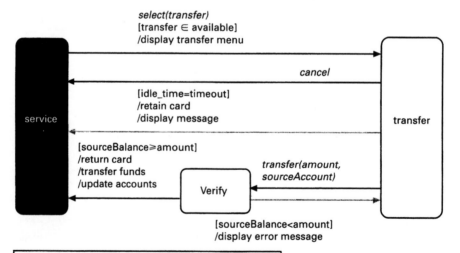

Note

transfer	= transfer service
available	= set of available services
sourceAccount	= source account
sourceBalance	= cash available in source account
idle_time	= system idle time
timeout	= maximum allowed idle time

9.2.7   User interface requirements

User interface considerations are important in formulating the requirements of interactive systems. However they are highly subjective and difficult to establish through a structured process of requirements analysis. In many cases, user interface requirements can only be determined through experiment and prototyping. We therefore do not intend to specify user interface requirements here, but briefly discuss their relationship to other viewpoint requirements.

In VORD the user interface requirements can be represented as constraints on viewpoint services. They describe the mode and presentation of viewpoint services. This process is, in turn, informed by viewpoint event scenarios which describe the interaction between the viewpoint (in this case the user) and the system.

Figure 9.19 shows the relationship between user interface requirements and event scenarios. A service is provided through the interaction between a viewpoint and the system. The interaction is described using a set of event scenarios. The viewpoint requiring the service may impose certain constraints on the way the service is presented. These may include constraints on the mode of the presentation and how the presentation is organised (layout).

User interface components (e.g. windows, buttons and icons) provide the medium through which the viewpoint interacts with the system. The system displays and accepts information through these components; in essence the event scenarios is re-enacted through these components. The user interface constraints reflect how the elements of this interaction are organised and presented to the user. The constraints and information from the event scenarios can be used as a starting point in the design of the user interface. It is important to note that prototyping is essential for user interface development. The prototype should be made available to users and the resulting feedback used to improve the design.

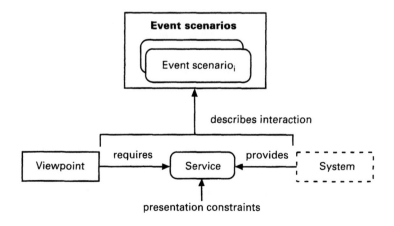

Figure 9.20
User interface requirements and event scenarios.

9.2.8 Requirements analysis

In Chapter 3 we discussed the process of requirements analysis. The objective of viewpoint requirements analysis is to establish that viewpoint requirements are correct and 'complete'. There are two main stages to this analysis.

1. Correctness of viewpoint documentation; the viewpoint documentation must be checked to ensure that it is consistent and that there are no omissions.

2. Conflict analysis; conflicting requirements from different viewpoints must be exposed and resolved.

9.2.8.1 Checking viewpoint documentation

Checking the correctness of viewpoint documentation involves verifying that it has been correctly and completely documented. In Chapter 7 a viewpoint was defined as a entity consisting of a set of attributes, requirements, event scenarios and specialisations. Although some of this information must appear on all viewpoints, other information may be omitted depending on whether the viewpoint is direct or indirect. Figure 9.21 shows relationship between a viewpoint type and the need for corresponding documentation.

The scheme may be used as a checklist for viewpoint documentation, and is explained as follows.

1. A 'yes' means that the documentation must be present in the viewpoint; for example, a viewpoint must be uniquely identified, labelled and traceable to abstract viewpoints.

Figure 9.21
Checklist for
viewpoint
information.

Information	Viewpoint type	
	Direct	Indirect
Identifier	yes	yes
Type (trace)	yes	yes
Attributes	yes	no
Event scenarios	yes	no
Service	yes*	no
Control	yes*	no
Non-functional requirements	optional	yes
Specialisations	optional	optional

2. A 'no' means that the corresponding documentation is not part of the viewpoint; for example, an indirect viewpoint does not receive services or provide control information.

3. An 'optional' means that the documentation may optionally be present in the viewpoint. For example, viewpoints may or may not have special-isations; and direct viewpoints may or may not have non-functional requirements. Where optional documentation is present, it must be checked against other related documentation (see viewpoint information structure in Figure 9.22).

4. A 'yes*' denotes a set of information, at least one of which must be docu-mented in the viewpoint. In other words the set refers to information that may be present in whole or part, in the viewpoint. For example, some direct viewpoints receive services and provide control information, others provide only control information.

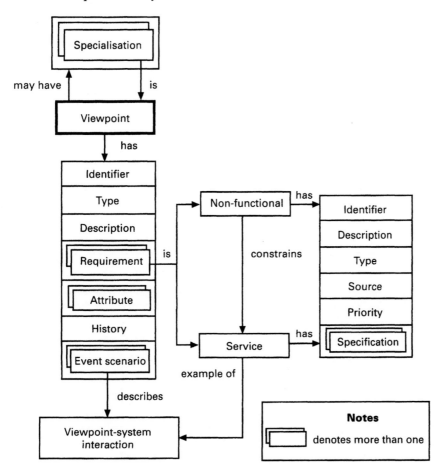

Figure 9.22
Viewpoint information structure.

Lastly, the relationship between various viewpoint information components is provided in Figure 9.22. This can be used for verifying the completeness of the viewpoint documentation.

9.2.8.2 Conflict analysis

Viewpoints have differing stakes in and interactions with the intended system and have requirements that are closely aligned with these interests. Conflicts may arise from contradictions among individual viewpoint requirements. Some related work in this area includes the work on domain-independent conflict resolution by Easterbrook and Nuseibeh (1996) and the work on rule-based software quality engineering by Hausen (1989).

Earlier we mentioned how non-functional requirements tend to conflict and interact with other system requirements. This kind of conflict may be quite specific, as in the following two cases:

- where the service provision across viewpoints is associated with different constraints of the same general type; for example, where the reliability of a service is specified in terms of its availability in one viewpoint, and in terms of its probability of failure on demand (POFOD) in another viewpoint

- where the provision of a service across viewpoints is associated with similar constraints but differing constraint values; for example, where the reliability of a service, specified in terms of its availability, has a value of 999/1000 in viewpoint and a value of 90% in another viewpoint.

It is may also be the case that a requirement in one viewpoint contradicts a requirement in another viewpoint; for example, the bank viewpoint requirement that the system must have a complete maintaince once every month conflicts with the availability requirement for the home customer that the cash withdrawal service is available in 999/1000 requests.

These types of conflict can be exposed by analysing the constraints associated with a particular service, for consistency, and by analysing one viewpoint's requirements against other viewpoint requirements for contradictions. In addition to these specific viewpoint requirements, there are high-level organisational and other global requirements that define the general quality attributes of the intended system. All other individual requirements must be analysed against these. At this level, we are interested in establishing whether specific viewpoint requirements augment or contradict general organisational goals.

Software quality goals are normally generated by indirect viewpoints such as those of the organisation purchasing the software system. The aim of these goals is to maximise certain product attributes, efficiency and reliability, within the constraints of cost, schedule, and technical feasibility. These problems are characterised by the presence of multiple, conflicting goals accompanied by a large candidate solution space. The goals conflict because they are somehow interrelated. In software development, there are several quality characteristics, or software quality factors, that inherently conflict. For example, efficiency and maintainability frequently conflict. The objective of maintainability is to improve code understandability, and efficiency frequently requires reliance on exceptional code. The same is true for expandability and reliability (increased risk to acquire more functionality), safety and availability (fail-soft/fail-safe requirements reduce the set of available system capabilities).

Requirements conflict resolution and management is the subject of on-going research. There is no simple way of automating all the aspects of conflict resolution. We are sceptical about the usefulness of automated semantic analysis. The checking model adopted by VORD is based on ensuring that information can be presented in a way that manual analysis is simplified.

Individual requirements are checked against each other, and against the global requirements. Conflicting requirements go through a negotiation process where their weightings, rationale and relation to global quality goals are taken into account. The negotiated requirements are added to the list of acceptable requirements. Changes in requirements may necessitate a repeat of the process. Figure 9.23 shows part of a table of the ATM requirements indicating some conflicting requirements. Five relationships are indicated: empty (–), no obvious contradiction (✓), augments (a), contradicts(×) and constraints (c). Global goals are italicised.

Figure 9.23 identifies two requirements, 4.1 and 4.2, conflicting with the non-functional requirement 2.3. The conflicts can be resolved by studying the weightings and rationale associated with the requirements. It is also important to carefully study the coverage of the 'offending' requirements. Change in one requirement tends to ripple through the system and all affected requirements must be analysed, even if they have previously been considered.

The non-functional requirement 2.3, has a weighting of 5 and is generated by the bank customer viewpoint. A weighting of 5 indicates a moderately significant requirement. The requirement 4.1 is generated by the bank view-point and has a weighting of 6. Apart from this, the requirement affects all other system services. Requirement 4.2 also comes from the bank viewpoint but affects only the cash withdrawal. As requirement 4.1 has a greater weighting than requirement 2.3, we can alter requirement 2.3 to conform to 4.1. In the case of requirement 4.2, it is clear that both regular maintenance and a reliable service provision are vitally important. A compromise may be to do the maintenance late at night when the likelihood of customers using the ATM is remote. This could also be shifted to weekends, for example, Sunday. The altered requirement could read, 'complete system maintenance will be done once every month, on the last Sunday of the month at 2:00 a.m. in the morning'.

Requirement 1 / Requirement 2	Reference	2.3	4.1
	Description	Cash withdrawal service should be available in 999/1000 requests	Complete system maintenance must be done once every month
Reference	**Description**		
2.3	Cash withdrawal service should be available 999/1000 requests	–	×
2.4	Cash withdrawal service should have a response time of no more than 1 minute	✓	×
2.5	At least 50% of the currency notes in the ATM should be 5 and 10 dollar bills	✓	✓
2.1.3	Provide for balance enquiry by bank customers	✓	?
3.1	*All system security risks must explicitly identified, analysed and minimised according to the ALARP (as low as is reasonably possible) principle.*	c	✓
4.1	Complete system maintenance must be done once every month	×	–
4.2	Cash withdrawal service should be available in 90% requests for the service	×	×
4.3	Cash withdrawal should have a response time of no more than 2 minutes from the time of request	✓	×
4.4	*System must be operational in 6 months*	c	✓
4.5	System should accommodate all current currency notes	✓	✓

Figure 9.23
Part of ATM conflict identification table.

9.2.9 Service specification

VORD supports the specification of viewpoint services in a variety of notations. This is particularly important for two reasons.

1. One of the major problems associated with software development is the lack of adequate communication between the requirements engineer and the system's potential users due to the differences in their experience and education. The ability to represent the same requirement in different notations which are familiar to different people enhances communication and aids understanding.

2.   No one requirements notation can adequately articulate all the needs of a system. More than one specification language may be needed to represent the requirement adequately.

We illustrate these aspect of VORD by specifying a simplified version of the ATM's cash withdrawal service using a formal and informal notation. We will use a simplified form of the formal notation Z and an informal notation to specify the service. In both cases we will assume that the customer has a valid cash-card and has entered the correct Personal Identification Number (PIN). Figure 9.24 shows an informal specification of the case withdrawal service.

There are clearly a number of ambiguities in this description but it is expressed at a level which can easily be understood by non-technical staff. A more precise specification can be developed and linked to this informal description (as shown in Figures 9.25–9.27). Of course, we recognise that the problem with multiple representations of a service is the demonstration that these representations are equivalent. Finkelstein, et al. (1992) have identified a comparable problem in the VOSE approach and they discuss methods of equivalence demonstration.

More precisely, the cash withdrawal service can be specified as a disjunction (OR) of two other Z schemas; *PermitWithdrawal* and *RefuseWithdrawal* (see Figure 9.25).

This is based on the free types shown in Figure 9.26. FundStatus represents the stock of the ATM funds. An inAdequate status indicates that the ATM funds have fallen below 1000, represented by criticalLevel. AccountStatus represents the status of the customer account, which is in one of two states; overdrawn or in goodStanding. The information on the customer account details and the level of the ATM is contained in the specification for the entity Bank (see Figure 9.27).

The names and types for the Bank are declared in the top half and the predicates set out in the lower half of the schema. The ∀ notation used in the

Figure 9.24
An informal specification of a simplified cash withdrawal service.

Customer requests cash withdrawal
>   If any of the following conditions are true refuse withdrawal:
>   **condition1**: The requested amount exceeds customer balance.
>   **condition2**: The funds in ATM are less than requested amount
>   **else** do the following:
>>   dispense cash
>>   update customer account
>   **endif**

Figure 9.25
Specification for
cash withdrawal.

```
┌─ CashWithdrawal ──────────────────────────┐
│                                            │
│  PermitWithdrawal ∨ RefuseWithdrawal       │
│                                            │
└────────────────────────────────────────────┘
```

Figure 9.26
Free types for
cash withdrawal.

```
┌────────────────────────────────────────────┐
│ FundStatus::= adequate | inAdequate        │
│ AccountStatus ::= overdrawn | goodStanding │
│ criticalLevel = 1000                       │
│ accountNumber:0..10⁵                       │
└────────────────────────────────────────────┘
```

accountNumber:$0..10^5$

predicate section is known as the universal quantifier. The universal quantifier is always followed by a declaration and a heavy dot before the predicate that is being quantified. The notation ⇔ is known as the equivalence notation and is used to show that two predicates are equivalent.

For a cash withdrawal to be permitted (see Figure 9.28) two conditions must be fulfilled:

- the customer account must be in goodStanding (i.e. not overdrawn)
- the ATM must contain adequate funds.

After a cash withdrawal the customer account is updated. This is illustrated in the separate specification of PermitWithdrawal and RefuseWithdrawal.

The PermitWithdrawal schema shown in Figure 9.28 specifies the operation for a cash withdrawal. The △ Bank notation means that the operation changes the state of the bank. The predicates set for the withdrawal are:

- the amount required must be less or equal to the funds in the customer's account

- the funds in the customer account after the withdrawal are equal to the previous funds minus the amount withdrawn.

Figure 9.27
Specification of
Bank.

```
┌─ Bank ──────────────────────────────────────────────┐
│ atmFunds: ℕ                                          │
│ fundStatus:FundStatus                                │
│ customerFunds:accountNumber ⇸ ℝ                      │
│ customerStatus:accountNumber ⇸ accountStatus         │
├──────────────────────────────────────────────────────┤
│ ∀c:AccountNumber•                                    │
│    (fundStatus = inAdequate ⇔ (atmFunds≤criticalLevel)│
│    (customerFunds(c)<0) ⇔ (customerStatus(c) = overdrawn│
└──────────────────────────────────────────────────────┘
```

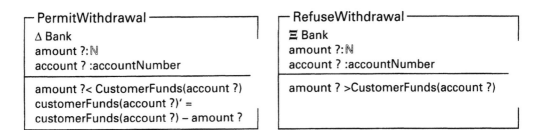

Figure 9.28
Specification of
PermitWith-
drawal and
RefuseWith-
drawal.

Similarly the RefuseWithdrawal schema describes the operation for refusing a cash withdrawal. No withdrawal is permitted if the amount requested is greater than the customer balance. The ΞBank notation means that this operation leaves the bank unchanged.

9.2.10   The requirements specification document

The final product of the requirements definition process is a requirements document. A requirements document has a number of sections. The IEEE standard 830–1993 recommends that the requirements document should have 3 main sections. Section 1 introduces the purpose and scope of the requirements document. This section also provides a glossary of the definitions, acronyms and abbreviations used in the requirements document. Section 2 is concerned with the description of the factors that affect the intended system and its requirements.

Section 3 describes the software requirements. Each requirement must include a unique identifier. Essential requirements must be marked as such. For incremental delivery, each software requirement must include a measure of priority so that the developer can decide the production schedule. References that trace the software requirements back to the user requirements document must accompany each requirement. Any other requirements sources must be stated. Each software requirement must be verifiable. The standard requires that functional requirements (services) be structured top-down in this section. Non-functional requirements can appear at all levels of the hierarchy and of functions, and by the inheritance principle apply to all functional requirements below. Non-functional requirements may be attached to functional requirements by cross-references or by physically grouping them together in the document. The general organisation of the IEEE recommended requirements document is shown in Chapter 1.

For most requirements documents, the structure of section 1 and section 2 is largely independent of the requirements approach used, hence is unlikely to differ significantly from that recommended in the IEEE standard. However, the organisation of section 3 may differ depending on the requirements approach used and the intention of the specifier. In the case of VORD, viewpoints are explicitly included in the specific requirements section. The aim of this is twofold; firstly, viewpoints help in the structuring and organisation of the requirements. Secondly, viewpoints augment the traceability of the requirements. A sample VORD template for the specific requirements section is shown in Figure 9.29.

The requirements are structured in the context of viewpoints to maintain traceability with viewpoints. Section A provides a short description of the viewpoint and section B the viewpoint type. Section C lists all viewpoint attributes while section D lists all viewpoint specialisations in terms of their references. Section E provides the development history of the viewpoint

Figure 9.29
VORD
requirements
document
template.

REQUIREMENTS DOCUMENT
SPECIFIC REQUIREMENTS SECTION

3. SPECIFIC REQUIREMENTS
Viewpoints
Identifier   *(reference and name of viewpoint)*
   A Description
   A short description of viewpoint
   B Type
   This section defines the viewpoint type.
   C Attributes
   This section lists viewpoint attributes
   D Specialisations
   This section provides a list of viewpoint specialisations
   E History
   This section describes the evolution of the viewpoint and its requirements
   F Requirements
     F1 Services
     Identifier   *(unique service identifier)*
       Description   *(short description of service)*
       Source   *(source of service)*
       Priority   *(measure of importance of service)*
       Event scenario   *(reference to event scenario)*
       Specification   *(reference to various specs)*
     F2 Non-functional Requirements
     Identifier   *(unique requirement identifier)*
       Description   *(short description of non-functional requirement)*
       Source   *(source of non-functional requirement)*
       Priority   *(measure of importance of requirement)*
       Affected Services *(list of service reference affected or constrained by non-functional requirement)*

including its components). Section F describes the viewpoint requirements (functional and non-functional). Each requirement has a unique identifier, a description, a source and a priority. In addition services have an event scenario and specification. The description of non-functional requirements includes references to affected services. Figure 9.30 shows the template being used to describe some the requirements of the Home customer viewpoint.

9.3 Transition to object-oriented design

One of the objectives of VORD is to support the object-oriented development process. VORD can be thought of as a two layered approach to requirements definition. The first layer, the viewpoint layer, is concerned with formulating viewpoint requirements. This layer identifies viewpoints, captures and structures their requirements. The second layer, the system layer, reconciles and interprets these requirements into a cohesive object-oriented framework.

Detailed object-oriented design is outside the scope of this book; however, we can illustrate, using part of the ATM example described, an object-oriented design which can be developed from a set of viewpoint requirements. The description provided here focuses on object identification, and is only intended to form the initial transition to a more detailed object-oriented design.

In the object-oriented sense, a viewpoint service can be viewed as the product of the interaction between system-level objects. Mapping a viewpoint service to objects involves identifying objects responsible for its provision. VORD proposes an approach for identifying relevant problem domain objects that is closely related to the viewpoints and their requirements.

Viewpoints represent classes of objects that constitute the system and its environment. Direct viewpoints represent entities that map directly onto system level objects and represent the first level of object identification. Additionally, objects can also be identified by exploding viewpoint attributes.

Viewpoint attributes very often are not atomic, but may have attributes themselves. In some cases the attributes may be aggregate structures and may lead to the discovery of other objects. For example, in relation to the ATM system, all bank customers have a cash-card as an attribute. The cash-card itself has a number of attributes, including type, number, customer name, account-no, and expiry-date.

Indirect viewpoints represent entities that may generate non-functional requirements that constrain the way services are provided and the way the system is developed. Because they are restrictions or constraints on system services, non-functional requirements greatly influence the design solution.

Figure 9.30
Section of
VORD
requirements
document.

REQUIREMENTS DOCUMENT
SPECIFIC REQUIREMENTS SECTION

3. SPECIFIC REQUIREMENTS
Viewpoint
2.Bank Customer
A   Description
The home customer viewpoint represents the customers who belong to the bank.
B   Type
/Direct/Operator/Bank customer
C   Attributes
1.   Cash-card
2.   Account
3.   PIN
D   Specialisations
None
E   History

Reference	Date	Change Description	Rationale
2.1 Viewpoint	23/4/97	component created	N/A

F   Requirements
  F1 Services
   2.2   Cash withdrawal
  Description:
  The ATM should provide a cash withdrawal service to all its customers.
  Source: 4 Bank
  Priority: 9
  Event scenario: (see page 232–234)
  Specification: 1. Informal (see page 241)
                 2. Formal (see page 242–243)

  F2   Non-functional Requirements
  2.3 Cash withdrawal availability
  Description:
  Cash withdrawal service should be available in 999/1000 requests
  Source: 2 Bank customer
  Priority: 5
  Affected Services: 2.2 Cash withdrawal

  Description:
  Cash withdrawal service should have a response time of no more that 2 minutes.
  Source: 2 Bank customer
  Priority: 5
  Affected services: 2.2 Cash withdrawal

9.3.1   Identifying objects from viewpoints

A number of guidelines for identifying objects have been proposed (see chapter 6). There is no doubt that these are all useful ways for determining relevant problem domain objects. The approach described here is not intended to replace these traditional approaches, but to complement them. It is important that objects identified using the VORD approach, are verified using the more traditional object identification techniques. The object notation used here is a simple extension of the viewpoint notation shown in Figure 9.2.

The basic VORD notation comprises a rectangle representing a viewpoint and square brackets representing the viewpoint attributes. For object-oriented analysis, we have extended this notation to represent the basic object structures as shown in Figure 9.31. An object is indicated with a rectangular box and a label. Aggregation is indicate by a vertical line dropping from the left hand side of the object box to join another object. A square bracket and a label indicates an atomic attribute. Generalisation (inheritance) is indicated with a line joining the right hand centre of the parent object to the left hand centre of the sub-class object.

Based on the viewpoint identification diagram of the ATM (see Figure 9.9), we can identify the initial object structure for the bank customer viewpoint shown in Figure 9.32. The object structure shows the aggregation structure for the bank customer. The cash-card and account objects have been developed to show their internal structures.

This process can be repeated for other direct viewpoints. It is also important to note that additional relevant objects can be identified by studying the user interaction with a service; this can be done by inspecting viewpoint event scenarios for relevant problem domain abstractions. We believe that the approach is useful because it provides a means of tracing design artifacts and decisions to viewpoint requirements. At a more detailed level, event scenarios can be mapped to messages and operations used in object interaction.

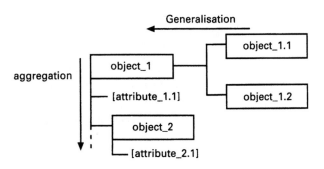

Figure 9.31
Object notation.

Figure 9.32
Bank customer
viewpoint object
structure.

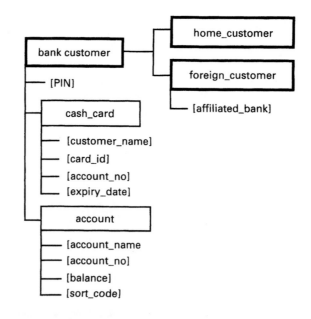

◆ **Key Points**

◆ Interactive systems can be defined as systems whose operations involve a significant degree of interaction with end-users.

◆ The requirements definition process for such systems must address important system properties such as user interface development, user classes, indirect system concerns, quality of service and other systems interfaced.

◆ A natural way to specify interactive systems is to specify the services which they provide for end-uses and other systems

◆ VORD is based on the viewpoints that focus on user issues and organisational concerns. It defines requirements as services.

◆ VORD defines two types of viewpoint, direct and indirect. Direct viewpoints correspond directly to clients in that they receive services from the system and send control information and data to the system. Indirect viewpoints range from engineering, through organisational to external viewpoints. Indirect viewpoints may generate requirements which constrain the services delivered to direct viewpoints.

◆ System behaviour is defined in VORD using event scenarios. Exceptions and normal behaviour may defined.

◆ Exercises

9.1 Explain the notion of viewpoints used in the VORD method. Why are indirect viewpoints very important? Illustrate your answer with an example.

9.2 Suggest giving reasons possible viewpoints for a university students records system.

9.3 Suggest services which such a records systems should provide.

9.4 Use the notion of viewpoints in VORD to identify the possible requirements for a web-based requirements tool to support collaboration among its users. Explain why viewpoints help to ensure that all stakeholder perspectives are identified.

9.5 Suggest possible viewpoints that need to be taken into account when developing word processing software. Identify some possible requirements for these viewpoints.

9.6 Consider a system intended to provide a video-on-demand service. Subscribers will be provided with a cable connection and decoder unit, which they can use in conjunction with their television sets to access a remote video library. Suggest possible viewpoints for the system and their possible requirements/concerns.

9.7 Use event scenarios to model a possible video provision scenario in 9.5.

9.8 Suggest possible viewpoints and service requirements for an Airline ticket reservation system

◆ References

Easterbrook, S., and Nuseibeh, B. (1996). Using viewpoints for inconsistency management. *Software Engineering Journal*, **11**(1): 31–43.

Finkelstein, A., Kramer, J., Nuseibeh, B., and Goedicke, M. (1992). Viewpoints: a framework for integrating multiple perspectives in systems development. *International Journal of Software Engineering and Knowledge Engineering*, **2**(10): 31–58.

Hausen, H. L. (1989). Rule-based handling of software quality and productivity models. *Software Engineering Lecture Notes*, **387**: 376–394.

◆ Further reading

Requirements engineering with viewpoints (G. Kotonya and I. Sommerville, *Software Engineering Journal*, **11**(1), 5–18, 1996). This paper describes the VORD method and its uses.

10 Case Study

◆ **Summary**

This chapter describes a case study that we have been closely involved in. The Electronic Document Delivery project (EDDIS), is concerned with developing the next generation library systems for the UK higher education. EDDIS is intended to be a 'one-stop shop' for most library needs. Its main function is to manage the process of identifying, locating ordering and supplying documents. In this chapter we will demonstrate how a viewpoint-oriented method VORD, described in Chapters 7 and 9, was used to document, analyse and specify the requirements for EDDIS. Using VORD to formulate the requirements for EDDIS has revealed that viewpoints can be an effective mechanism for eliciting and structuring varied stakeholder requirements and expectations. It has also demonstrated the practical utility of a viewpoint-based requirements approach on medium-sized system.

The system described here is an electronic document delivery and interchange system (EDDIS). EDDIS is an Electronic Library Programme (ELIB) project whose objective is to develop a Web-based library system for the United Kingdom Higher Education sector. The main function of EDDIS is to manage the process of identifying, locating, ordering and supplying documents. Although the initial proposal for EDDIS was conceived in the context of delivery of documents electronically, EDDIS is also required to manage the request and supply of printed documents, and is not restricted to digitised documents. It is intended that EDDIS will have the full functionality of an ILDRMS (Interlending and Document Request Management Systems).

It is obviously impossible to provide all the details of the case study here, but we will provide sufficient detail to illustrate the complex issues that need to be considered when formulating the requirements for real systems. These issues include:

- the ability to separate and prioritise stakeholders concerns
- the ability to structure and trace requirements with varying levels of detail
- the ability to expose incomplete and inconsistent requirements.

This is important not only for ease of understanding, but also for managing requirements change. Although EDDIS is primarily an end-user system, it was recognised that, because of financial constraints, many of the functions in EDDIS would be mediated by an administrator. It was anticipated that the system would be administered by the local library, but this would not always be the case. Furthermore, some of the administrator's functions could be devolved to other users. For example EDDIS could be configured so that departments have control of their own budgets.

The requirements for EDDIS can be summarised thus:

- identifying documents

- locating documents

- ordering documents

- receiving documents (digitised and non-digitised)

- providing access to documents received

- managing the receipt, lending and return of non-digitised documents

- acting as a supplier in response to orders for documents from other agents (including EDDIS servers)

- keeping track of appropriate management account informing.

10.1 EDDIS requirements

This section describes the EDDIS requirements as outlined in the original EDDIS user requirements document.

1.   EDDIS will provide a range of services available only to the system administrator. This are primarily:
     (i)   specific administrative services, for example management information
     (ii) management of non-digitised documents.

2.   EDDIS will support the management of ordering and supplying of all types of documents, both digitised and non-digitised. In the case of the receipt of non-digitised documents, EDDIS will support the receipt and subsequent management of both returnable and non-returnable items, that is, EDDIS will have a circulation system with the following features:
     (i)   lending documents
     (ii)   returning documents
     (iii) recalling documents
     (iv)   renewing documents
     (v)   fines
     (vi)   overdues.

3.   In addition to requesting documents, EDDIS will manage incoming request for documents from other agents, including other EDDIS servers; that is, it will act as a supplier.

4.   EDDIS will be configurable so that it will comply with the requirements of all UK and (where relevant) international copyright legislation. Minimally this means that EDDIS must provide a form for the user to sign the copyright declaration statement. It also means that EDDIS must keep track of copyright declaration statements which have been signed/ not signed. Under no circumstances must an order be sent to the supplier if the copyright statement has not been signed.

5.   EDDIS will keep track of all data required by the relevant copyright licensing agencies. This means that EDDIS must be able to supply details of all copies of documents received in a certain period.

6.   EDDIS will have a financial/accounting system, which will be configurable so that the accounts of all transactions can either be managed by a single accounting authority, for example, the Library, or distributed over multiple accounting authorities or individual.

7.   The prototype EDDIS is required to be operational by 1 June 1997.

8.   User interface
     (i)   The user interface will be html. Users will access EDDIS via standard Web browsers such as Netscape and Internet Explorer.

(ii) EDDIS will be primarily an end-user system. Users will use the system within the constraints of the permissions assigned by the administrator; to identify, locate, order and received documents.

9. Accounts

(i) Users will log onto EDDIS via accounts, which will be created by the administrator. There will be two types of accounts: individual and group accounts. In general, individual accounts will have access to more services than group accounts.

(ii) Individual accounts are intended for use by single users. All individual accounts will be password protected. Users of these accounts will be able to change the passwords in their accounts. group accounts are intended for groups of users, for example, members of the institution, faculty, department. Some of these will be password-protected, others will not. However only the administrator will be able to change group account passwords.

10. Services

(i) Users will have access to a range of services determined by the permissions associated with the accounts they use. The permissions will be set by the administrator. Services available within accounts will vary; some accounts could have access to most of the EDDIS services, but others could be severely restricted. For example, some accounts will be able to search all databases available to EDDIS, also to locate and order documents; whereas others might only be able to search a restricted set of databases and not be able to order documents.

(ii) There will be four primary services available to users.

- Document search will allow users to search for and identify documents which interest them. A document search is initiated by a search criterion and the output will be a set of document-ids which act as input for document locate and order services.
- Document locate will allow users to determine the location of documents. A document locate is initiated by a set of document-ids and the output is a set of location-ids.
- Document order will allow users to order documents. A document order is initiated by a set of document-ids and location-ids. The output is initially a set of order-ids and eventually the documents.
- Document read will allow users to read, and where appropriate, print documents.

(iii) There will be various secondary services.

- Status enquiry will allow users to check the status of document orders.

- ◆ Order feedback will allow users to provide necessary feedback for document orders to be fulfilled.
- ◆ Mail services will provide SMTP/MIME email tailored for EDDIS services.
- ◆ User statistics will provide the administrator with information about the performance and use of EDDIS.
- ◆ Non-digitised documents will allow access to non-digitised documents: books, photocopies, films, fiche, etc.

(iv) When users access EDDIS they will be presented with Web pages, and all the services available to them.

(v) When connected to EDDIS, users will not be permitted to work outside the html environment. However this restriction does not apply to the administrator.

(vi) The administrator will have an account which will access all services available to users.

(vii) Additionally, the administrator will have access to a range of administrative services via an administration module which will not be available to other users.

11. Communication

(i) Users will communicate with EDDIS mainly via the html interface.

(ii) User input to EDDIS will be via the html interface.

(iii) EDDIS out to the user will be via the html interface, email and print. The print output will mainly be documents supplied, which because of copyright restrictions must be printed and deleted immediately upon receipt. The email output will be documents, messages from the system and other output.

The requirements expressed in natural language are typical of the requirements for real systems. Careful study shows that there are several anomalies and inconsistencies. Some will be highlighted as we develop the requirements in more detail using VORD. A detailed description of VORD is provided in Chapter 9. Briefly, VORD has 3 iterative steps:

1. viewpoint identification
2. viewpoint documentation
3. viewpoint analysis and requirements specification

Based on these method steps, we will identify the viewpoints associated with EDDIS, document their requirements, analyse the requirements and discuss some of those conflicts between requirements which may have emerged during this analysis.

10.2 Identifying EDDIS viewpoints

In Chapter 7 we discussed how viewpoints can be used to represent users, systems and stakeholders. We also demonstrated that viewpoints have diverse requirements and constraints that need to be discovered and documented. Using the abstract set of viewpoints shown in Chapter 9 and the requirements described in section 10.1, the EDDIS viewpoints shown in Figure 10.1 can be identified.

To discover the specialised viewpoints, we need to decompose these general classes into specific viewpoints. The EDDIS user viewpoint, for example, has several specialisations, all of which share certain common attributes. In many ways the ability to structure and document viewpoint requirements in this way is one of the major strengths of the method, as it allows the specifier to be quite specific about the requirements of a viewpoint. It is possible, for example, to model different viewpoints requiring similar services but with differing constraints. It is also possible to model similar constraints with varying levels of restriction, as has been described in Chapter 9.

The EDDIS user viewpoint represents the class of system operators or users, and is an instance of the abstract class, Operator. The Document

Figure 10.1
EDDIS
viewpoints.

Identifier	Label	Description
1	Eddis user	This viewpoint represents the general EDDIS user. These include people who operate or use the system in some way.
1.1	Academic	This viewpoint is largely concerned with using EDDIS for academic purposes. Academic users include: staff, students and users outside the University
1.2	EDDIS administrator	This viewpoint is concerned with the administration of EDDIS. This viewpoint will be responsible for operating the administrative services.
2	Supplier	This viewpoint is concerned with the receipt of orders and supply of documents
3	EDDIS consortium	Represents the organisation responsible for commissioning EDDIS
4	Document Standards	Represents the standards associated with the format and delivery of documents
5	Copyright legislation	Represents the United Kingdom and international copyright restrictions

supplier viewpoint represents a class of document suppliers with which EDDIS will communicate. The Copyright legislation viewpoint is concerned with issues relating to copyright restrictions. The EDDIS consortium viewpoint comprises the EDDIS management who have the responsibility for defining the development policies for EDDIS. These policies translate to requirements and constraints that affect the product and development process, and include such diverse concerns as system delivery date, system costs and development platform. The Document standards viewpoint represents a class of document delivery and management standards. It is worthwhile to look at EDDIS from this perspective to establish that these non-functional requirements have been taken into account.

In the next sections we will provide a detailed structure and documentation for the viewpoints described in Figure 10.1. Briefly, the viewpoint structure is based on a class hierarchy. The viewpoint class hierarchy is decomposed according to viewpoint attributes and requirements. The generic viewpoint class contains attributes and requirements common to viewpoint specialisations or sub-classes. Viewpoints are first decomposed by attributes then by requirements. For *indirect* viewpoints, the first step is not essential, as these types of viewpoint are mainly concerned with non-functional requirements rather than direct interaction with the intended system. For this class of viewpoint, the decomposition should be by requirements.

10.2.1 Requirements for EDDIS user viewpoints

The EDDIS user viewpoint is a direct viewpoint and it comprises two main groups of users; those who intend to use the system for academic purposes (academic viewpoint) and those who intend to intend to use the system for administrative purposes (administrative viewpoint). The academic viewpoint comprises members of university staff, students and users outside the university community (external users). Administrative staff comprise the EDDIS administrator.

The structure of the EDDIS user viewpoint is shown in Figure 10.2, the more general viewpoints (on the left) represent requirements and attributes common to their specialisations. General EDDIS user requirements include the need to log onto the system and to access appropriate services. In addition to this, academic users require to be able to access 'item locate' and 'item search' services, and the administrator will want to access administrative services. The lower viewpoints will progressively require specific services. The level of service provided will depend on the access privileges accorded the specialisation. The sub-classing criteria is based on the services received by a particular viewpoint. In the next section, we will describe the EDDIS User requirements and the constraints affecting the requirements.

The next step is to document the requirements of the EDDIS user viewpoint. Viewpoint documentation includes the viewpoint identifier, label,

Figure 10.2
Structure of
EDDIS user
viewpoint.

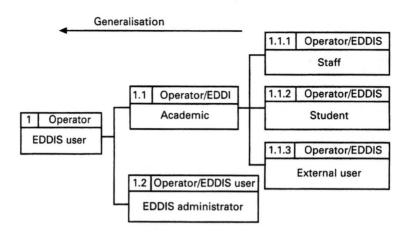

viewpoint description, attributes (described later), viewpoint requirements and event scenarios. Event scenarios are described in section 10.3. The requirement documentation comprises the requirement identifier, label, description type, source, the level of priority (weighting) attached to the requirement and specification.

Figure 10.3 shows a summary the service requirements for the EDDIS user viewpoint. The services have been extracted from the requirements described in section 10.1. In addition to inheriting the requirements of their parent classes, viewpoints can define specific requirements. The management service, for example, is provided only to the EDDIS administrator. The rationale, priorities and the constraints associated with inherited services may also differ from viewpoint to viewpoint. The academic viewpoint has no specific requirements of it own but inherits the requirements of the EDDIS user viewpoint. Similarly, the student and external user viewpoints inherit the requirements of the academic viewpoint.

VORD uses the simple scheme described in Chapter 9 to compute requirement priorities based on the relative importance of the requirement, the resources needed to deliver the requirement and the risk associated with the requirement. A requirement is weighted as high (H), medium (M) or low (L) in relation to each of the three factors. For this application the 3 factors were weighted equally on a scale of 1 to 3, as shown in Figure 10.4. However the factors may be weighted differently for other applications.

10.2.2 Supplier viewpoint requirements

The document supplier has direct interaction with the intended system, but receives no services from EDDIS. Its role is limited to providing control information. The control information provided may be an event that triggers some system operation; this may optionally be accompanied by data. It may also be data that is required to satisfy some precondition. The supplier receives

Viewpoint		Requirement			
Identifier	Label	Identifier	Description	Source	Priority
1	EDDIS user	1.1	Provision of a system access service.	EDDIS con.	9
		1.2	Provision of a document search service	EDDIS con.	9
		1.3	Provision of a document locate service	EDDIS con.	9
		1.4	Provision of facility to print and store documents	EDDIS con.	7
1.1	Academic				
1.1.1	Staff	1.1.1.5	Provision of a document status enquiry service.	EDDIS con.	6
		1.1.1.6	Provision of a document order service	EDDIS con.	6
1.1.2	Student				
1.1.3	External user				
1.2	EDDIS administrator	1.2.7	Provision of system management services, these include:	EDDIS con.	9
		1.2.7.1	ability to register users	EDDIS con.	9
		1.2.7.2	ability to remove users	EDDIS con.	9
		1.2.7.3	ability to edit user attributes	EDDIS con.	6
		1.2.7.4	system usage information	EDDIS con.	6
		1.2.7.5	restricted database access information	EDDIS con.	6
		1.2.7.6	restricted catalogue access information	EDDIS con.	6
		1.2.8	provision of non-digitised document service	EDDIS con.	

Figure 10.3
EDDIS user
requirements.

requests for documents from the users through the document order service. Documents sent by the supplier are received by EDDIS and passed on to the user. The user can send the supplier messages to request the status of the order, the supplier may in turn request for additional information. The supplier requirements are modelled as part of the event scenario for the order service (see section 10.2.6). The data required for the control information can be traced to viewpoint attributes.

Weighting / Factor	High(H)	Medium(M)	Low(L)
Importance	3	2	1
Resources required	1	2	3
Risk involved	1	2	3

The supplier receives requests for documents from the user through the document order service. Documents sent by the supplier are received by EDDIS and passed onto the user. Because the supplier provides control information, it is worth considering the constraints under which this information may be provided. Figure 10.5 shows the viewpoint documentation for the Supplier. The documentation includes: the viewpoint identifier, viewpoint label, attributes, the control information provided by the viewpoint, and associated priorities.

10.2.3 Requirements for indirect viewpoints

EDDIS has three indirect viewpoints: EDDIS consortium, Document standard and Copyright legislation, shown in Figure 10.6.

The EDDIS consortium viewpoint comprises four United Kingdom universities. The EDDIS consortium viewpoint is concerned with issues affecting the system development. Most of the constraints on the EDDIS user services originate from this viewpoint. The Document standards viewpoint is concerned with search, ordering and delivery standard requirements. The Copyright legislation viewpoint is concerned with issues relating to UK and international copyright requirements. The requirements are shown in Figures 10.7 and 10.8.

10.2.4 Viewpoint attributes

Viewpoint attributes represent values that characterise the viewpoint in the problem domain. They are things 'contained' or 'owned' by the viewpoint; for example, a customer viewpoint in a banking environment may have a

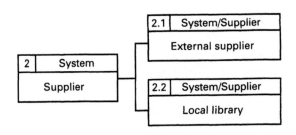

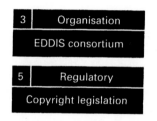

Figure 10.6
Indirect
viewpoints.

Viewpoint		Requirement			
Identifier	Label	Identifier	Description	Source	Priority
3	EDDIS	3.8	Development to be on UNIX platform	EDDIS con.	9
	consortium	3.9	C++ to be development language	EDDIS con.	9
		3.10	Proof of concept system to be delivered by 1/6/97	EDDIS con.	7
		3.11	System must be robust, system should have built in mechanism to allow for graceful degradation of services	EDDIS con.	9
		3.12	Data stored by user determined by account and set by system administrator	EDDIS con.	7
		3.13	Inputs to search and locate services to be stored in account's current work area	EDDIS con.	5
		3.14	Output results kept for duration of session	EDDIS con.	5
		3.15	Printing of search results will be only to authorised printers	EDDIS con.	5
		3.16	Variable search criteria, including: author, title, ISBN, ISSN & keyword	EDDIS con.	8

Figure 10.7
Requirements
for indirect
viewpoints.

name and an account as attributes. Attributes are important because they encapsulate data that is consumed by the system operations. In VORD, attributes are documented for direct viewpoints because they may be reflected in system objects (see Chapter 9). An attribute and its identifier are enclosed in square brackets and they appear as shown in Figure 10.9.

As with ordinary requirements, viewpoint attributes are also generalised from right to left. All EDDIS user viewpoints have a username and a password to facilitate access to EDDIS. In addition, all the Academic viewpoints have a registration and the EDDIS administrator viewpoint has an administration password. The Supplier viewpoint has a name, a postal, email and IP address, phone number and the set of documents held. Many external suppliers also have a charging scheme for the documents supplied. When

Viewpoint		Requirement			
Identifier	Label	Identifier	Description	Source	Priority
3	EDDIS consortium	3.17	Document location codes will be based on the current edition of British Library Document Supply, Directory of Library Codes	EDDIS con.	8
		3.18	Output format to indicate: total number of items found, how many already in output set, how many new items.	EDDIS con.	7
		3.19	Supplier terms to accompany document	EDDIS con.	4
		3.20	Orders will have unique numbers	EDDIS con.	9
		3.21	Information management services will be available 99% of the time	EDDIS con.	9
		3.22	EDDIS must maintain a reasonable quality of service to users	EDDIS con.	8
		3.23	Provision of appropriate viewers for	EDDIS con.	3
		3.24	EDDIS users	EDDIS con.	9
			Report format for usage to indicate the following over defined periods of time (i.e. daily, on specified dates, weekly, monthly): 1. document searches executed 2. document locations executed 3. documents supplied 4. pages supplied 5. document orders not supplied 6. document orders cancelled Ordered by: 1. use 2. cost centre 3. institutional level		
4	Document standards	4.25	Document interface standard to be Z39.50	Document standards	9
		4.26	Document ordering standard to be ISO 10160-1	Document standards	9
5	Copyright legislation	5.27	EDDIS must comply with the requirements of all UK and international copyright legislation. EDDIS users must sign a *copyright declaration* form for all document orders	Copyright legislation	9

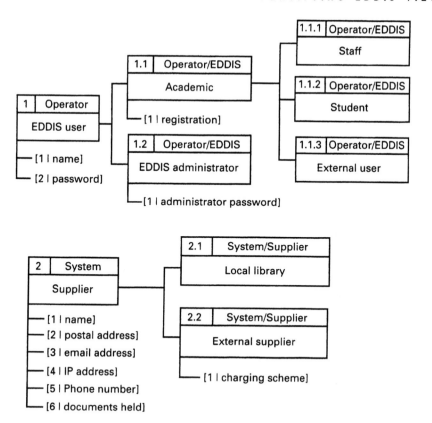

Figure 10.9
EDDIS
viewpoints with
attributes.

referring to a specific attribute, the attribute identifier should indicate the viewpoint (identified by a bold part) followed by a unique attribute number (non-bold part). For example, the registration attribute on the 'Academic' viewpoint has the unique identifier, '**1.1**.1'. The same identification scheme is used for requirements and other viewpoint information.

10.2.5   Viewpoint constraints

10.2.5.1   Constraints on viewpoint services

Non-functional requirements arising from viewpoints translate to constraints on system services, and may also constrain the development process. Requirements generated by one viewpoint may translate to constraints on another viewpoint's requirements. This section identifies and documents the constraints affecting the services provided by EDDIS and the control information. Figures 10.10 and 10.11 show the constraints on the EDDIS user services and the affected services. Constraints can be traced to non-functional requirements through their identifiers. For example, the constraint 3.18 specifying output format can be traced to the non-functional requirement 3.18.

Figure 10.8
Requirements
for indirect
viewpoints
(continued).
(OPPOSITE
PAGE)

Constraint				Affected Service
Identifier	Description	Source	Type	Identifier
3.8	Development to be on UNIX platform	EDDIS con.	Platform	All
3.9	C++ to be development language	EDDIS con.	Platform	All
3.10	Proof of concept system to be delivered by 1/6/97	EDDIS con.	Delivery	All
3.11	System must be robust, system should have built in mechanism to allow for graceful degradation of services	EDDIS con.	Reliability	All
3.12	Data stored by user determined by account and set by system administrator	EDDIS con.	Access	1.2, 1.3
3.13	Inputs to search and locate services be stored in account's current work area	EDDIS con.	Storage	1.2, 1.3
3.14	Output results kept for duration of session	EDDIS con.	Storage	1.2, 1.3
3.15	Printing of search results will be only to authorised printers	EDDIS con.	Access	1.2, 1.3

Figure 10.10
Constraints on
EDDIS services.

10.2.5.2 Constraints on viewpoint attributes

Like viewpoint requirements, attributes are also affected by constraints generated through non-functional requirements. Constraints on control information can be traced to the non-functional requirements that generate them via the constraint identifiers which match those of the non-functional requirements. Figure 10.12 shows the constraints on viewpoint attributes. The way in which control information is delivered affects the provision of services and must be considered when developing the system. The EDDIS documents must, for example, be compliant with the ISO 10160–1 document standard and must include supplier terms.

10.2.6 Describing system behaviour

In this section we describe how event scenarios were used to model the behaviour of the EDDIS system. We illustrate this aspect of the system by describing a broad spread of user and administrative services covering most viewpoints. The event scenarios described are:

- system access service
- document search service
- document locate service

Constraint				Affected Service
Identifier	Description	Source	Type	Identifier
3.16	Variable search criteria, including: author, title, ISBN, ISSN & keyword	EDDIS con.	Flexibility	1.2
3.17	Document location codes will be based on the current edition of British Library Document Supply, Directory of Library Codes	EDDIS con.	Standards	1.3
3.18	Output format to indicate: total number of items found, how many already in output set, how many new items.	EDDIS con.	User interface	1.2, 1.3
3.19	Supplier terms to accompany document	EDDIS con.	Format	1.4
3.20	Orders will have unique numbers	EDDIS con.	Standards	1.4
3.21	Information management services will be available 99% of the time	EDDIS con.	Reliability	1.2.1
3.22	EDDIS must maintain a reasonable quality of service to users	EDDIS con.	Performance	All
3.23	Provision of appropriate viewers for EDDIS users	EDDIS con.	User interface	All
3.24	Report format for system usage	EDDIS con.	User interface	1.2.1.4
4.25	Document interface standard to be Z39.50	Document standards	Standards	1.2, 1.3, 1.4
4.26	Document ordering standard to ISO 10160-1	Document standards	Standards	1.4
5.27	EDDIS must comply with the requirements of all UK and international copyright legislation. EDDIS users must sign a *copyright declaration* form for document orders	Copyright legislation	Legal	1.1.1.6

Figure 10.11
Further constraints on EDDIS services.

- document order service
- user registration service

A detailed description of the event scenarios and the notation used is provided in Chapter 9. Very briefly, an event scenario is defined as a sequence of events together with exceptions that may arise during the interchange of information between a viewpoint and the system. A normal sequence of events may

Constraint			Affected Control	
Identifier	Description	Source	Type	Identifier
3.19	Include supplier terms that is: date of delivery, copyright restrictions, charges and delivery format	EDDIS con.	Format	2.6
4.26	Document ordering standard to ISO 10160-1	Document standards	Standards	2.6
5.27	Copyright legislation	Copyright legislation	Legal	2.6

Figure 10.12 Control information and associated constraints.

have exceptions at various points in the event sequence. At the system level, exceptions cause a transfer of control to exception handlers. An extended state transition model is used to model event scenarios. Exceptions are shown by grey lines. A transition is triggered by an event and/or preconditions which must be satisfied before the transition can take place. An event may include an optional set of parameters, and may be accompanied by a set of actions.

10.2.6.1 Event scenario for system access

The system access service is concerned with providing the user with access to EDDIS services and setting up of the default environment parameters. The start-up service provides the first level of control when the user logs onto EDDIS. Figure 10.13 shows the event scenario for the system access service. The service described by the event scenario is associated with the EDDIS user viewpoint, hence the identifier '1.1'.

The system is initially in idle state until the user logs in with a valid username and password (collectively referred to as login). A valid username and password causes the system to go into a ready state where it displays a menu of the available EDDIS services. The system also opens a session and sets up the user's permissions. The permissions contain a list of services and other system facilities allowed to the user.

The user can select the desired service by pointing and clicking on it, this is equivalent to sending the system a *select(service)* event. If the user is allowed the service, then the system goes into the service state, where it displays a menu for the selected service. The user can move from the service state to the ready state by sending the system a *quit* event, and from the ready state to the idle state by logging out.

The ready state forms the common point for accessing all other EDDIS services. A user is allowed to access only those services set in the user's permission vector. The service state refers to the system when it is in one of the following service states:

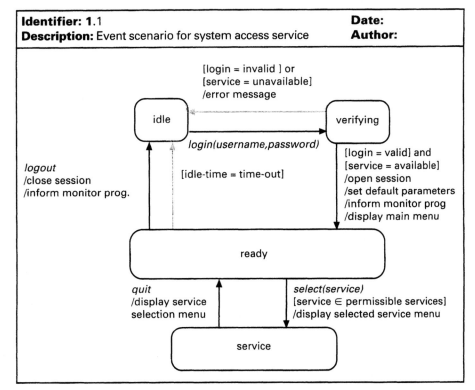

Figure 10.13
Event scenario
for system
access service.

1. document search service
2. document locate service
3. document order service
4. document read service
5. management information services

We shall describe each of these services in the following sections.

EDDIS provides two types of user-account: individual and group. Users of individual accounts are allowed to alter the environment of the selected service, for example, to select the initial set of databases and catalogues to be searched. The *setParameters* event allows users with individual accounts to do this. Users with group accounts are not permitted to do this.

10.2.6.2 Event scenario for search service

The document search service allows the user to search a set of databases, D, to obtain details of documents which match a search criterion. The set of databases searched is determined by the permissions (P_{db}) set in the permission vector. The event scenario for the search service is shown in Figure 10.14. The user initiates the search by entering a search criteria. If the search criterion is valid, the system responds by searching a set of databases selected by the

Figure 10.14
Event scenario
for search
service.

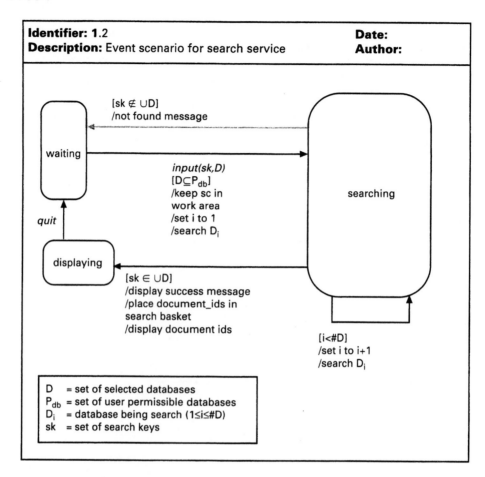

Identifier: **1**.2   Date:
Description: Event scenario for search service   **Author:**

waiting

[sk ∉ ∪D]
/not found message

input(sk,D)
[D⊆P$_{db}$]
/keep sc in
work area
/set i to 1
/search D$_i$

searching

quit

displaying

[sk ∈ ∪D]
/display success message
/place document_ids in
search basket
/display document ids

[i<#D]
/set i to i+1
/search D$_i$

D   = set of selected databases
P$_{db}$ = set of user permissible databases
D$_i$ = database being search (1≤i≤#D)
sk = set of search keys

user. The result from the search is placed in the search basket and displayed as a set of document_ids.

The search criteria include the following elements:

- author
- title
- ISBN
- ISSN
- keyword

Document ids will comprise the following:

1. document type
2. call number
3. author
4. title
5. sub-title
6. sponsoring body
7. place of publication
8. publisher series title or number

9. volume number   10. issue number

11. edition   12. date of publication

13. author of article   14. title of article

15. pagination   16. national bibliography number

17. ISBN   18. ISSN

19. system number(e.g. accession number)

10.2.6.3 Event scenario for locate service

The document locate service allows users to locate documents from a set of catalogues C. The accessible set of catalogues is determined by the permission (P_{cat}) set in the permission vector. The locate service is initiated by the user entering a set of document_ids. The system verifies the ids and displays the result of locating a set of documents. A locate basket is used to hold the results of the locate operation. Figure 10.15 shows the event scenario for the locate service.

10.2.6.4 Event scenario for order service

The document order service allows users to order documents from suppliers. The set of suppliers accessed by a user is determined by the permission vector. The service is initiated by an *input(document_id, location_id)* event. Each

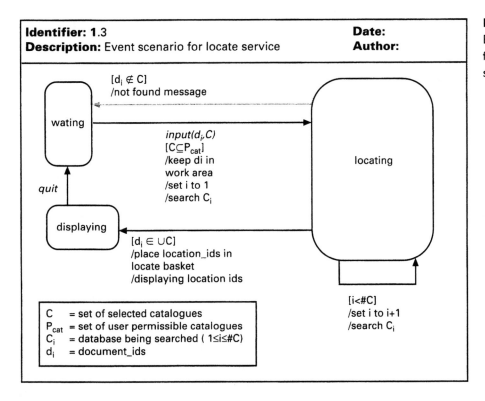

Figure 10.15 Event scenario for locate service.

document order is assigned a unique order_id which is stored in the user's work area. The output from this service is initially a set of order-ids, and later documents.

The document order service allows users to receive and store documents from suppliers. The documents are stored at locations determined by the user's permission vector. When the system is in the displaying state the user can print and forward documents. Figure 10.16 shows the event scenario for the document order service.

An important requirement of EDDIS is that it is able to transfer requests from a supplier to the user for additional information relating to an order. It

Figure 10.16
Event scenario
for order
service.

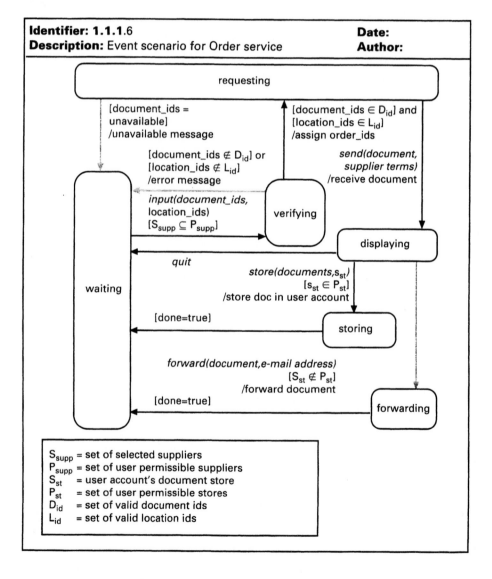

Identifier: 1.1.1.6   Date:
Description: Event scenario for Order service   Author:

requesting

[document_ids = unavailable] /unavailable message

[document_ids ∈ D_{id}] and [location_ids ∈ L_{id}] /assign order_ids

[document_ids ∉ D_{id}] or [location_ids ∉ L_{id}] /error message

send(document, supplier terms) /receive document

input(document_ids, location_ids) [$S_{supp} \subseteq P_{supp}$]

verifying

displaying

waiting

quit

store(documents,s_{st}) [$s_{st} \in P_{st}$] /store doc in user account

[done=true]

storing

forward(document,e-mail address) [$S_{st} \notin P_{st}$] /forward document

[done=true]

forwarding

S_{supp} = set of selected suppliers
P_{supp} = set of user permissible suppliers
S_{st} = user account's document store
P_{st} = set of user permissible stores
D_{id} = set of valid document ids
L_{id} = set of valid location ids

is also required that the user be able to respond via EDDIS. When the user places an order it may be the case that the document can only be delivered in a non-digitised form, or it may be the case that additional information is required by the supplier. In the first case, the supplier responds by sending an email message to the user and the document to the Librarian. In the second case the supplier responds by sending an email message to the user.

10.2.6.5 Event scenario for information management services

Information management services are concerned with the management and organisation of the information kept by EDDIS. This includes registering new users, editing user details and removing users, keeping track of the document searches, ordering and locating, and keeping track of system usage statistics. The event scenario for some management services is described below.

Only the system administrator will be allowed to register, remove and modify user parameters in EDDIS. These services must therefore be included in the System Administrator's list of permissions. The 'register user' service is concerned with adding users to EDDIS. This service is accessed from the main services menu. A new user is registered via the event *register(details)*. The system administrator is informed via a system message whether the operation has been a success. The parameters associated with the register event comprises a number of data items required to register a new user on EDDIS, these include:

1. username
2. password
3. userID
4. name
5. title
6. email address
7. postal address
8. billing address
9. institutional status
10. student no./staff no.
11. expiry date
12. cost centre
13. institutional affiliation level (1–4)
14. account type
15. financial account no.
16. search permissions
17. order permissions
18. order limit
19. cost limit of single order
20. expenditure limit
21. default delivery format

Figure 10.17 shows the register user event scenario. The 'Remove user' service is concerned with removing users from EDDIS. This service is accessed from the main services menu. A new user is removed via the event *remove(userID)*. The system administrator is informed via a system message if the operation has been successful or not.

The 'Edit user' service is concerned with modifying user details once they are on EDDIS. This service is accessed from the main services menu. User details are accessed via the event *Edituser(userID)*. If the userID is valid the system goes into an editing mode and displays the user details. Editing the user details

Figure 10.17
Register user
event scenario.

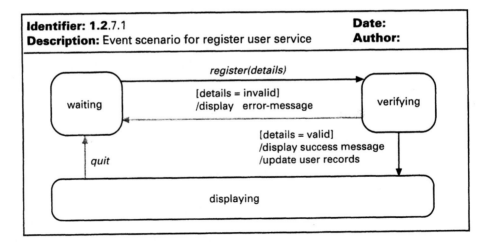

results in the user database being updated and the system reverting to the original service state. It is also possible for the system administrator to cancel the editing process.

10.2.7 Tracing events to viewpoints

The provision of a viewpoint service is subject to control influences from several sources in the system environment. The document order service, for example, is initiated by the 'Staff' viewpoint, but involves the participation of the 'Supplier' viewpoint. The complete description of the events that affect a service provision requires that all the viewpoints participating in the service provision are identified. It is also important to note that some viewpoints, for example databases, may only provide control information.

Figure 10.18 shows a summary table of events arising from the five event scenarios described previously. This type of table helps identify the role of viewpoints in the provision of services and to trace the impact of change.

10.3 Analysis and evolution of EDDIS requirements

In Chapter 9 we described the requirements analysis process used by VORD and mentioned that the main objective of the analysis process was twofold:

◆ to establish that viewpoint documentation is complete and consistent
◆ to identify and resolve conflicting requirements

In this section we will not go into the details of how the EDDIS requirements were checked for completeness and how the conflicts were identified

Service Described		Event Scenario	
Identifier	Label	Event	Viewpoint originating event
1.1	System access	1. login(username, password)	EDDIS user
		2. logout	EDDIS user
		3. select(service)	EDDIS user
		4. quit	EDDIS user
1.2	Document search	1. input(sk, D)	EDDIS user
		2. quit	EDDIS user
1.3	Document locate	1. input(d_{i}, C)	EDDIS user
		2. quit	EDDIS user
1.1.1.6	Document order	1. input(document_ids, location_ids)	Staff
		2. send(documents)	Supplier
		3. store(documents)	Staff
		4. forward(document, e-mail address)	Staff
		5. quit	Staff
1.2.7.1	User registration	1. register(details)	System administrator

Figure 10.18
Event trace table.

and resolved (this is described in Chapter 9). Instead we will provide a summary of some of the problems encountered during the requirements formulation and the changes that were proposed. The aim here is to give the reader some idea of the varied nature of the problems encountered in the process of defining software requirements. Figure 10.19 shows some EDDIS requirements changes.

When a requirement is modified in VORD, its identifier is modified to indicate level of change. A requirement n.m, for example, becomes n.m(1) after a single change, and n.m(2) with a second change, and so on. This reduces the number of artificial versions. The number of changes and the extent of change determines the point at which a new version of the requirement is created.

10.4 Specifying EDDIS requirements

VORD supports the specification of viewpoint services in a variety of notations. This is particularly important for two reasons.

Item				
Affected items and proposed action				
Identifier	Description	Problem	Identifier	Proposed action
1.1.1.6	Document order event scenario	It is a requirement that all document order must be accompanied by a signed copyright acceptance form. This information is missing from the event scenario.	1.1.1.6 1.1.1.6(1)	No change The event shall be modified thus: *input(document_ids,location_ids)* modified to read: *input(document_ids,location_ids, ©)* where © is a signed copyright acceptance form.
3.22	EDDIS must maintain a reasonable quality of service to users	Need for a clearer. requirement	3.22(1)	EDDIS must be able to automatically monitor and control the number of people logged onto the system at anytime to maintain a reasonable quality of service to its users. The program will monitor the users logged on against a preset maximum and prevent additional users when the preset a maximum is reached.
1.2.8	Non-digitised receipts	There was no means of incorporating this requirement given the tight project time scale	1.2.8(1)	The requirement was deferred to the next release of EDDIS
3.10	Proof of concepts system to be ready by 1/6/97	It was discovered that it was not going to be possible to meet this deadline due to the restrictive schedule.	3.10(1)	The proof of concepts date was put forward to 1/12/97
3.23	Provision of appropriate viewers	This requirement was found not to be necessary	3.23(1)	Requirement was deleted

Figure 10.19
Summary of analysis and changes.

1. One of the major problems associated with software development is the lack of adequate communication between the requirements engineer and the system's potential users due to the differences in their experience and education. The ability to represent the same requirement in different notations which are familiar to different people enhances communication and aids understanding.

2. No one requirements notation can adequately articulate all the needs of a system. More than one specification language may be needed to represent the requirements adequately.

The requirements document used in VORD is adapted from the recommendations of the IEEE standard 830–1993. Figure 10.20 shows part of the EDDIS requirements document. The VORD requirements document is structured using viewpoints to maintain traceability with viewpoints. Section A provides a short description of the viewpoint and section B the viewpoint type. Section C lists all viewpoint attributes while section D lists all viewpoint specialisations in terms of their references. Section E provides the development history of the viewpoint including its components). Section F describes the viewpoint requirements. In addition, services have an event scenario and specification. The description of non-functional requirements includes references to affected services.

Figure 10.20
Part of EDDIS requirements specification document.

REQUIREMENTS DOCUMENT
SPECIFIC REQUIREMENTS SECTION

---

3. SPECIFIC REQUIREMENTS
Viewpoint
1. EDDIS User

    A Description
    //brief description of viewpoint
    The EDDIS user viewpoint represents the general system user.
    Users will include; academic users and administrative staff.

    B Type
    //this section defines the viewpoint
    /Direct/Operator

    C Attributes
    1. Name
    2. Password

    D Specialisations
    //this section provides a list of viewpoint specialisations
    1.1 Academic
    1.2 EDDIS Administrator

    E History
    //References to the development history of viewpoint components

    F Requirements
    //viewpoint requirements are described in this section

    F1 Services
    //viewpoint services or functional requirements are described here
    1.1 System access
    Description:
    The system will provide its users with the ability to access
    EDDIS services based on a set of user access permissions.
    Source: 3 (EDDIS consortium)
    Priority: 9
        Importance: 3
        Resources: 3
        Risk: 3   (Continued overleaf)

Figure 10.20
(*Continued*).

> Rationale: A primary service, all other services are
>   dependent on it
>
> **Event scenario:**   1.1
> **Specification:**   <Object-oriented specification >
>
> 1.2 Document search
>   :
>
> 1.3 Document locate
>   :
>
> 1.4 Document print and store
>   :
>
> 1.5 Document status enquiry
>   :
>
> 1.6 Document order
>   :
>
> **F2 Non-functional Requirements**
> *//Non-functional requirement associated with viewpoint go here*
> *//each non-functional requirement has a unique identifier,*
> *//description, source, priority and a list of affected services*

♦ **Key Points**

♦ Viewpoints are an effective mechanism for eliciting and structuring user requirements and expectations.

♦ The requirements definition process should be guided by multi-perspective techniques that take into account the varied stakeholder requirements, conflicting opinions and possibilities error and omissions.

♦ Requirements expressed in natural language are typical for real systems.

♦ Conflict analysis and resolution is a difficult problem, especially for real systems where requirements may need to be represented in several varied ways. There is no simple way of automating all the aspects of conflict resolution.

♦ The explicit identification of viewpoints with services in VORD has made it possible create a framework where stakeholder concerns and other aspects of requirements can be integrated.

◆ Exercises

10.1 Model the EDDIS requirements shown in Figure 10.3 using one of the other viewpoint methods described in Chapter 7. Contrast the strengths of the method with the one used in Chapter 10.

10.2 Making appropriate assumptions, construct event scenarios for the remaining EDDIS services.

10.3 What are the participating viewpoints in provision of the services described in 10.2?

10.4 Identify two conflicting requirements from Figures 10.7 and 10.8 and suggest how they could be resolved.

10.5 Using the EDDIS user viewpoint as a starting point, identify possible objects associated with the viewpoint.

10.6 Model the EDDIS system using the method described in Chapter 6 SADT.

10.7 Why is the non-functional requirement 3.11 (Figure 10.10) ambiguous? How can it be rewritten to remove the ambiguity?

10.8 Suggest one way to incorporate a scheme for charging EDDIS users. Illustrate the charging scheme using an event scenario.

◆ Acknowledgements

The EDDIS project is part of the UK Electronic Libraries Programme funded by the Joint Information Systems Committee of the Higher Education Funding Councils. The members of the project consortium are the University of East Anglia (lead site), Lancaster University, the University of Stirling and the Bath Information and Data Service. Further information can be found in 'Project EDDIS: an approach to integrating document discovery, location, request and supply.', David Larbey, Interlending & Document Supply Vol 25, No 3, 1997 pp 96–102; and 'Electronic Document Delivery Including Overviews of Network Standards GEDI, ISO ILL and Z39.50.'

Index